The Domestication
of Transcendence

Other Westminster John Knox books
by William C. Placher

A History of Christian Theology: An Introduction

Narratives of a Vulnerable God: Christ, Theology, and Scripture

Readings in the History of Theology,
Vol. 1: From Its Beginnings to the Eve of the Reformation
Vol. 2: From the Reformation to the Present

Unapologetic Theology: A Christian Voice in a Pluralistic Conversation

Belonging to God: A Commentary
on "A Brief Statement of Faith"
with David Willis-Watkins

THE DOMESTICATION
OF TRANSCENDENCE

How Modern Thinking about God Went Wrong

William C. Placher

Westminster John Knox Press
Louisville, Kentucky

Book design by Jennifer K. Cox
Cover design by Kim Wohlenhaus
Cover illustration: S. Bravo in Haarlem (AFTER CLEANING) by Saenredam, Pieter Jansz (Dutch 1597-1665). Courtesy Philadelphia Museum of Art: The John G. Johnson Collection.

First edition

Published by Westminster John Knox Press
Louisville, Kentucky

This book is printed on acid-free paper that meets the American National Standards Institute Z39.48 standard. ♾

PRINTED IN THE UNITED STATES OF AMERICA

96 97 98 99 00 01 02 03 04 05—10 9 8 7 6 5 4 3 2 1

Library of Congress Cataloging-in-Publication Data
Placher, William C. (William Carl), 1948–
    The domestication of transcendence : how modern thinking about God went wrong / William C. Placher. — 1st ed.
        p.   cm.
    Includes bibliographical references (p.   ) and index.
    ISBN 0-664-25635-X (alk. paper)
    1. God—History of doctrines.   2. Theology, Doctrinal—History—Modern period, 1500–   3. Philosophy, Modern.   4. God.   I. Title.
BT98.P55   1996
231'.09'03—dc20
                                                                            95-46686

To the Yale-Washington Theology Group

The power of God . . . must not be confounded with any high, exalted force, known or knowable. . . . Being completely different, it is the KRISIS of all power, that by which all power is measured, and by which it is pronounced to be both something and—nothing, nothing and—something. . . . The power of God stands neither at the side of nor above—supernatural!—these limited and limiting powers. . . . It can neither be substituted for them nor ranged with them, and, save with the greatest caution, it cannot even be compared with them.

—Karl Barth, *The Epistle to the Romans* (1922)

She saw the streak as a vast swinging bridge extending upward from the earth through a field of living fire. There were whole companies of white trash, clean for the first time in their lives, and bands of black niggers in white robes, and battalions of freaks and lunatics shouting and leaping like frogs. And bringing up the end of the procession was a tribe of people whom she recognized at once as those who, like herself and Claude, had always had a little of everything and the God-given wit to use it right. She leaned forward to observe them closer. They were marching behind the others with great dignity, accountable as they had always been for good order and common sense and respectable behavior. They alone were on key. Yet she could see by their shocked and altered faces that even their virtues were being burned away.

—Flannery O'Connor, "Revelation"

Contents

Preface

The beginning of chapter 1 explains two of the reasons that led to the writing of this book. Others are more idiosyncratically personal. My theological instinct has been that the writing of Christian theology ought to begin with Christology, but—to make an obvious point—it is difficult to talk about Christology without making reference to God, thereby assuming your readers know what you mean by "God." Such an assumption seems problematic for contemporary theology. The problems of greatest concern to me are not the modern world's famous inability to believe in God—I'm willing, as a theologian, to take my chances there—but the world's characteristically trivial images of God. When the culturally dominant pictures of God have come to be simplistic, it becomes hard to arouse much excitement about the news of divine incarnation—or much sense of its meaning. I sensed this problem even as I was writing my last book, *Narratives of a Vulnerable God*. I wouldn't back off from my efforts there to speak in the language of Christian faith about God's vulnerability in love, but I worried—and continue to worry—that in the contemporary context God-talk too could seem a little too comfortable and domestic. Perhaps this book can help redress the imbalance.

One of my roles in life seems to be that of unofficial historian of postliberal theology, or "the Yale school"—even though my skepticism about the existence of such a "school" makes the role a somewhat uncomfortable one. But in an earlier book, *Unapologetic Theology*, I did try to explain the philosophical context for a way of doing theology characteristic of a number of us who taught or studied at Yale, and I have reviewed the work of the "school" in a number of articles. In most of this work I emphasized the work of Hans Frei, the influence of Barth and Wittgenstein, and topics related to hermeneutics. But George Lindbeck's *The Nature of Doctrine*, the one book that most put "postliberal theology" on the table for discussion, has at least as much to say about our language about God as about hermeneutics. And Lindbeck has always been more a Thomist than a Wittgensteinian or a Barthian. Though I am not yet fifty, I already see a remarkable group of scholars younger than I and trained at Yale—Kathryn Tanner, Bruce Marshall, Eugene Rogers, and Serene Jones, among others—who are exploring this side of postliberal theology. Among other things, this book means to salute and engage in conversation with that younger generation.

I continue to worry about appropriate Christian language for God, given contemporary concerns I share about the masculine bias of that language in the tradition. My own practice has been to avoid pronouns with reference to

God and to use even *Father* and *Son* sparingly, supplemented by alternative terms for the first two Persons of the Trinity. But I quote my sources and standard translations without much reference to their often very male language about God. This all seems like an awkward and tentative compromise; I continue to struggle with the problem. In this book, I am proposing a critical retrieval of some aspects of traditional Christian theology. Some readers will feel that, along the way, I am not nearly critical enough of the male bias of that tradition. Perhaps so. But it would never occur to me to consult Aquinas or Luther or Calvin for the best guidance about the relations between women and men or gender sensitivity in language. On those issues it seems to me obvious that we have better ideas than they did, but I often find that they had richer insights than we into God and God's grace. I find it so difficult to think about God that I am eager to get help wherever I can, so I find myself taking for granted the faults of earlier theologians and eagerly pursuing what I can learn from them.

The invitation to give the T. V. Moore Lectures for 1995 at San Francisco Theological Seminary provided the chance to try out a preliminary version of several chapters of this book. Timothy Staveteig was a helpful and supportive editor. Michael Root read several chapters and particularly helped me rethink what I had said about Luther. My Wabash colleague Stephen Webb's reflections about excess and divine gifting continue to influence me.

I wrote the book during a productive year at the Center of Theological Inquiry in Princeton, and I am grateful to Daniel Hardy, the director of the Center, for the invitation to come and his generous encouragement and to Kate LeVan and the rest of the Center's marvelous staff for all their help. William Harris, archivist extraordinaire, helped me pretend to be a real historian. Nearly all the other members of the Center were congenial and generous colleagues. James Keenan was a good neighbor, a model of scholarly energy, and a real help in thinking about the Puritans. It was a particular pleasure to spend the year with two old friends. George Hunsinger's insights into the nature of theology lie somewhere in the background of much of this book. William Werpehowski read most of it in manuscript and continues to teach me not only about theology and ethics but also about friendship.

Roughly fifteen years ago, a number of us who were in graduate school together decided to begin meeting at least once a year to discuss theology and go to movies. The "Yale-Washington theology group" has been one of the centers of my intellectual life, and to my comrades in it this book is affectionately dedicated.

1 Introduction
Theology and Modernity

The writing of this book emerged in part out of two frustrations—frustrations that developed as I read in recent Christian theology. One was that theology, like many other fields, has come to be flooded with talk of *postmodernism* and with claims to represent *the* authentically postmodern theology. But *postmodernism* seems to mean so many different things to different people that one wonders if it has any clear meaning at all. Part of the problem is that the meaning of *modern* is so unclear, and thus it is hard to know what *post*modernism is supposed to be following, rejecting, or transcending.[1]

The second frustration was that many contemporary theologians attack the Christian tradition, or *classical Christian theism,* for its picture of a distant, lordly deity, incapable of being affected by the things of the world, standing at the summit of metaphysical hierarchies, and reinforcing their oppressive structures. My frustration arose because this did not seem to be the way Aquinas or Luther or Calvin, for instance—or the Bible, for that matter—talked about God, and so I began to wonder just what *classical Christian theism* really meant.

Both these concerns led me back to the seventeenth century. The beginning of the modern era has been dated everywhere from the origin of the Renaissance to the French Revolution, but somewhere around the seventeenth century, when new technology and new patterns of thinking, as well as the growth of capitalism and the nation-state, came to center stage in Western Europe, seems the most natural starting point. Certainly a historian of theology, contrasting how things stood when Calvin died in 1564 with the eighteenth century's debates over Deism, cannot help feeling that a dramatically different era had begun sometime in the interim. Thus to understand modern theology, to figure out (among other things) whether we are now postmodern and what that might mean, the seventeenth century seemed a good place to begin. As I

---

1. A number of philosophers, for such reasons, have recently been exploring the beginnings and meanings of modernity. See Hans Blumenberg, *The Legitimacy of the Modern Age,* trans. Robert M. Wallace (Cambridge, Mass.: MIT Press, 1983); Jürgen Habermas, *The Philosophical Discourse of Modernity,* trans. Frederick G. Lawrence (Cambridge: MIT Press, 1987); Stanley Rosen, *The Ancients and the Moderns: Rethinking Modernity* (New Haven: Yale University Press, 1989); Stephen Toulmin, *Cosmopolis: The Hidden Agenda of Modernity* (New York: Free Press, 1990).

There has been less such work among theologians, though, for an admirable exception, see Louis Dupré, *Passage to Modernity* (New Haven: Yale University Press, 1993). Dupré looks at the issues from a Catholic perspective, with particular insight into the relations between theology and spirituality. Jeffrey Stout, *The Flight from Authority* (Notre Dame, Ind.: University of Notre Dame Press, 1981) discusses interrelated issues in philosophy, religion, and ethics.

started to read the theology of that time and contrast it with what went before it, I began to conclude that some of the features contemporary critics find most objectionable in so-called traditional Christian theology in fact came to prominence only in the seventeenth century. Some of our current protests, it turns out, should not be directed against the Christian tradition, but against what modernity did to it.

To relieve any suspense, let me report at the start that this research has not yielded a clear definition of postmodernism, and indeed the question of whether I want to lay claim to writing postmodern theology, never very urgent, now strikes me as unimportant.

Any contemporary theologian is to some extent a product of the modern age. Its insights are not baggage we could leave behind; they are a part of us. But modernity need not imprison us. On individual points, we are free to think that much of theology in the modern era took a wrong course. To take an example from outside the direct concerns of this book, while we may celebrate the increase in religious tolerance that followed the religious wars of the seventeenth century, we can also regret how little check remained on nation-states' claims to call on their citizens to kill each other.

To say this—or to make any other criticism of some turn modernity took—is not to propose a simple return to the premodern. We could not go back to that world if we wanted to, and we would not want to if we could. It was a world of terrible injustice and violence, and some aspects of its theology both reflected and even contributed to those horrors. Christian theologians supported oppressive social structures and all sorts of bigotry; the male bias of the tradition is only one of its most obvious faults. If contemporary theology engages in critical retrievals of insights from premodern theology, then the retrievals must indeed always be critical, keeping in mind that what we retrieve was often embedded in contexts we can no longer accept. To engage in such critical retrievals while acknowledging our debts to modernity is to synthesize something new. As already noted, I am not much interested in whether the results should be labeled postmodern. What matters is that we find, from whatever sources, ways of speaking about God as faithfully and truthfully as we can.

A Sketch of the Project

This book selects from all the issues Christians faced at the beginning of the modern era one set of interrelated questions: How did theologians and philosophers think about God? How did they define their language about God? What was God's relation to the created world and human moral efforts?[2] I will argue

---

2. I am not claiming that these are the only important questions. Hans Frei, for instance, brilliantly considered changes in biblical hermeneutics beginning in roughly the same period, which had equally momentous effects. See Hans W. Frei, *The Eclipse of Biblical Narrative* (New Haven: Yale University Press, 1974).

that seventeenth-century thinkers grew more confident about human capacities—about their ability to understand God and God's role in the world and to contribute to human salvation—and narrowed their understanding of what counted as reasonable articulation of and argument for faith. That combination of a kind of confidence in human abilities and constricting definitions of acceptable reasoning led theology astray. Broad generalizations about the Christian tradition are dangerous, so I will be contrasting seventeenth-century developments with three particular earlier theologians—Aquinas, Luther, and Calvin. The three of them certainly would not have agreed about everything, but they did manifest patterns of theological thinking that often got lost in the seventeenth century. They can thus provide a kind of control group against which to measure modernity's innovations. Thus, chapters 2, 3, and 4 will consider what they said about some particular problems: Aquinas on our knowledge of God, Luther on divine grace, and Calvin (in a way that combines themes from the other two chapters) on the language of Christian faith. Then chapters 5 and 6 will discuss how ways of thinking about God exemplified by these earlier figures broke down in the seventeenth century—chapter 5, with respect to language about God; chapter 6, in regard to understandings of grace. Since no theologians of that period have the stature of Aquinas, Luther, and Calvin, I will have to make claims about general trends and representative figures, in the process probably giving less than their due to those who best preserved older theological virtues. My story concerns how much of the talk about God among Christian intellectuals changed its form and how those changes even came to dominate theology and philosophy. Readers should remember that there were always some to resist the changes or turn in different ways that found less support.

These five chapters having considered some issues about God, the next three will take up God's relation to the world—chapter 7, reviewing some themes in Aquinas, Luther, and Calvin; chapter 8 (in parallel to chapter 5), discussing seventeenth-century changes on the scientific and metaphysical side; chapter 9 (in parallel to chapter 6), on the ethical side. The decreasing emphasis on revelation and grace in the seventeenth century went hand in hand with decreasing attention to the Trinity, and that shift to Christian reflection on a simply unitary God will be the subject of chapter 10. The final two chapters will then draw some constructive conclusions from all this for contemporary theology—chapter 11, about our understanding of God; chapter 12, about God's relation to the world, with particular attention to the problems of evil and human sin. I mean to urge on theologians today virtues like caution, modesty, and reticence: learning to rest more content with how little we can understand about God and to be more willing to live with ambiguities and puzzles than much of modern thinking about God has been.

My teacher Hans Frei used to say that he tried to stay out of trouble by claiming to be a theologian when he was talking with historians and to be a historian when he was talking with theologians. I am neither as good a historian nor as good a theologian as he was, and therefore I am in far greater need of offering apologies and cautionary notes. My efforts to bring some historical matters into contemporary theological discussion will no doubt sometimes strike historians of the relevant periods as dangerously oversimplifying or saying the obvious. On the other hand, philosophically trained theologians will sometimes be frustrated that I allow matters that contemporary debates would push to clarification to remain in ambiguity. Sometimes resolving ambiguities distorts the historical reality of a time that had not yet arrived at our questions. I can only plead in defense of my project that few theologians these days know anything about, for instance, Francisco Suárez or Samuel Rutherford, who turn out to be key figures in the story I will be telling, and that even thinkers as important as Aquinas or Calvin often get misunderstood in contemporary debates. Moreover, histories of seventeenth-century thought have tended to put philosophy and theology (and even Catholic and Protestant theologies) into separate intellectual boxes. When thinking about the Middle Ages or the nineteenth century, we usually recognize that philosophical and theological developments are parts of an interconnected story. But we forget that a Catholic philosopher like René Descartes and a Protestant theologian like Francis Turretin were roughly contemporaries, facing many of the same historical circumstances, and both deeply influenced by the Catholic theologian Suárez.

If I can, at risk of oversimplification, make some connections among these folk and make them seem intriguing enough to drive readers to consult the original texts or the historical work of scholars more learned than I, then this book will have achieved one of its purposes. Another purpose would be served if I can encourage some historical work on issues that would be particularly helpful to constructive theologians—a heartfelt hope, given that some of the most important texts in respect to these issues remain untranslated or unavailable in modern editions.

One limitation in what follows may be particularly frustrating: I will be writing intellectual history generally in isolation from social history, and as a result, often talking about *what* happened without much reflection on *why* it happened. Theology grows out of social contexts, and understanding those contexts often can help us understand theology better. For example, as I have said, seventeenth-century thinkers, in theology as in other fields, often seem to have grown more confident, more optimistic about the capacities of human reason. Indeed, one of the standard versions of the contrast between modernity and postmodernism talks about the end of modernity in the failure of confidence in human progress and reason (and in European culture as the supposed vanguard of those ideals) in the aftermath of the trenches of World War I, the Holocaust, and threats of nuclear and ecological catastrophe. A certain bleak anxiety, or ironic defense mechanisms for dealing with it, might indeed seem one of the characteristics of postmodernism.

But what about that modern optimism? It is a psychological commonplace that superficially vigorous confidence often covers up underlying insecurities, and something of the sort may be true of intellectual trends in seventeenth-century Europe. In much of Europe it was a dreadful time. Thirty years of warfare, motivated in substantial part by religious differences, led to the death of a third of the population of Germany and to substantial if lesser disasters elsewhere on the Continent.[3] Civil war brought worse conflict than England had known since the Norman Conquest six hundred years earlier. A severe depression, starting about 1619, ended the economic expansion characteristic throughout the sixteenth century. The plague ran through France from 1630 to 1632 and again from 1647 to 1649, and the famous English plague of the 1660s was only the last and worst of a whole series. In a time when most people lived less protected from nature than we are, it was cold—a "little ice age," worse than anything since or for centuries before.[4]

People's minds as well as their bodies must often have seemed under assault in the seventeenth century. For nearly a millenium, most Western Europeans had been able to take their religious beliefs for granted, as fostered by the dominant social structures around them and shared by nearly all their neighbors. Now their neighbors in the next territory might hold quite different religious views and be threatening military invasion over the difference. Ordinary folk could naturally begin to wonder how sure they were of the truth of their own beliefs, not to mention how willing they were to die for them.[5] At the same time, the scientific discoveries of what Whitehead called "the century of genius,"[6] which often strike historians today as cause for growing cultural confidence, must often have seemed to their contemporaries unnerving undercuttings of their most basic beliefs—imagine that the earth does not rest solidly beneath our feet but goes hurtling around the sun![7]

In such a context, the modern appeal to reason, rigorously defined, can appear less a matter of confident optimism than a kind of desperation. In a world full of so much uncertainty, one would want to be able to argue compellingly for one's beliefs, including one's beliefs about God, and to be clear about the relation of one's own moral efforts to one's salvation. Stephen Toulmin has recently made a counter-intuitive but often persuasive case for the seventeenth century as a time of *diminishing* intellectual tolerance on the part of everyone

---

3. See E. A. Beller, "The Thirty Years War," in *The New Cambridge Modern History*, vol. 4, ed. J. P. Cooper (Cambridge, Mass.: Cambridge University Press, 1970), 357.
4. Toulmin, *Cosmopolis*, 17–18.
5. John Bunyan, *Grace Abounding to the Chief of Sinners* (Oxford: Clarendon Press, 1962), 31.
6. Alfred North Whitehead, *Science and the Modern World* (New York: Free Press, 1967), 39.
7. Surveying a whole range of issues, Theodore Rabb concludes that the period from the 1630s to the 1670s saw the greatest change in Europe of any time between the Reformation and the French Revolution. It was, he says, centrally a crisis of the location of authority: "In a world where everything had been thrown into doubt, where uncertainty and instability reigned, could one attain assurance, control, and a common acceptance of *some* structure where none seemed within reach?" Theodore K. Rabb, *The Struggle for Stability in Early Modern Europe* (New York: Oxford University Press, 1975), 33.

from counter-Reformation Catholics to Protestant scholastics to Cartesian philosophers, a sad decline from the more open-minded days of Renaissance humanism.[8] Such historical analysis has interesting affinities with recent postmodern analyses of the tyrannical hegemony of Enlightenment reason.[9] Maybe the "Age of Reason" was not such a time of intellectual independence as we have been taught to think. Since my own concern lies primarily in drawing lessons for contemporary theology, I will here not much explore such social forces and other underlying causes, though I judge them important and am eager to learn more about them from others. But we too live in a time of defensiveness and insecurity, and politics—including church politics and academic politics—these days presses many people toward positions that reject ambiguities and draw sharp lines. Seeing the problems such strategies created in seventeenth-century theology might foster a bit more caution in our own time.

To conclude this opening section, a word about the book's title—first, about *domestication*. In the 1630s, when the Massachusetts Bay Colony condemned and exiled Anne Hutchinson for teaching too radical a doctrine of grace (and for, as a woman, teaching at all), Thomas Hooker, one of the organizers of the campaign against her, insisted that her picture of God's unpredictable and excessive grace was too dangerous to the social order. "I know there is wilde love and joy enough in the world," Hooker wrote, "as there is wilde thyme and other herbes, but we would have garden-love and garden-joy, of God's own planting."[10] The passage offers a wonderful metaphor for how seventeenth-century theology tended to go wrong, as Christians concerned about both intellectual and social order domesticated an earlier awe in the face of divine mystery and boldness in envisioning the possibilities of grace.

Transcendence is a more complicated word. It has come to be a technical term in philosophy and theology, referring to God's distance from and independence of the created world, in contrast to *immanence*. But the *Oxford English Dictionary* records its first usage with that meaning only in 1848, where it refers to the view of Deists, and such usage in French began even later. Using the word at all of the seventeenth century or the centuries before it therefore risks, I admit, problematic anachronism. What I want to convey—and *transcendence* seemed a relatively neutral way of doing it—is this: before the seventeenth century, most Christian theologians were struck by the mystery, the wholly otherness of God, and the inadequacy of any human categories as applied to God. That earlier view never completely disappeared, but in the seventeenth century philosophers and theologians increasingly thought they could talk clearly about God.

They therefore shifted to what Kathryn Tanner calls a "contrastive" under-

---

8. Toulmin, *Cosmopolis,* x, 169.

9. See Theodor W. Adorno and Max Horkheimer, *Dialectic of Enlightenment,* trans. John Cummings (New York: Herder & Herder, 1972), 6, 24; Michel Foucault, *Histoire de la folie à l'âge classique* (Paris: Editions Gallimard, 1972), 41–47.

10. Thomas Hooker, *The Soules Implantation into the Natural Olive* (London: R. Young, 1640), 180.

standing of transcendence—more about this in chapter 7. Though the terms would emerge only later, they were already explaining God's difference from created things by saying that God was *transcendent* (distant, unaffected) in *contrast* to *immanent* (close, engaged). Rather than explaining how all categories break down when applied to God, they set the stage for talking about transcendence as one of the definable properties God possesses—a quality we could understand and that many writers today could then come to find deeply unattractive. In that sense, transcendence got domesticated, and theology suffered as a result.

In Search of Postmodern Theology

To claim that a critical retrieval of some premodern ways of talking about God can provide a helpful theological resource for our putatively postmodern time is thoroughly unfashionable. A good many recent discussions of postmodern theology scarcely attend to the differences between modern and pre-seventeenth-century theology—it is all "classical Christian theism" and all a bad thing. The historical account that will fill most of this book challenges that assumption, claiming that we can even derive resources for correcting some of the errors of modernity by learning from some earlier theology. But what about current claimants to "postmodern" status among theologians? Have they already solved the problems? The rest of this chapter will argue that several of the most prominent strategies in fact continue some of the problematic features of modern theology. Process theology, for instance, offers a good example of continuing the seventeenth-century project of trying to get clear on the categories we use to speak of God, to subject the divine to the structures of human reason, and thereby, I believe, to domesticate the transcendent. Various forms of theological functionalism also domesticate God by explicitly seeking to design God to serve our purposes—just the sort of idolatry that most directly contrasts with a full respect for divine mystery. The a/theology of Mark C. Taylor, in contrast, provides a case of a self-consciously "postmodern" theology that seeks to honor the radical otherness of the divine. But, in continuity with theological trends that began in the seventeenth century, Taylor has little to say about revelation or grace, and therefore, I will argue, his respect for the transcendent risks leaving him with nothing to say about God at all.

For two or three generations now, process theology has posed one of the strongest intellectual challenges to what process theologians generally call "classical theism."[11] David Ray Griffin has, in numerous books and articles, recently been pressing the claim of process thought to represent the authentic

---

11. It is worth noting in passing Langdon Gilkey's remark that, "What process philosophers of religion call 'classical theism' is a strange hodgepodge that bears little historical scrutiny." Langdon Gilkey, "A Theology in Process: Schubert Ogden's Developing Theology," *Interpretation* 21 (1967): 449.

voice of "postmodern theology."[12] Griffin and others contrast their view with
the classical model in which "all creative power belongs to God alone.
Whether the world has any power depends on God's will. . . . Even if the world
does have such power, God is free to interrupt this power or cancel out its effects at any time." On their process model, the universe is a more collaborative affair: "Creative power inherently belongs to the realm of finite existents
as well as to God. . . . God is not an eternal being to whom the basic principles of existence do not apply, and who can, therefore, interrupt the causal
processes of the world at will. God is more the soul of the universe."[13] God
works by persuasion rather than coercion, and one can specify the sorts of
things such a God can and cannot do.

Its adherents claim both moral and intellectual advantages for the process
model. Morally, they argue, the classical model pictures God as a distant tyrant,
defined in terms of absolute power and ultimately inconsistent with Christian
affirmations about God's love and tender care.[14] Moreover, "The traditional
concept of God is in many ways stereotypically masculine. God was conceived
to be active, unresponsive, impassive, inflexible, impatient, and moralistic. . . .
This has led to a one-sided and hence unhealthy Christianity,"[15] whereas the
process model, according to its advocates, shares insights to be learned from
contemporary feminism.[16] On the classical model at its most consistent, Griffin maintains, "the idea of 'cooperating' with God" is "the worst sin, because
it denies that God has already done everything for us." Thus it fosters no forms
of spiritual discipline, and those in search of such disciplines today have found
themselves turning from Christianity to Eastern traditions.[17]

Even more seriously, in Schubert Ogden's words, "as some three hundred
years of careful criticism have shown, the main assertions of classical theists are
utterly incapable of satisfying" basic conditions of "logical self-consistency."[18]
If God is omnipotent in the way that classical theism describes, how can

12. Griffin argues that deconstructionists and others more usually identified with postmodernism
in fact press characteristic modern premises to their logical conclusions and thus might better be
called "ultramodernism," while the process picture of naturalistic theism, nonsensationalist em-
piricism, and a nonmechanistic, nondualistic view of nature marks a new start that has a better
claim to be postmodern. For some characteristic passages, see David Ray Griffin, *God and Religion in the Postmodern World* (Albany: State University of New York Press, 1989), x, 4–5; "Liberation Theology and Postmodern Philosophy: A Response to Cornel West," in David Ray Griffin,
Varieties of Postmodern Theology (Albany: State University of New York Press, 1989), 143–44.
13. David Ray Griffin, "Postmodern Theology and A/Theology: A Response to Mark C. Taylor,"
in Griffin, *Varieties of Postmodern Theology*, 48.
14. See Schubert Ogden, *The Reality of God* (New York: Harper & Row, 1966), 18; Alfred North
Whitehead, *Process and Reality* (New York: Free Press, 1969), 404.
15. John B. Cobb, Jr., and David Ray Griffin, *Process Theology: An Introductory Exposition*
(Philadelphia: Westminster Press, 1976), 61.
16. See for instance Marjorie Hewitt Suchocki, "God, Sexism, and Transformation," in Rebecca
S. Chopp and Mark Lewis Taylor, eds., *Reconstructing Christian Theology* (Minneapolis: Fortress
Press, 1994), 27–30.
17. Griffin, *God and Religion in the Postmodern World,* 116.
18. Ogden, *The Reality of God,* 17.

human beings (or any other creatures) have freedom? If God has such power and is good, why is there evil? Classical theists have had centuries to solve such problems, and they have failed; it is time to look for something better.

David Griffin admits that "adequacy to the facts of experience is a greater virtue than logical consistency." Therefore theologies that affirm the existence of evil and admit they cannot reconcile it with their claims about God are preferable to those that try to deny that evil exists. But living with inconsistency is "a drastic step," and it would be better to find a way of avoiding it.[19] One can, in a pinch, live with saying, "P and not P, which must fit together in some way that I cannot understand," if there are compelling reasons for saying both P and not P. But if P is "God exists," then people today, Griffin claims, do not have sufficiently compelling reasons for affirming it in the face of logical difficulties:

> Throughout most of Christian history in Europe (roughly the fourth to the eighteenth centuries), the cultural situation was such that the reality of God seemed overwhelmingly obvious to most people. . . . In such a situation the theologian could simply appeal to "mystery" without defaulting on the theological task. . . . But in our day, all of this has changed.[20]

If we lack a good enough argument for the existence of the God of traditional theism or a cultural context in which the existence of that God seems so self-evident as to need no argument, then, since there have to be very good reasons for living with inconsistencies, the conceptual problems that classical theism faces count as decisive reasons for rejecting it.[21]

Process thinkers thus tend to define the issues in terms of a debate between rival metaphysical systems, with the utterly transcendent, omnipotent God of classical theism set against the more immanent, collaborative God of process thought, who is (for Whitehead) an actual occasion or (for Hartshorne, Ogden, Cobb, and Griffin) a society of actual occasions, but at any rate one of the things in the world in genuine interaction with the others. They tend to assume that all reasons for belief in God have to be publicly accessible. But I have suggested already, and will argue in more detail in later chapters, that transcendence has often functioned in the Christian tradition, not to make a metaphysical proposal, but as a kind of agnosticism about certain sorts of metaphysical questions. It is not that God is transcendent and therefore distant, unrelated, and not at all immanent, but that our human categories of closeness, distance, relatedness, standoffishness, and the like radically break down when we try to apply them to God. Against certain modern metaphysi-

---

19. David Ray Griffin, *God, Power, and Evil: A Process Theodicy* (Lanham, Md.: University Press of America, 1990), 222–23.
20. David Ray Griffin, "Creation Out of Chaos and the Problem of Evil," in John B. Cobb, Jr., ed., *Encountering Evil: Live Options in Theodicy* (Atlanta: John Knox Press, 1981), 118.
21. See Griffin, *God, Power, and Evil*, 141–42, 255–56.

cians in the Christian tradition, process thinkers may be able to score points and even win the game, but many Christian thinkers before the seventeenth century would ask whether such a game was even worth playing.

Arguments so fundamental are hard to adjudicate. Griffin, for instance, says that moral goodness and the power to affect the world "are essential to the meaning of the term 'God' in our tradition," but omnipotence is not, even though "many may, because of cultural-psychological conditioning, find it difficult to worship" the nonomnipotent God defined by process theology.[22] But how do we decide what is essential to make God really God and what merely seems such because of our cultural-psychological conditioning?

The proposal this book will develop is that God is not one of the things in the world, to be analyzed and compared with categories appropriate to the other things in the world. I will try to show that proposal's internal coherence, faithfulness to the tradition, and richness in helping Christians understand their world—the only ways of arguing I know for such matters. "God does not belong to the class of existing things," John of Damascus wrote; "not that God has not existence but that God is above all existing things, no even above existence itself."[23] As Paul Tillich elaborated the point,

> The being of God cannot be understood as the existence of a being alongside others or above others. If God is a being, he is subject to the categories of finitude, especially to space and substance. Even if he is called the "highest being" in the sense of the "most perfect" and the "most powerful" being, this situation is not changed. When applied to God, superlatives become diminutives.[24]

Something we can understand and adequately account for in terms of our human categories is not God. And therefore, the deity of process thought who, in Whitehead's words, "is not to be treated as an exception to all metaphysical principles" but as "their chief exemplification" is not the God of Christian faith.[25] Transcendence that fits our categories has been domesticated. When process theologians make proposals about how much power God has, and how God interacts with other societies or actual occasions, "classical" Christian theologians will often not make counterproposals but will rather deny that we can know that much about God or fit God that clearly into *any* conceptual categories. In doing so, incidentally, they may adapt better to many characteristically "postmodern" assumptions about the fragmentariness and ambigu-

---

22. Ibid., 21, 274.

23. John of Damascus, *Exposition of the Orthodox Faith* 1.4, trans. S.D.F. Salmond, *Nicene and Post-Nicene Fathers,* 2nd ser., vol. 9 (Peabody, Mass.: Hendrickson Publishers, 1994), 4, translation altered.

24. Paul Tillich, *Systematic Theology* (Chicago: University of Chicago Press, 1951), 1:235.

25. Whitehead, *Process and Reality*, 405. I think, incidentally, that Whitehead understood that he was doing metaphysics and not doing Christian theology. He developed a metaphysical system in which creativity is the ultimate principle, and in which he used "God" as the name for one of the actual occasions in the world in which creativity works itself out.

ity of all knowledge than does the epistemological optimism of process thought.

Mark C. Taylor's a/theology, on the other hand, stands near the center of what usually gets called "postmodernism," drawing theological implications from a philosophical tradition that runs from Kierkegaard and Nietzsche through Heidegger to Derrida. Taylor has no objections to contradictions—he revels in them—and it would be hard to find a more fragmentary, oblique theological project. It is a project for which I must confess more sympathy than I can find for much of process theology. Taylor sets up "transcendence" and "immanence" as polar opposites and then searches for the subversive Other that both these categories leave out.[26] The object of his search could be that more radical alternative to "contrastive" notions of transcendence which I am claiming tended to get lost in the seventeenth century. "The Holy is Other—Wholly Other," he writes. "Philosophy's exclusion of this Other is no accident; to the contrary, philosophy constitutes itself by *not* thinking the Other."[27] "This elusive mean, disruptive limen, odd third is . . . unnameable." "Every name must be erased as soon as it is articulated. It is precisely this play of inscription and erasure that insinuates the different difference and other other that solicits the errant thinker."[28] But many theologians before the beginning of the modern era shared such a respect for divine otherness. Errant thinkers like Taylor might therefore find themselves unexpectedly joined in their wanderings by the likes of Aquinas, Luther, and Calvin.

But the story is not that simple. My sympathies often lie with Taylor when he is criticizing what he is against; I am less sure what he is *for*. He is against something that he too, alas, calls "classical theism":

> According to the tenets of classical theism, God, who is One, is the supreme Creator, who, through the mediation of His divine Logos, brings the world into being and providentially directs its course. . . . Utterly transcendent and thoroughly eternal, God is represented as totally present to Himself [*sic*]. He is, in fact, the omnipresent fount, source, ground, and uncaused cause of presence itself.[29]

"Transcendence" here functions as a metaphysical category, meaning "eternally *beyond,* always *elsewhere.*"[30] "Classical theism" labels a metaphysical system, which imposes a rational order on both thought and reality.[31] Taylor is attacking precisely the patterns of thought I will argue came to dominate Christian theology in the seventeenth century. I share his opposition to them, and so, I will argue, did many earlier Christian thinkers.

26. Mark C. Taylor, *Tears* (Albany: State University of New York Press, 1990), 79.
27. Ibid., 106.
28. Ibid., 81.
29. Mark C. Taylor, *Erring* (Chicago: University of Chicago Press, 1984), 7. The "[sic]" is Taylor's.
30. Ibid., 72.
31. Ibid., 53–54.

It is harder to know what Taylor is *for*. He celebrates a shift from *mimesis* to *poiesis*—from thinking of language as mirroring or representing some external reality to thinking of it as a creative, human construction.[32] Thus on several occasions he quotes with approval Wallace Stevens's remark, "The final belief is to believe in a fiction, which you know to be a fiction, there being nothing other. The exquisite truth is to know that it is a fiction and that you believe it willingly."[33] But he also writes:

> Poiesis becomes mimesis when the creative production of the artist imitates the creative production of God. . . . The identification of human action with divine action marks the end of theology beyond which— or the "beyond" of which—we are now called to think. This beyond is, strictly speaking, unrepresentable. . . . Insofar as constative, expressive, performative, and poetic strategies of signification remain bound to and by the structure of representation, they cannot think the strange nothing that remains to be thought after the end of theology.[34]

This passage reminds us that, if the object of our talk turns out to be something we have made for ourselves, then it is hardly the radically Other. But Taylor provides no clue of how, by human efforts, *poiesis* might become *mimesis* and the imagination reach beyond its own creations.

The celebration of *poiesis* pursued consistently, in other words, betrays Taylor's project. If our language about God is merely a story we tell, an imaginative construction, a fiction, then the otherness of the Wholly Other has disappeared. God is simply one of the artifacts of human culture, thoroughly amenable to our manipulation and control. Second Isaiah was right to ridicule the man who takes a piece of cedar, uses half of it to warm himself and cook his dinner, and makes the other half into a God (Isa. 44:15–17). Such a thoroughly domesticated God, so much the product of human effort and imagination, is an idol, one of the things we use, like the firewood on the hearth, for our human purposes, and therefore is not really God at all. But in the passages when Taylor rejects the idolatrous implications of exclusive emphasis on *poiesis,* he is left with literally nothing to say. A God who lies beyond every human grasp without qualification is a God about whom we can literally know, think, or say nothing at all. As Taylor himself admits, "Gradually—perhaps all too gradually—I am coming to suspect that the only book worth writing is the book I cannot write."[35] And neither, of course, can anyone else.

At least no human author can tell the tale for which Taylor is beginning to long. Is the key to the problem that Taylor's theology has no place for God's self-revelation? He powerfully reminds us of the futility of all human efforts to reach God, to turn God into an object. But the possibility that God, as subject,

---

32. Mark C. Taylor, *Deconstructing Theology* (Chico, Calif.: Scholars Press, 1982), 90.
33. Ibid., 81; *Tears,* 212.
34. Taylor, *Tears,* 215.
35. Mark C. Taylor, *Nots* (Chicago: University of Chicago Press, 1993), 7.

might reach toward us does not seem to arise. Taylor is a justly famous interpreter of Kierkegaard, and an odd feature of his interpretation of Kierkegaard illustrates my point. In *The Point of View for My Work as an Author,* Kierkegaard explained that he had written his pseudonymous works as a means of breaking through the defenses of his contemporaries. It doesn't work, he said, simply to occupy a Christian standpoint and lecture people on the errors of their ways. One has to begin where one's readers are and show, from the inside, as it were, the problems in their positions, the way their forms of life break down, in order to begin to create the possibility that they might hear the gospel.[36] The works published under his own name, Kierkegaard explained, represented his own views; the pseudonymous works are imaginative constructions of various other points of view.[37]

Taylor, however, discusses only the pseudonymous works (and the passages in the *Journals* that serve as preliminaries for them), and he regularly attributes their conclusions to "Kierkegaard."[38] He finds a dark and enigmatic theology indeed: "Indirect communication says the unsayable in and through the *failure* of language. The 'name' of this failure is the unnameable and the pseudonym of the unnameable is 'God.'"[39] But Kierkegaard's point was that, from outside Christian faith, it does look incomprehensible—the pseudonymous authors like Johannes de Silentio keep telling us they cannot understand. But to one addressed by God, who has encountered God's grace—someone like Søren Kierkegaard—Christian faith *does* make sense. That, however, is a voice Taylor does not let us hear "Kierkegaard" speak. The resulting interpretation can get perverse:

> Throughout this pseudonymous authorship, Kierkegaard refuses to speak in his own name; he always writes as an other. Never identifying with any of his personae, the author forever withdraws, thereby allowing an other Other to "speak" by *not* speaking. Kierkegaard's aesthetic education does not reveal the presence of the divine here and now but stages an unrepresentable retreat that leaves everyone gaping.[40]

Well, yes, one wants to say—in the *pseudonymous* authorship Kierkegaard (tautologously) does not speak in his own name. But there are also numerous

---

36. Søren Kierkegaard, *The Point of View for My Work as an Author,* trans. Walter Lowrie (London: Oxford University Press, 1939), 27–29.

37. Ibid., 12.

38. See the discussion of *Fear and Trembling* in Mark C. Taylor, *Altarity* (Chicago: University of Chicago Press, 1987): "Kierkegaard maintains . . ." (p. 345), "Kierkegaard insists . . ." (p. 347), ". . . according to Kierkegaard . . ." (p. 348). In *Nots* Taylor is more careful: "Kierkegaard, or more precisely his pseudonym, Johannes de Silentio . . ." (p. 76), "Johannes de Silentio insists . . ." (p. 79).

39. Mark C. Taylor, *Disfiguring: Art, Architecture, Religion* (Chicago: University of Chicago Press, 1992), 314.

40. Taylor, *Nots,* 80.

nonpseudonymous books, and there is even one book (*The Point of View*) that explains that they represent Kierkegaard's own position. Why ignore them?[41]

The issue reaches beyond Taylor's interpretation of Kierkegaard. He is heroically attempting a theology that fully acknowledges the radical otherness of God, the inaccessibility of God from the human side, but lacks revelation or grace from God's side. He is left, like Kierkegaard's pseudonym Johannes de Silentio, who cannot understand Abraham, with silence—if sometimes with the pretense that silence, surrounded with enough paradoxes, can speak.[42]

Still, Taylor stands out among contemporary theologians for his respect for God's otherness. He may end up with nothing at all, but he has generally resisted making an idol. Many of his contemporaries have been less cautious. Gordon Kaufman, because of the clarity of his position, provides a good example. Opposition to idolatry would seem to lie at the heart of Kaufman's theological method. "God is never available to us as an object we can directly inspect and examine," he insists.[43] Indeed, to cling to *any* particular symbol, name, story, or image as necessary to talk about God is a form of idolatry.[44] "To the extent that we try significantly to control this mystery—for example, through particularly favored theological ideas or religious practices—we become idolators who *sin* against God."[45] Therefore, we should choose what we say about God in terms of its "function," its usefulness to our best purposes of encouraging human flourishing and the flourishing of everything in the world around us.[46]

> Theology also serves human purposes and needs and should be judged in terms of the adequacy with which it is fulfilling the objectives we humans have set for it. "The sabbath was made for man," Jesus said, "not man for the sabbath" (Mark 2:27). That is, all religious institutions, practices and ideas—including the idea of God—were made to serve human needs and to further our humanization.[47]

humaine intent ≠ self-serving

41. Taylor offers an analogous interpretation of Karl Barth as advocating an "essentially other-wordly" salvation and a radical picture of transcendence that finally leads to nihilism. Taylor, *Disfiguring*, 316. It is the odd construction of what Barth's theology would be if it contained no Christology.

42. I am fascinated by the following passage: "Anselm's address *to* God is an appeal to be addressed *by* God. The efficacy of Anselm's language in relation to both self and others presupposes an intervention from 'beyond' that takes place through the discourse of an Other. For Anselm, the name of this Other is, of course, God. But the name 'God' is a strange name. As the condition of the possibility of the efficacy of language, God, whose discourse is always the discourse of the Other, eludes the very linguistic structures he, she, or it nonetheless makes possible. To address this Other is always already *to be addressed by* the Other. The form of address in which the Other approaches is prayer." Taylor, *Nots*, 23.

This sounds pretty much right to me, but it also sounds like the beginning of a theology different from what Taylor has yet developed.

43. Gordon Kaufman, *In Face of Mystery* (Cambridge, Mass.: Harvard University Press, 1993), 28.

44. Ibid., 43.

45. Ibid., 355.

46. Ibid.

47. Gordon Kaufman, *The Theological Imagination: Constructing the Concept of God* (Philadelphia: Westminster Press, 1981), 264.

If Kaufman wants us to design our thinking about God to serve our human purposes and needs, however, how can that not leave us with a God who is the product of our manipulation?

Consider Kaufman's critique of transcendence. Sometimes, he says, "transcendence" means "God's radical otherness from all creatures," with a "sharp dualism between God and the world."[48] But such a view is harmful. It assigns positive value to domination and oppression; it has fostered destructive attitudes toward the environment and encouraged oppression. If God's greatness lies in God's unassailable distance and power over others, and we should try to be like God, then disastrous consequences will follow.[49] In contrast to this dangerous interpretation,

> the notion of transcendence is sometimes developed with an extreme emphasis on God's mysteriousness and unknowability, God's wholly otherness. This sort of interpretation . . . has had the consequence for many of reducing God to a completely unknown "X," the ultimate Mystery which bounds all experience and knowledge but which we can never grasp or understand. Such a totally distant God, one emptied of all content and meaning, eventually becomes perceived, however, as one essentially irrelevant to the day-to-day concerns of human life, and thus one which can safely be ignored or neglected.[50]

If the first interpretation of transcendence Kaufman cites sounds like the pattern I am arguing grew prominent in the seventeenth century ("contrastive transcendence"), then the second has features in common with the earlier view I am seeking to recover—or with Mark C. Taylor. Like Taylor, but unlike the premodern views of interest to me, however, Kaufman's own alternative offers no revelatory move from God to us. Identifying any such divine initiative would, for him, constitute idolatry, since it would identify something particular as distinctively the revelation of God.[51] Therefore, oddly, he has to fall back on human moves toward God for human purposes. If Taylor reduces us to silence, then Kaufman uses the images and stories he finds humanly useful—which seems to me a worse form of idolatry, of bringing the divine under our control, than what he seeks to avoid. Yet such theological functionalism has grown so widespread that in some quarters it grows hard to explain that there might be an alternative to it.[52]

Indeed, I have singled Kaufman out for discussion simply because he is

---

48. Kaufman, *In Face of Mystery,* 303.
49. Ibid., 305.
50. Ibid., 315.
51. "If the story of Jesus . . . provides significant insight and orientation for today's human life and problems, christology can and should continue to have an important place in our theological reflection and our religious devotion; if not, it should be allowed to fall away." Ibid., 382.
52. For classic critiques, see H. Richard Niebuhr, "Utilitarian Christianity," *Christianity and Crisis* 6 (8 July 1946): 3–5; and George Hunsinger, "Where the Battle Rages: Confessing Christ in America Today," *Dialog* 26 (fall 1987): 264–74.

characteristically clear and honest about his functionalism. The theological world seems full of functionalists these days, and the attraction is easy to understand. Most of us have causes we believe in with some passion. We would like to think that God is on our side. It is therefore tempting if we are told that we can design God to fit our specifications.

If the causes in which we believe concern struggles against oppression, then the effort to get God on our side may be particularly tempting. In the current political climate, for one thing, such struggles need all the help they can get. And the biblical witness provides some considerable warrant for claiming that God *is* on the side of the struggle against oppression. My own conviction is that Christians engaged in the search for justice ought to pursue those biblical warrants, with all their ambiguities, rather than falling victim to theological functionalism. In wrestling with scripture, we have to deal with many hard sayings and much that rightly makes us deeply uncomfortable or angry. But we also find a resource that can challenge the dominant values of our age, which are often in desperate need of challenging. Functionalism opens the door to idolatry, and the dominant idols are, in the end, those of the powerful. If we let human beings design God, then the socially dominant result will not be a deity fitted to the needs of the oppressed of the world.

On the other hand, it is too easy for more conservative Christians to fulminate against the functionalist strategies they perceive among feminists or other theologians of liberation. "Those people," they say, are distorting the gospel to serve their own agendas—as if the God of American nationalism or free-market capitalism or male hegemony were not at least as much the product of theological functionalism and therefore equally a form of idolatry.

It is disappointing that the very interesting projects of "French feminism" often turn, in theology, to rehashes of Feuerbach and Freud. What begin as fascinating reflections on the "other" sometimes turn into the conclusion that women ought to construct divinities in their own image. This may be fair return for men's having done the same, but it seems to lose the otherness of the other that was putatively at the heart of the project. See Luce Irigaray, *This Sex Which Is Not One*, trans. Catherine Porter (Ithaca, N.Y.: Cornell University Press, 1985), 77–78, 97. For critiques like my own, see Cleo McNelly Kearns, "Kristeva and Feminist Theology," in C. W. Maggie Kim, Susan M. St. Ville, and Susan M. Simonaitis, eds., *Transfigurations: Theology and the French Feminists* (Minneapolis: Fortress Press, 1993), 71, and especially Serene Jones, "This God Which Is Not One," in *Transfigurations*, 125, 137–38.

Some feminists, influenced by process thought or deconstructionism, engage in attacks on the overemphasis on transcendence or binary thinking they identify with more traditional theology. See, for instance, Sallie McFague, *Models of God* (Philadelphia: Fortress Press, 1987), 62–67; Marjorie Hewitt Suchocki, "God, Sexism, and Transformation," 40–42; Julia Kristeva, "Women's Time," trans. Alice Jardine and Harry Blake, in *The Kristeva Reader*, ed. Toril Moi (New York: Columbia University Press, 1986), 209. Here I would be more sympathetic, but would argue that the real enemy is often themes that came in with modernity.

I have rarely addressed feminist issues directly in this book, in part out of a conviction that in debates over feminism men often need to do less talking and more listening. To the extent that I can make a contribution, as one sympathetic to many of the goals of some feminists, it is perhaps to raise objections to the work of (male) theologians on which some feminists have heavily depended in their work, and invite them to think of looking for alternative theological allies.

We have to try to hear God speak to us, if we are to escape worshiping an idol. That means we cannot simply fit God in as one component of our intellectual systems, or think only of a God who fits our categories and purposes. But we cannot climb to heaven on a pile of negatives and paradoxes either. God has to come to us, and, when that happens and we manage to notice, we will find all our intellectual, moral, and social orders mightily upset. Christians have always, in one degree or another, failed to notice God's initiatives toward the world, sought to move to God under their own power, and thereby fallen into idolatry. But certain ways of doing so became more pervasive, I believe, in the seventeenth century, as an earlier sense of the divine mystery, the wonder of grace, and the inadequacy of all human talk about God tended to get lost. How that happened is the story I want to tell in hopes that we might learn from those mistakes.

good summary paragraph

Part 1

Three Premodern Theologies

2   Aquinas on the Unknowable God

A few pages into his massive *Summa Theologiae,* in the preface to question 3 of part 1, Thomas Aquinas stated, "Now we cannot know what God is, but only what He is not; we must therefore consider the ways in which God does not exist rather than the ways in which he does."[1] This seems a very odd thing for Aquinas to say. After all, he is nearly everyone's favorite example of "classical theism." We know about Aquinas, or think we do: in question 2 of the *Summa,* he proved the existence of God in five different ways, and then, beginning in question 3, he defined God's attributes—God is simple, perfect, good, infinite, immutable, and so on. The resulting picture puts a clearly defined God at the peak of a grand metaphysical hierarchy. Social historians quickly note analogies to the hierarchical structure of medieval society, and many contemporary readers have heard enough to infer that Aquinas stood for all the hierarchical, patriarchal, onto-theological thinking they most dislike.

So what can it mean when Aquinas says, "We cannot know what God is"? A great many interpreters have simply ignored the passage. This century's most vigorous critic of "classical theism," Charles Hartshorne, simply assumes that Aquinas defined God's positive attributes, and in all his discussions of Aquinas, never so much as mentions this rather dramatic denial of any such intent.[2] Frederick Copleston, an admirer of Aquinas and author of the most widely

---

1. Thomas Aquinas, *Summa Theologiae* 1a.3, pref., trans. English Dominican Fathers (London: Blackfriars, 1963–).The comment has many parallels in Aquinas. See for instance Aquinas, *On the Power of God: Quaestiones Disputatae de Potentia Dei* 7.5 ad 14, trans. English Dominican Fathers (Westminster, Md.: Newman Press, 1952); *Commentary on Boethius' "De Trinitate"* 1.2, in *The Trinity and the Unicity of the Intellect,* trans. Rose Emmanuella Brennan (St. Louis: B. Herder Book Co., 1946), 29; *Summa Contra Gentiles: On the Truth of the Catholic Faith* 1.14.2, trans. Anton C. Pegis (Garden City, N.Y.: Hanover House, 1955). "The better we know God the more we understand that he surpasses whatever the mind grasps." *Summa Theologiae* 2a2ae.8.7.
The reading of Aquinas presented in this chapter may represent the most controversial part of this book, but it would be hard at this point to give a noncontroversial reading in Aquinas. I have resisted carrying on a running argument with alternative interpretations but tried to document my own with some care. I am persuaded enough by Michel Corbin's arguments for development in Thomas's thoughts that I have tried to support the key points with evidence from the last period of life, when he was writing the *Summa Theologiae.* (See Michel Corbin, *Le Chemin de la Théologie chez Thomas D'Aquin* [Paris: Beauchesne, 1972].) My debts especially to the work of Victor Preller and David Burrell for pointing me in the right directions go far beyond what these notes indicate. I have also benefitted from conversations with Bruce Marshall and J. A. DiNoia and from the opportunity to read in manuscript Eugene F. Rogers, Jr., *Thomas Aquinas and Karl Barth: Sacred Doctrine and the Natural Knowledge of God* (Notre Dame, Ind.: University of Notre Dame Press, 1995).
2. At least David Burrell reports he has never been able to find such a reference. David B. Burrell, *Aquinas: God and Action* (Notre Dame, Ind.: University of Notre Dame Press, 1979), 80.

respected recent history of philosophy, reviews what he takes to be Aquinas's account of God's attributes and concludes, "Obviously we have here a hierarchic conception of the universe, ranging, if one may so express it . . . up to God . . . at the top."[3]

The Attributes and Existence of God

Suppose, however, that Aquinas, a remarkably careful writer, meant what he said. Question 3, from whose introduction this puzzling passage comes, discusses the "simplicity" of God. On most interpretations, it considers the first of a series of divine attributes. This adds another puzzle, for "simple" is hardly the first thing most of us would think of if we were listing the properties we think God possesses. For Aquinas's project, however, saying that God is "simple" does constitute a good starting point, for reflecting on simplicity offers a good way of introducing a range of things we *cannot* say about God—just what Aquinas promised he would be doing.[4] Most of the articles of question 3 thus actually work through a list of the ways in which we ordinarily understand things, and conclude that none of them works when applied to God.

I might, for instance, ordinarily think about something by distinguishing its component parts. A carburetor has a tube through which air flows, and a jet that sprays fuel into it. But God, as simple, has no component parts, so we cannot understand God in that way. Again, I might understand the carburetor in terms of its form and matter: take some tempered steel and shape it into a large tube with a small jet entering it. But, Aquinas says, God is not "composed of" form and matter, since God is not a material body, so we cannot use such distinctions to understand God. I might think about my carburetor in terms of potency and act—that is, I might say something like, "Here is how you make a carburetor, and then, when you pump fuel and air through it, here is what it does." But divine simplicity, Aquinas says, does not admit of potency, so that distinction is likewise of no use. Yet again, if we had a carburetor on the table in front of us and I were trying to explain it to you, you might ask about some

---

3. F. C. Copleston, *A History of Medieval Philosophy* (London: Methuen & Co., 1972), 187. To be sure, Copleston states in a footnote, "This is, it is true, an unfortunate way of putting things," but it *is* the way he chooses to put them. Nor is Copleston alone. For instance: "According to Thomas Aquinas and his predecessors, the structure of the universe is hierarchical. At the top is God, at the bottom *materia prima,* and between them the things, each on its own level." Hampus Lyttkens, *The Analogy between God and the World* (Uppsala: Almqvist & Wiksells, 1952), 171.

4. "When applied to God, 'simple' is not primarily a metaphysical description for Aquinas, but rather a metalinguistic stipulation rooted in the conviction of God's transcendence. It serves to qualify the application of all creaturely discourse to God, who is, so the faith maintains, the beginning and end of creatures but not himself a creature." Bruce D. Marshall, "Aquinas as a Postliberal Theologian," *The Thomist* 53 (July 1989): 382.

For alternative interpretations of simplicity in Aquinas, see William E. Mann, "Divine Simplicity," *Religious Studies* 18 (1982): 451–71; Peter Burns, "The Status and Function of Divine Simpleness in Summa Theologiae Ia, qq 2–13," *The Thomist* 57 (1993): 1–26.

piece sticking out of the top, and I'd reply, "Oh, that must be how it fastens to the rest of the engine. That doesn't really have anything to do with being a carburetor." In other words, I would distinguish its essence from something distinct from that essence. But this also does not work with respect to God, who has no properties distinct from the divine essence.

The list goes on. It seems that none of the ways we would ordinarily go about understanding something work with respect to God. We human beings know things "by combining and separating."[5] But composition and separation do not exist in God, and therefore any of the understandings we might have of God, it seems, will not correspond to how God really is.[6] Beginning with simplicity thus shapes the discussion of "divine attributes" that follows; in this context, they turn into reminders of the limitations and inadequacies of what we can say about God.[7] A decade or so before writing the *Summa,* Aquinas covered much of this same ground in his *Disputed Questions on the Power of God,* and concluded, "Wherefore man reaches the highest point of his knowledge about God when he knows that he knows him not, inasmuch as he knows that that which God is transcends whatsoever he conceives of him."[8]

On the other hand, Aquinas himself elsewhere admitted, "We cannot know of the existence of something without also knowing its essence in some way."[9] It seems meaningless to say, "X exists," if we can give no account whatever of what sort of thing X might be. If question 3 insists that we cannot know *what* God is, what then are we to make of the arguments in question 2 *that* God exists?

Nearly every anthology of readings from the history of philosophy includes "Aquinas's five proofs of the existence of God," a selection from question 2 of the *Summa,* often with a title and introduction that completely misinterpret the passage in at least two ways. First, the standard interpretation says that later on, in his discussions of the Trinity, Christ, and the sacraments, Aquinas was operating in the context of Christian faith, but here he was speaking as a philosopher, laying out arguments generally available to reason.[10] But in question 1 Aquinas explicitly distinguished the project in which he was engaged (which he called "sacred doctrine" and which depends on "what God has revealed") from "philosophical researches" (which are "pursued by human

---

5. Aquinas, *Summa Theologiae* 2a2ae.1.2.

6. Ibid., 1a.13.4.

7. See Burrell, *Aquinas,* 27–41, for the working out of this in detail.

8. Aquinas, *On the Power of God* 7.5 ad 14.

9. Aquinas, *Commentary on Boethius' "De Trinitate"* 6.3.

10. For instance: "The existence of God is a philosophical problem. . . . The position of a theologian on this point unavoidably consists in collecting philosophical evidence, in sifting it, in weighting it and ordering it in view of his own theological purposes. . . . On this problem . . . a theologian cannot do much more than apply to the philosophers for philosophical information." Etienne Gilson, *Elements of Christian Philosophy* (Garden City, N.Y.: Doubleday & Co., 1961), 43.

reasoning").[11] Nothing in question 2 indicates that he had suddenly switched activities back to philosophy. Indeed, he began his discussion of the "five ways" with a biblical quotation: Does God exist? "The Book of Exodus represents God as saying, 'I am who am.' "[12] Aquinas, then, was already operating in the context of Christian faith.[13]

So the famous "proofs of the existence of God" are not really "proofs," if that means exercises in reason outside the context of faith—and neither are they really "of the existence of God." There is change in the world, Aquinas said in the first "way," and

> anything in process of change must be changed by something else.
> . . . Now we must stop somewhere, otherwise there will be no first
> cause of the change, and, as a result, no subsequent causes. . . . Hence
> one is bound to arrive at some first cause of change, not itself changed
> by anything, and this is what everybody understands by God.[14]

Similar arguments then appeal to (2) the series of efficient causes, (3) the contrast between contingent and necessary things, (4) the gradations found in things, and (5) the series of final causes. In every case the argument concludes with a similarly odd phrase: "to which everyone gives the name 'God,' " or "and this we call 'God.' " Aquinas could have said, "And therefore God exists," but he never did.

For one thing, as David Hume would point out centuries later, the conclusions of such arguments fall well short of what religious folk mean by God.[15] Assume that the world as we know it implies some intelligent designer and governor; the evidence surely falls far short of showing that designer to be perfect. Indeed, on the face of it, one might think that the world looks like the product of a rather unskilled architect; just looking around us, most of us tend to think that we could find room for improvement. Similarly, perhaps the world we see requires a powerful something-or-other to get it moving, but the evidence need not imply that that first mover is actually infinite. And so on. Aquinas already knew this. The effects we see, he admitted, are not adequate to the power of their cause "so that one could arrive at a knowledge of the quiddity of the cause."[16] He acknowledged that in some weak sense, "practi-

11. Aquinas, *Summa Theologiae* 1a.1.1.

12. Ibid., 1a.2.3.

13. Otto Pesch at one point worried about a "falling back" into philosophy in question 2. Otto Hermann Pesch, *Theologie der Rechtfertigung bei Martin Luther und Thomas von Aquin* (Mainz: Matthias Grünewald Verlag, 1967), 865. But he elsewhere concluded that this whole section represented "the judgment of the Christian faith concerning the results of the philosophical efforts." Otto Hermann Pesch, *The God Question in Thomas Aquinas and Martin Luther,* trans. Gottfried G. Kordel (Philadelphia: Fortress Press, 1972), 7.

14. Aquinas, *Summa Theologiae* 1a.2.3.

15. David Hume, *Dialogues concerning Natural Religion,* part 5, *David Hume on Religion* (Cleveland: Meridian Books, 1963), 139.

16. Aquinas, *Commentary on Boethius' "De Trinitate"* 6.3.

cally all" people have "a common and confused knowledge of God," since they "see that things in nature run according to a definite order" and "perceive in most cases that there is some orderer" of things that have an order. But this is not really to have knowledge of God, since they do not know "who or what kind of being, or whether there is but one orderer of nature."[17] Even if arguments such as these get us somewhere, they do not get us to God.

Nor is it obvious that they all get us to the same place. The first "way" roughly paraphrases Aristotle, who used the argument that a series of movers must have a first member to argue for the existence of an "unmoved mover." But Aristotle's God, that "unmoved mover," was utterly indifferent to the world—Aristotle thought that knowing about the world would get God caught up in change and imperfection.[18] Aquinas's fifth "way," by contrast, implies a designer and governor who watches over and guides the world. The fourth "way," with its references to gradations of perfections, sounds more Platonic than Aristotelian, and Aquinas seems unconcerned about how to fit together this jumble of philosophical contexts.[19] Elsewhere in the *Summa*, moreover, Aquinas acknowledged that reason cannot prove that the world is not eternal; only explicitly theological arguments establish that it was created at a point in time.[20] So it seems that, just on the basis of arguments about movers and efficient causes, there *could* be an infinite series, and there is no reason to posit a first.[21]

So what is going on here? Is the collection of arguments just badly confused? Or was Aquinas engaged in a different sort of project? Victor Preller makes a persuasive case for the latter explanation:

---

17. Aquinas, *Summa Contra Gentiles* 3.38.1. Nicholas Wolterstorff notes how close this is to Calvin's view. Nicholas Wolterstorff, "The Migration of the Theistic Arguments: From Natural Theology to Evidentialist Apologetics," in *Rationality, Religious Belief, and Moral Commitment,* ed. Robert Audi and William J. Wainwright (Ithaca, N.Y.: Cornell University Press, 1986), 58.

18. Aristotle, *Metaphysics* 12.9.15–34, trans. W. D. Ross, in *The Basic Works of Aristotle,* ed. Richard McKeon (New York: Random House, 1941).

19. The fourth way also seems to assume that God is the highest instance in a general class of existent and good things, just as fire is the highest in a general class of hot things. But God, Aquinas elsewhere insists, is not a member of any general class. See Victor Preller, *Divine Science and the Science of God* (Princeton: Princeton University Press, 1967), 133.

20. Aquinas, *Summa Theologiae* 1a.46.2.

21. The standard reply to this objection is to say that Aquinas was here arguing the impossibility of an infinite series of *presently existing* causes, not an infinite series running back into the past. So a machine in which gear A is turned by gear B, which in turn is turned by gear C and so on, could not have an *infinite* series of gears turning each other with no initial source of motion. See for instance Reginald Garrigou-Lagrange, *God: His Existence and His Nature,* trans. Bede Rose (St. Louis: B. Herder Book Co., 1949), 264–65; F. C. Copleston, *Aquinas* (Baltimore: Penguin Books, 1955), 118–19. But Victor Preller points out that such an argument implies that no created thing could itself be a cause of motion, that, in other words, all created things are passive. And this Aquinas elsewhere denies. See Aquinas, *Commentary on Aristotle's "Physics"* 8.22.1163, trans. Richard J. Blackwell, Richard J. Spath, and W. Edmund Thirlkel (New Haven: Yale University Press, 1973), and Preller, *Divine Science and the Science of God,* 109–13.

For Aquinas to say, "There are five ways in which the existence of God may be demonstrated," is not for him to say, "There are five ways in which *I* can demonstrate, on the basis of *my* philosophy, that God exists." It is merely to say that there are five ways in which philosophers have traditionally proved the existence of God. It happens to be the case . . . that the *rationes* [reasons] on which the five *viae* [ways] are based are mutually inconsistent. . . . It happens further to be the case that none of the five ways as they now stand is compatible with Aquinas' understanding of the logic of "God." Such an observation would not disturb Aquinas in the least. The theological point that he wishes to make is that the mind of man is ordered to its Creator as to One Unknown. Aquinas expects to find indications of that ordering in all philosophical traditions.[22]

So Aquinas's claim runs roughly like this: From the standpoint of Christian faith (which is where he began) one of the things we can notice is that in a variety of ways human efforts to make sense of the world in its own terms break down. If we try to make sense of the things we encounter in experience, and understand what makes them all run, or why they should exist at all, or what the ultimate perfection of the things we value would be, or how the world seems to work according to some purpose, we always find we have unanswered questions left over.[23] The project of understanding the world in its own terms remains always frustratingly incomplete; once we have seen what there was to see and understood what there was to understand about the world, we are left still puzzled. And it happens to be the case that various people, realizing this limitation of reason's project of understanding the world in its own terms, have given the name "God" to that "beginning and end of all things"[24] toward which reason puzzledly and unsuccessfully reaches without ever grasping.

To say this is not, however, to make "God" the name for the culmination of a metaphysical system. It is much more nearly to use the name "God" as a reminder that metaphysical systems cannot have culminations. As Aquinas put it, from the standpoint of faith,

> God as an unknown is said to be the terminus of our knowledge in the following respect: that the mind is found to be most perfectly in pos-

22. Preller, *Divine Science and the Science of God,* 24–25.

23. "Yet others arrived at a knowledge of God from the incomprehensibility of truth." Aquinas, *Commentary on the Gospel of St. John,* prologue, trans. James A. Weisheipl and Fabian R. Larcher (Albany, N.Y.: Magi Books, 1980), 24.

24. Aquinas, *Summa Theologiae* 1a.2 pref.

25. Aquinas, *Commentary on Boethius' "De Trinitate"* 1.2 ad 1. "The God at whom we would have arrived by tracing back the causal regress would be a God far too closely tied to his creation to satisfy Christian demands for this 'otherness' or transcendence. . . . Paul Tillich is perfectly right when he says that that Cosmological Argument degrades God to the level of the world itself. . . . [it] finds a place for God as the one who completes the world's pattern: he is the missing piece of the cosmic jigsaw—a crucial piece no doubt, but not so utterly different from all the other pieces as piety requires him to be." Ronald W. Hepburn, *Christianity and Paradox* (New York: Pegasus, 1958), 166–67. I am agreeing with Hepburn and adding (as he would not) that in that sense Aquinas is not offering a "cosmological argument."

> session of the knowledge of God when it is recognized that His essence is above everything that the mind is capable of apprehending in this life.[25]

In this life, as Aquinas wrote later, "revelation does not tell us what God is, and thus joins us to him as to an unknown."[26]

Analogy

Can we therefore say anything at all about this Unknown? If not, then what does it even mean to say that it or she or he exists? Aquinas, as already noted, used "simplicity" to fence off what lies beyond our capacity to understand, as a reminder of all the normal strategies for understanding that do not work in this case. By his time philosophers and theologians had already been thinking a good bit about what one can say and not say about the utterly simple. Most concluded that a plurality of *negative* attributes or of certain kinds of *relational* attributes was compatible with simplicity. Thus if X is "not red," "not white," "not a football," and so on, those negative attributes need not in themselves introduce complexity into X. A single simple thing can "not be" a whole list of things. Similarly, if I am thinking about X, if X appears in several books as a philosophical example, and so on, then X could still be utterly simple. These relational attributes would not of themselves introduce complexity into it. If, however, X has a plurality of *positive, nonrelational* attributes (X is white *and* tall *and . . .*), then it is hard to see how we could continue to think of X as utterly "simple."[27] And, if X is not simple, then even if X is the Unknown that is "the beginning and end of all things," it would turn out we could use some of our usual categories and conceptual strategies to understand it.

Predecessors of Aquinas had picked up both possible alternatives as a way of preserving God's simplicity. A century before, Moses Maimonides had pro- *apodictic* posed that all the predicates we attribute to God are in fact negative. Thus to say that God is "living" is only to say that God is not lifeless, to say God is "wise" is only to say that God is not foolish, and so on. Maimonides's contemporary Alan of Lille had tried to make all the predicates of God relational: *relational* if God is "living," that means only that God is the cause of life; if God is "wise," that means only that God is the cause of wisdom. Neither says anything about what or how God is.[28] Either strategy could preserve God's simplicity. While using "God" simply as a name to point toward that which, beyond the world of our experience, somehow accounts for the origin and structure of that

---

26. Aquinas, *Summa Theologiae* 1a.12.13 ad 1.
27. See Marilyn McCord Adams, *William Ockham* (Notre Dame, Ind.: University of Notre Dame Press, 1987), 2.910.
28. David B. Burrell, *Exercises in Religious Understanding* (Notre Dame, Ind.: University of Notre Dame Press, 1974), 131.

world, either strategy would preserve our inability in any sense to grasp God through our understanding.

Aquinas, however, developed a position more complex than either of these proposals. Against Maimonides, he argued that, if all God's predicates are negative, then "no reason could be given why one name is assigned to God rather than another." If "living" just means "not dead," then why not say God is "short," meaning "not tall," or "tall," meaning "not short," or even "dead," meaning "not living"?[29] Against a position like Alan of Lille's he denied that we can *simply* say that "God is X" means "God is the cause of X," with no implications at all about what God is actually like. Both views, Aquinas thought, broke too radically with what religious people mean when they talk about God. "This is not what people want to say when they talk about God. When a man speaks of the 'living God' he does not simply want to say that God is the cause of our life, or that he differs from a lifeless body."[30]

To be sure, some of the things we say about God only express what God is not: *immutability* means that God does not change, *infinity* means that nothing we say can limit God, *simplicity* means that there is no sense in which God is complex. Even *unity* "adds nothing real to any existent being, but simply denies division of it."[31] Still, Aquinas thought that it fails to be honest to "God-talk" if we try to explain all of it in purely negative terms.

As an alternative, he introduced a famous distinction between *univocal, equivocal,* and *analogical* predication. Two things are said *univocally* if we mean the same thing in both cases. If I say that the Sears Tower is tall and that the Empire State Building is tall, then, while the two structures are different in other ways, and one may be taller than the other, I mean the same thing by "tall" both times. By contrast, two usages are *equivocal* if they simply happen to use the same word for completely different meanings. I refer to the "bark" of a tree and the "bark" of a dog, but there is no mysterious relation between the two kinds of "bark." The use of the same word is pure accident. *Analogical* prediction lies somewhere in between the other two classes. Aquinas's example was that we speak of a person as "healthy," a diet as "healthy," and urine as "healthy." These are not just different examples of "health" used in the same sense, even in quite different degrees. It would make no sense to ask if my fruit-and-bran-muffin breakfast is more healthy or less healthy than I am—it is healthy in a quite different way. Yet it is not just arbitrary that we use the same word in both cases, as it was with the two kinds of bark. A healthy diet helps cause a person's health; a healthy urine is a sign of it, and therefore these uses of "healthy" are somehow related.[32] But can we clarify that "somehow"? Aquinas was cautious.

---

29. Aquinas, *Summa Theologiae* 1a.13.2. I am extrapolating from Aquinas's own example, which is: Why not say that God is "a body," meaning not merely potential, the way Aristotle's primary matter is? See Adams, *William Ockham*, 2:911.

30. Aquinas, *Summa Theologiae* 1a.13.2.

31. Ibid., 1a.11.1.

32. See ibid., 1a.13.10. The Blackfriars translation cleans up Aquinas here; the English replaces "urine" with "complexion."

"Aquinas," David Burrell has written, "is perhaps best known for his theory of analogy. On closer inspection it turns out that he never had one."[33] If "theory of analogy" means that Aquinas offered an account that enables us to understand what predicates mean when applied to God, then he did not offer such a theory. Notice, first of all, that in his example "health" in the sense in which a diet is healthy is not roughly like "health" in the sense in which a person is healthy, the way viciousness in a dog is roughly like viciousness in a person. If I knew what "vicious" meant as applied to a person, I would have a rough idea about the character of a vicious dog, even if I had no idea what the word "dog" meant—a snarling, hostile something-or-other. But suppose I came from some planet where the inhabitants do not need to eat or drink, though they do from time to time get sick. I could understand what it meant for earthlings to be healthy, drawing on my own experience of health and its absence. But at the notion of a "healthy diet," I would be stumped. I would not understand the concept of "diet," let alone its relation to human health. If a more experienced space traveler offered to explain, I would ask, "You mean this diet-thing, whatever it is, grows more active, feels better, becomes likely to live longer, and that's what you mean by saying it's 'healthy'?" "No," the reply would come, " 'healthy,' as applied to a diet, doesn't mean that sort of thing at all." "So this is just equivocation?" "No, there is a connection, but since I've failed to explain to you how it works that these humans eat food, you don't understand the relation of a diet to one's well-being, and so I really can't explain what that connection is."

Similarly, one might say—and Aquinas did say—that the use of words like "wise" and "good" of both God and things in the world is not just arbitrary, as equivocal use would be. But it is not that God is wise like Einstein and good like Gandhi, only more so. While the predicates we apply to God are somehow connected to the way we use the same words of other things, we cannot understand what the connection is. To use Aquinas's terms, whose importance Victor Preller and George Lindbeck have emphasized, there is some connection between the "thing signified" in our experience and the "thing signified" in God. If we understood God, we would realize the appropriateness of using a term like "wise" of God. Indeed, "wise" would then seem *most* appropriately used of God, with every human application but a pale reflection. But, situated as we are, we cannot understand the "mode of signifying" that any term has as applied to God, and hence we simply cannot imagine how such terms would turn out to be appropriate.[34]

Someone might object that this argument has made the issue too difficult. After all, we have lots of experience of one thing causing another. Even our

33. Burrell, *Aquinas*, 55.
34. Aquinas, *Summa Theologiae* 1a.13.3; *Summa Contra Gentiles* 1.30.2. See Preller, *Divine Science and the Science of God*, 173; George A. Lindbeck, *The Nature of Doctrine: Religion and Theology in a Postliberal Age* (Philadelphia: Westminster Press, 1984), 66–67.

imaginary space traveler, without experience of digestion, presumably knows something about some forms of causation. Thus we could say to the space traveler, "Well, 'health' in respect to a diet means that a diet *causes* health in a person." And we could say of God, " 'Good' in God means that God *causes* good in the world we experience." In contrast to Alan of Lille's view, moreover, this account would claim really to tell us something about God's nature. Many of Aquinas's interpreters think that this makes things much clearer; one can even set up a series of ratios:

$$\frac{\text{cause}}{\text{effect}} = \frac{\text{God}}{\text{world}} = \frac{\text{God's good}}{\text{created good}}$$

But two problems need to be noted. First, such an abstract knowledge of causation would in any event fail to help us understand the "mode of signifying" of terms as applied to God unless we already knew more about God. I might have been told, for instance, that there is *something* in a certain sort of strong electrical current that *causes* a magnetic field, but, if I do not understand anything about electricity, this still leaves me quite in the dark about how electrical currents work. Secondly, in the case of God, Aquinas stated quite specifically that these ratios do not work. " 'To become' and 'to make,' " he insisted, "are used *equivocally* in reference to this universal production of all things and in reference to other productions."[35] That is, the way God causes the universe is not the same as, or even at all like, the way causes in the world we experience produce their effects. To take one obvious example, most of the kinds of causing we know about involve taking some raw material and doing something to it; but God, Aquinas believed, creates "out of nothing." Our causal activity follows rules already in place as to what will work and what will not. God presumably makes up the rules. To say such things ("God creates out of nothing," "God makes up the rules") is not, however, to describe the mode of God's causation but simply to indicate that it is not like any kind of causation we know anything about or can imagine. Therefore the following analogy does not help us understand how goodness applies to God, since we do not know how God functions as a cause:

$$\frac{\text{God's goodness}}{\text{creaturely goodness}} = \frac{\text{cause}}{\text{effect}}$$

We can use words of God that "simply mean certain perfections without any indication of how these perfections are possessed."[36] But, "so far as the way

---

35. Aquinas, *Commentary on Aristotle's "Physics"* 8.2.974, emphasis added.
36. Aquinas, *Summa Theologiae* 1a.13.3 ad 1.

of signifying these perfections is concerned, the words are used inappropriately [of God], for they have a way of signifying that is appropriate to creatures."[37] "Analogy" thus does not provide a neat alternative between univocity and equivocity that solves the problems. It is, Aquinas admitted, itself a type of equivocation.[38]

Aquinas used two particular devices to keep reminding us that our language never quite works when applied to God. First, in insisting on God's simplicity, he claimed that the predicates we apply to God are not distinct in God. If I say that Socrates is living and wise and good, then I mean three different (though perhaps interrelated) things; his wisdom is different from his goodness and different still from his life. But since God is simple, there cannot be such distinctions within God, and what they refer to in God must not be distinct: "Thus the different and complex concepts that we have in mind correspond to something altogether simple which they enable us imperfectly to understand."[39] Second, in our ordinary talk about the world around us, we distinguish between abstract properties, like wisdom, and their particular instantiations, like this wise person. But Aquinas uses both terms about God: he says that God is "wise" and that God is "wisdom."[40] Now that is simply not the way the word "wisdom" works in our ordinary usage—even Einstein or Socrates cannot become so wise as to become wisdom itself.

Aquinas might have tried to develop an account of what it is about God such that all God's attributes are somehow identical in God, and such that both the particular and the general term fit in the case of God. But he did not. He therefore offered, not a *metaphysical system* that would place God within our understanding of the world and specify the meaning of our language about God, but *metalinguistic rules* that remind us of the limitations of our language about God and thereby make it clear that we *cannot* place God within the world we can understand.[41] Setting rules for Christian language, he never claimed too much for what that language can tell us about God: "What it signifies in God is not confined by the meaning of our word but goes beyond it."[42]

37. Ibid., 1a.13.3.

38. Ibid., 1a.13.10 ad 4.

39. Ibid., 1a.13.4. They are not different as far as the thing is concerned (*secundum rem*) but they are different as far as the *ratio*, the way we understand them, is concerned (*secundum rationem*). Ibid., 1a.13.12. The Blackfriars translation seems to me here to make the point less clear.

40. See ibid., 1a.3.4 ad 1, for a defense of the general principle.

41. See Marshall, "Aquinas as Postliberal Theologian," 382. "The reason why no created species can represent the divine essence is plain: for nothing finite can represent the infinite as it is; but every created species is finite. . . . Further, God is his own *esse;* and therefore his wisdom and goodness and anything else are the same. But all those cannot be represented through one created thing. Therefore, the knowledge by which God is seen through creatures is not a knowledge of his essence, but a knowledge that is dark and mirrored, and from afar." Aquinas, *Commentary on the Gospel of St. John* 1:18 (no. 211).

42. Aquinas, *Summa Theologiae* 1a.13.5.

Faith

It follows that, when we try to apply our understanding to claims about God, our capacities fail. Aquinas even wanted to use a different word: we can have knowledge (*scientia*) of human things, he said, but we have wisdom (*sapientia*) with respect to divine things. Such wisdom "knows the highest cause and thereby is able to judge all relevant matters," but it rests on "faith."[43] Knowledge depends on "seeing" the truth of principles that are self-evident to us, or conclusions we can derive from them. Faith lacks this "vision," and so Aquinas could describe it as "mid-way between science and opinion."[44] But just as analogy turned out not to represent a clear category halfway between equivocity and univocity, so faith is not simply a mean between knowledge and opinion. It is like opinion in that it lacks any clear evidence to prove it— indeed, we can believe something without really understanding it—and yet it has the same kind of certainty that science has.

How can that be possible? How can we be "certain" of what we cannot "see"? Aquinas offered two related explanations, which appeal to trust in authority and to the roles of the will and of grace.[45]

First, authority: we believe things *about* God, he explained, because we believe (trust *in*) God—we accept God's authority.[46] Having made faith sound like a second-best sort of thing, lacking vision, Aquinas now turned the tables and said, "Anyone is far surer of what he hears from the infallible God than of what he sees with his own fallible reason."[47] Even with human authorities, after all, hearing an authoritative word can yield more certainty than intellectually "seeing" for myself.[48] If I have been reading about quarks, for instance, I may think I have figured out that each electron consists of three quarks, and even think I "see" why. But if a distinguished physicist had simply told me that each electron consists of three quarks, I would have been *more* confident— even if I had not been reading in such matters and did not really understand what the language meant.

> All things being equal, seeing is more certain than hearing. But if the one from whom something is heard far exceeds the sight of one who sees, then hearing is more certain than seeing. An example: a person with scant learning is far surer of something he hears from an expert than he is of any insight of his own. Thus anyone is far surer of what

43. Ibid., 2a2ae.9.2.
44. Ibid., 2a2ae.1.2.
45. Ibid., 2a2ae.2.9 ad 3.
46. Ibid., 2a2ae.2.2.
47. Ibid., 2a2ae.4.8 ad 2.
48. "Faith has a knowledge that is more like hearing than vision. Now, a man would not believe in things that are unseen but proposed to him by another man unless he thought that this other man had more perfect knowledge of these proposed things than he himself who does not see them." Aquinas, *Summa Contra Gentiles* 3.40.4.

he hears from the infallible God than of what he sees with his own fallible reason.[49]

We read the Bible, for instance, and it "makes God's will known."[50] Truth about God comes to us, on God's authority, "not to be understood, but to be believed as heard."[51]

But why do I believe that some set of words speaks with divine authority? The physicist can produce advanced degrees and a list of professional publications. The case of the Bible, or of any form of Christian witness, is more complex. Here Aquinas turned to his second point, the role of will and grace. He said that the certainty of faith comes through a will to assent: "the act of faith is . . . fixed on one alternative by reason of the will's command."[52] If I am looking at an elephant and a mouse, I do not have to *decide* to believe that the elephant is larger: I just *see* that this is the case. Believing even a Nobel Prize-winning physicist, however, involves thinking about it and making a decision to rely on this person's authority.[53]

In the case of God, faith rests ultimately on such a relationship of trust in God, but in actual practice we end up trusting in propositions—from the Bible or elsewhere—that speak of God.[54] In this case, as in other cases of faith, the truth of these propositions is not compelling simply on inspection; we have to decide to believe in them. But in this case—the crucial difference—that decision does not result from our own efforts, but comes as a gift of God's grace. Faith is thus "an act of mind assenting to the divine truth by virtue of the command of the will as this is moved by God through grace."[55] Grace transforms me into being a person of faith, such that, confronted with the authority of God, I believe it. The external element—the words I read or hear—does not suffice to generate belief; there has to be an internal cause as well. But the Pelagians were wrong, Aquinas argued, simply to identify that internal cause as human free will: "Since in assenting to the things of faith a person is raised above his own nature, he has this

---

49. Aquinas, *Summa Theologiae* 2a2ae.4.8 ad 2.

50. Ibid., 3a.1.3. See Stephan Pfürtner, *Luther and Aquinas: A Conversation,* trans. Edward Quinn (London: Darton, Longman & Todd, 1964), 49–50.

51. Aquinas, *Summa Contra Gentiles* 4.1.4.

52. Aquinas, *Summa Theologiae* 2a2ae.4.1.

53. Interestingly, Aquinas at one point asked whether you could still have faith in something, even after it had been proven. In a way, he admitted, faith would now be redundant, but, "Conclusive proofs . . . do not . . . take away from the presence of charity whereby the will is prepared to believe such matters even were they not evident." (*Summa Theologiae* 2a2ae.2.10 ad 2.) The commitment to a personal relationship would remain even if it were no longer needed as a warrant for belief.

54. "From the perspective of the reality believed in . . . the object of faith is something non-composite, i.e., the very reality about which one has faith. . . . from the perspective of the one believing . . . the object of faith is something composite in the form of a proposition." *Summa Theologiae* 2a2ae.1.2.

55. Ibid., 2a2ae.2.9.

assent from a supernatural source influencing him; this source is God. The assent of faith, which is its principal act, therefore, has as its cause God, moving us inwardly through grace."[56]

More specifically, "the revelation of mysteries" and "to teach inwardly" are both the work of the Holy Spirit.[57] When a human being "becomes a sharer in the divine Word and in the Love proceeding, so that he has at his disposal a power to know God and to love him rightly, . . . he cannot . . . come to this by his own resources; it must be given to him from above."[58] And that gift is the inner presence of the Holy Spirit, which transforms those in whom it dwells so that they can see and love in this new way.

What we thereby see and love, Aquinas believed, is God as revealed in Christ: "In other men we find many participated truths, insofar as the First Truth gleams back into their minds through many likenesses; but Christ is Truth itself."[59] It is easy to read the *Summa Theologiae* in ways that minimize the importance Christology plays in it: Aquinas's christological emphases often come in a passing phrase, and, in such a massive work, many readers simply never get to the end, where he turned explicitly to Christology. Yet his signals are clear enough. In the preface to the second question of the *Summa Theologiae*, he outlined the structure of the whole that will follow:

> So because . . . the fundamental aim of holy teaching is to make God known, not only as he is in himself but as the beginning and end of all things, and of reasoning creatures especially, we now intend to set forth this diverse teaching by teaching
>
> first, of God,
> secondly, of the journey to God of reasoning creatures,
> thirdly, of Christ, who, as human, is our road to God.[60]

The three major parts of the *Summa* in fact followed just that plan. In the midst of the crucial section on faith in part 2, Aquinas reminded readers that the mystery of Christ's incarnation provides "the way of all to come to blessedness."[61] The prologue to part 3 then identified Christ as "the completion of the entire theological discourse," and again stated that Christ is "the path of truth."[62] The Blackfriars translation obscures a particularly pointed feature of these remarks: "road" and "path" are both, in the Latin, *via*, the word used of the five "ways" of arguing for God's existence back at the beginning of the *Summa*. There may be a number of ways of making arguments that point toward God, in other words, but *our* way, *the* way, lies in Christ.

56. Ibid., 2a2ae.6.1.
57. Aquinas, *Summa Contra Gentiles* 4.17.
58. Aquinas, *Summa Theologiae* 1a.38.1.
59. Aquinas, *Commentary on the Gospel of St. John* 1:14b (par. 188).
60. Aquinas, *Summa Theologiae* 1a.2 pref.
61. Ibid., 2a2ae.2.7.
62. Ibid., 3a pref.

Discussions of Aquinas (this one included) often spend nearly all their time on the first two parts of the *Summa,* treating the sections on Christ and the sacraments in part 3 as a kind of appendix. But in important ways part 3 represents the culmination of the whole. Aquinas diverged from the normal practice of his predecessors, for instance, in giving much more lengthy attention to the narratives of Christ's life.[63] Everything before part 3 remains an abstract possibility. It is in Christ, Aquinas believed, that Christians encounter the divine grace that makes it possible to see the world through the eyes of faith.[64] At the beginning of his commentary on the Gospel of John, he asked why the text begins with the Word—the Son—rather than the Father ("In the beginning was the Word . . ."). He conceded that one reason might be simply that the Father was already known in the Old Testament, so the Gospel appropriately begins with its distinctive content, the Son. But he then identified a more substantial point: "We are brought to know the Father through the Son. . . . And so, wishing to lead the faithful to a knowledge of the Father, the Evangelist fittingly began with the Son."[65] The self-revelation of God in Christ is the way we come to know God. More specifically, it is in the *humanity* of Christ that we come to know God, like doubting Thomas who "saw one thing and believed something else. He saw a man; he believed him to be God."[66] In encounter with Jesus—whether mediated through Gospel stories, credal affirmations, preaching, or sacraments—Christians believe that they encounter God, so that the character manifested *by* Jesus Christ and the teachings *of* Jesus Christ provide them with trustworthy authority for what to believe about God.

That conviction cannot be a matter of knowledge—what we *see,* after all, is only a human being—but must rest on faith that we are given by grace. Christ therefore becomes "the way of all to come to blessedness" not merely by revealing God but by making available the grace which makes that revelation accessible to human sinners. Even apart from our sin, we would need grace to enable us to reach beyond the limits of our human nature, and sin further blinds our understanding. Thus, Aquinas could even say, "the chief point in the doctrine of Christian faith is the salvation accomplished in the cross of Christ."[67] The end to which human beings are ordered is the vision of God, but we can only achieve that end through the work of Christ.[68] "He . . . has, by his passion—endured out of love and obedience—freed us, his members, from our sins."[69] In Christ our faith is grounded, since God in God's own self

---

63. Per Erik Persson, *Sacra Doctrina: Reason and Revelation in Aquinas,* trans. Ross Mackenzie (Philadelphia: Fortress Press, 1970), 87.

64. Aquinas, *Summa Theologiae* 3a.9.2.

65. Aquinas, *Commentary on the Gospel of St. John* 1:1–2 (par. 30).

66. Aquinas, *Summa Theologiae* 2a2ae.1.4 ad 1.

67. Aquinas, *Expositio in Omnes S. Pauli Epistolas: Epistola 1 ad Corinthos,* chapter 1, lecture 3, *Opera Omnia* (New York: Musurgia Publishers, 1949), 13:163. See Bruce D. Marshall, "Thomas, Thomisms, and Truth," *The Thomist* 56 (1992): 522.

68. Aquinas, *Summa Theologiae* 3a.9.2.

69. Ibid., 3a.49.1.

speaks to us; our hope is lifted up, since we see how much God loves us; and our love is enkindled, since we hasten to love in return.[70] The self-revelation of God in Christ shows us what to believe of God, and the salvific work of Christ raises us above the limits of our nature and breaks us loose from the bondage of sin that we might believe it. And the faith and love whereby we trust in this self-revelation comes to us as the gift of the Holy Spirit, so that what we know of God is inextricably in relation to the *Triune* God.

Faced with a world that makes no sense on its own terms, then, I read or hear the propositions of scripture or otherwise encounter Christian teachings, and I encounter the person of Christ. Nothing I see compels me to believe that this is the story of the self-revelation of God, and yet I am captured by its authority through a power not my own, the gift of the Holy Spirit, so that I find myself able to have faith in an unknown "beginning and end of all things" revealed in Christ.[71] I believe that the language I use about that mystery is somehow true, but I do not know how it properly applies. I am enabled to reach beyond any system, not brought to see it all fit together, trusting in language I have been given the faith to believe, and the God in whom I believe is the God revealed in Christ and known and loved by the gift of the Holy Spirit. In John Caputo's words, "In St. Thomas, metaphysics is meant to wither away. The whole elaborate texture of *disputatio* that he weaves is an exercise in showing the deficiency and infirmity of *ratio*, in showing that metaphysics is something to be overcome."[72]

70. Ibid., 3a.1.2.

71. See the objections of Terence Penelhum, "The Analysis of Faith in St. Thomas Aquinas," *Religious Studies* 13 (1977): 144. For a more positive account, see Marshall, "Aquinas as a Postliberal Theologian," 377–78.

72. John D. Caputo, *Heidegger and Aquinas: An Essay in Overcoming Metaphysics* (New York: Fordham University Press, 1982), 252.

3 Luther, the Cross, and the Hidden God

On April 9, 1518, Martin Luther set off to travel the several hundred miles across Germany from Wittenberg to Heidelberg for the triennial chapter meeting of his monastic order, the Augustinian Hermits. He walked the whole distance. The previous autumn his Ninety-five Theses criticizing the sale of indulgences had aroused a storm of controversy around this previously obscure thirty-four-year-old monk and professor. Many of his friends warned him against the trip to Heidelberg. He might be kidnapped along the way, they said, and rumor had it that plans were afoot to burn him at the stake within a few weeks. But Luther set off anyway, with another set of theses, these to be defended in the disputations at the chapter meeting.

Rather to his surprise, on his arrival at Heidelberg he was welcomed as a guest of honor by the Count Palatine and other dignitaries. His eloquence in the debates won the admiration of many in attendance, including a number of young men like Johannes Brenz and Martin Bucer, who would later become key leaders in the Reformation. Within a year, Luther would be famous over much of Europe, and the Reformation would have begun. The Heidelberg Disputation represented a crucial moment in his life and in the history of Christian theology.[1]

In the Twenty-first Thesis he had prepared to debate, at the culmination of his argument, Luther contrasted the "theology of the cross" with the "theology of glory": "A theology of glory calls evil good and good evil. A theology of the cross calls the thing what it actually is."[2] Luther rarely used the phrase "theology of the cross" after 1518,[3] and he seems to have associated the phrase with an emphasis on the importance of suffering in the Christian life particularly characteristic of his early thought. Still, the cross itself remained always central for him, and what he said about the theology of the cross at Heidelberg provides a key for understanding concerns—about justification, grace and works, faith and reason, and the hidden and revealed God—that shaped Luther's

---

1. See Roland H. Bainton, *Here I Stand* (New York: Abingdon-Cokesbury, 1950), 86; Martin Brecht, *Martin Luther: His Road to Reformation 1483–1521*, trans. James L. Schaaf (Philadelphia: Fortress Press, 1985), 213–15. I have not indicated in the notes to this chapter how much I owe to the standard scholarly treatments of Luther's theology for pointing me in the right directions. I am also indebted to an unpublished paper by Michael Root titled "Luther's Theology of the Cross between 1517 and 1520."

2. Martin Luther, "Heidelberg Disputation," trans. Harold J. Grimm, *Luther's Works*, vol. 31 (Philadelphia: Muhlenberg Press, 1957), 52–53.

3. See Jos. E. Vercruysse, "Luther's Theology of the Cross at the Time of the Heidelberg Disputation," *Gregorianum* 57 (1976): 524.

theology all his life. To understand why these issues mattered so much to him requires turning back a bit from that day in 1518.

The Road to Heidelberg

Luther had joined the Augustinian Hermits in 1505, when he was twenty-two. Like many of his contemporaries, he was preoccupied with the question of his justification before God. After all, how could anything else be as important as eternal salvation? But how could one be sure of gaining it? "I thought: Oh, if I enter a cloister," he reflected years later, "and serve God in cowl and tonsure, he will reward and welcome me."[4] But even the rigorous discipline of the monastery did not bring the assurance of salvation.

> When I was a monk, I made a great effort to live according to the requirements of the monastic rule. I made a practice of confessing and reciting all my sins, but always with prior contrition; I went to confession frequently, and I performed the assigned penances faithfully. Nevertheless, my conscience could never achieve certainty but was always in doubt and said: "You have not done this correctly. You were not contrite enough. You have omitted this in your confession."[5]

Luther thought of Christ as a judge, and before that stern judge he expected to find himself condemned.[6] "Though I lived as a monk without reproach," he wrote, looking back the year before he died, nearly thirty years later, "I felt that I was a sinner before God. . . . I could not believe that he was placated by my satisfaction. I did not love, yes, I hated the righteous God who punishes sinners."[7]

The theology of his time, and particularly the *via moderna*, the "modern way" in theology in which Luther had been trained, posed the problems with which he was struggling with special force.[8] These late medieval theologians like William of Ockham and Gabriel Biel tried to put God's role in justification

---

4. Martin Luther, *Sermons on the Gospel of St. John,* trans. Martin H. Bertram, *Luther's Works,* vol. 24 (St. Louis: Concordia Publishing House, 1961), 260.

5. Martin Luther, *Lectures on Galatians* (1535) (on Gal. 5:3), trans. Jaroslav Pelikan, *Luther's Works,* vol. 27 (St. Louis: Concordia Publishing House, 1964), 13.

6. "No matter how much we declared with our mouths that Christ had redeemed us from the tyranny and slavery of the law, actually we felt in our hearts that He was a lawgiver, a tyrant, and a judge more fearful than Moses himself." *Lectures on Galatians* (1535) (on Gal. 4:4–5), *Luther's Works,* vol. 26 (St. Louis: Concordia, 1963), 368. Martin Brecht notes that the Wittenberg churchyard contained a relief of Christ as judge of the world, with two swords coming out of his mouth; Luther would have known it well. Brecht, *Martin Luther: His Road to Reformation,* 76–78.

7. Martin Luther, "Preface to the Complete Edition of Luther's Latin Writings" (1545), trans. Lewis W. Spitz, Sr., *Luther's Works,* vol. 34 (Philadelphia: Muhlenberg Press, 1960), 336.

8. Even in 1520, in the midst of battles with the whole tradition of medieval Scholasticism, Luther could still, ironically but also seriously, describe himself as an "Ockhamist" who followed William of Ockham, the key philosopher-theologian of the *via moderna.* Martin Luther, "Responsio ad condemnationem doctrinalem per quosdam Magistros Nostros Lovanienses et Colonienses facta," *D. Martin Luthers Werke,* vol. 6 (Weimar: Hermann Böhlau, 1888), 195. "Adversus Execrabilem Antichristi bullam Mar. Lutherus," ibid., 600.

into a system—a system that also included an important place for human moral efforts. They did *not* believe that human efforts alone could win salvation. We are all sinners, they conceded, and we cannot be saved without God's grace, a grace which God was not required to give us. On the other hand, God does not, at least in the normal course of things, give grace to just anybody. Only if we do the best we can (*quod in se est*, "what is in one") will God give us grace.[9] It is not that we *earn* our salvation, but there *is* a kind of fittingness in God's willingness to accept our inadequate efforts as worthy of some sort of reward. Then, once we have grace, we can continue to make our best moral efforts, and God has promised that those who do so, aided by grace, will be rewarded with salvation. God is not required to do even this, except that God has—freely—promised to do so, and we can trust the promise.[10]

In a certain sense, all of this seems only fair and reasonable. Biel laid it out almost in a syllogism:

> God receives those who seek their refuge with him. Otherwise there would be iniquity in him. But it is impossible that there be iniquity in him. Therefore, it is impossible that he would not receive those who take refuge with him. But if one does what is in one, one does take refuge with him. Therefore it is necessary that God receive him. But this reception is the infusion of grace.[11]

Shouldn't God pay attention to those who are trying as hard as they can? Yet it is striking how much such a theory domesticates divine grace. The rules Biel described preserve places for grace and for divine freedom, but those places exist within a clearly structured system of human ethical struggle, in which God plays a rather carefully defined role and we can grasp the principles behind God's actions. Moreover, while the system requires grace for our salvation, it also requires our very best moral efforts. "If our merits would not complete those of Christ," Biel said, "the merits of Christ would be insufficient, yes, nothing."[12] It is respectable folk who will make it to heaven; "the righteousness of the Christian has to be greater than that of the scribes and Pharisees."[13]

9. Gabrielis Biel, *Collectorium circa quattuor libros Sententiarum*, book 2, dist. 27, q.1, a.3, concl. 4 (Tübingen: J.C.B. Mohr [Paul Siebeck], 1984). The term *facere quod in se est*, "to do what is in one," goes back to "Ambrosiaster," the late fourth-century text written by an unknown author and formerly attributed to Ambrose. (Heiko Augustinus Oberman, *The Harvest of Medieval Theology: Gabriel Biel and Late Medieval Theology* [Cambridge: Harvard University Press, 1963], 132. I am drawing on Oberman's book for most of my discussion of Biel.) Aquinas used it in roughly the way I have been describing in his early commentary on the *Sentences* of Peter Lombard, but modified his views considerably in his later works. But many in the later Middle Ages took the *Sentences* commentary as Aquinas's definitive position. See Heiko Augustinus Oberman, *The Dawn of the Reformation* (Edinburgh: T. &. T. Clark, 1986), 108.

10. For a good summary, see Luther, *Lectures on Galatians* (1535) (on Gal. 2:16), *Luther's Works*, 26:124.

11. Biel, *Collectorium circa quattuor libros Sententiarum*, book 2, dist.27, q.1, art.2, concl.4.

12. Gabriel Biel, *Sermones de Festivitatibus Christi*, 11G, quoted in Oberman, *The Dawn of the Reformation*, 117.

13. Gabriel Biel, *Sermones Dominicales* 60 BC, quoted in Oberman, *Dawn of the Reformation*, 117.

Biel himself admitted, however, that none of us can really know that we have done our best.[14] Who, after all, could say that we have done everything that was in us? Therefore none of us can be sure of our salvation. Luther found the thought terrifying. He never much studied Aquinas's theology, and so there is no way to know how he might have reacted to it.[15] But, taking the systems of late medieval theologians like Biel in deadly earnest, he was forever stuck confessing yet one more sin, engaging in yet one more penance, all in the hope that maybe at last this would add up to his best—but never sure. At the feast of Corpus Christi in 1515, Luther and some of his fellow monks had traveled to his hometown of Eisleben to celebrate the founding of a new monastery. In the midst of the ceremony, as the consecrated bread, the body of Christ, was being carried through the church, Luther found himself overcome with horror—for the bread represented Christ, and to him Christ represented condemnation.[16] Given the system of the *via moderna,* he had begun to wonder not merely whether anyone could be confident of salvation, but whether anyone could be saved.

By the time he wrote his *Disputation against Scholastic Theology* in 1517, Luther was ready to condemn the whole system—the church's system of demanding moral efforts and penances for moral failures on the road to justification, and the philosophical system that undergirded it. Nothing we do by our own efforts, he insisted, could have grace as a fitting reward. Theologians went wrong when they accepted a philosophical framework like that of Aristotle's *Ethics,* for which the aim of human life is to develop virtues through our own practice and hard work. We lose the freedom of divine grace if we try to fit it as one stage into such a process. God's transforming grace can seize us anywhere—if anything, more probably in the midst of despair than when we feel confident that we have been doing a pretty good job of morally improving ourselves. The morally confident are particularly susceptible to idolatrously putting themselves in the place of God. Moreover, in seeking security through trying to achieve salvation by their own efforts, they fall into radical *in*security, inevitably unsure that those efforts can ever suffice. Only throwing ourselves into complete trust in God's grace secures our hope.[17]

A few months after the *Disputation against Scholastic Theology,* Luther posted his famous Ninety-five Theses condemning abuses in the sale of indulgences. Among other things, he was simply applying the logic of the posi-

---

14. Biel, *Collectorium circa quattuor libros Sententiarum,* book 2, dist.27, q.1, art.3, dub.5.

15. For the classic argument that there is less difference between Luther and Aquinas than their interpreters have often claimed, see Otto Hermann Pesch, *Theologie der Rechtfertigung bei Martin Luther und Thomas von Aquin* (Mainz: Matthias Grünewald Verlag, 1967).

16. Martin Luther, *Table Talk,* trans. Theodore G. Tappert, *Luther's Works,* vol. 54 (Philadelphia: Fortress Press, 1967), 19, no. 137. The remark was recorded in 1531.

17. Martin Luther, "Disputation against Scholastic Theology," trans. Harold J. Grimm, *Luther's Works,* 1:9–16; see theses 17, 25, 30, 40, 41, and 54.

tion he had developed to a particularly egregious application of the *via moderna*'s system. After you had received grace, the logic ran, you had to continue to do the best that was in you. That included doing penance for your prior sins. Penance left incomplete in this life would have to be completed after death in purgatory. But the church needed money, and the cause of God would be served if the church got the money it needed. So repentent sinners could, by giving money, obtain an indulgence that let them out of all or part of an otherwise required penance. Thus, for instance, people unable to go on a crusade had been able to pay for the support of someone else who had gone on a crusade. As the logic of such a system developed one more stage, if money were needed to build a church, did it not make more sense for a penitent sinner to sacrifice some money rather than undergoing a personal penance?

While it still preserved the need for grace and required authentic repentance before an indulgence could be purchased, the very idea of indulgences pushed the late medieval system of obtaining justification to its limits. If one downplayed the need for authentic repentence, then it sounded as if one could simply buy one's way out of the consequences of sin. If one insisted on repentence as a necessary precondition for indulgences actually working, then, Luther said, no one would want to buy them, since they would not work except for the "exceedingly rare" person who was truly penitent, and such folk would gain forgiveness without an indulgence anyway.[18] The efforts of popular preachers to appeal to superstitious fears had gone far beyond anything theological theories warranted. But Luther was not just denouncing the excesses of the system; he had already condemned the system itself—the very idea that people could, even if only because of God's freely granted promises, even if only in a system that also required God's grace, in any sense at all earn their salvation. A new theology was taking form; six months after posting the Ninety-five Theses, Luther started walking to the Heidelberg Disputation.

Two Roads Not Taken

Late medieval thought offered two possible ways around the system Luther found so unsatisfactory: mysticism and the appeal to the absolute power of God. The Christian mystical tradition held out the hope of a direct encounter with God, and indeed many mystics were regularly under suspicion from ecclesiastical authorities who thought that such an encounter might render the usual paths of church and sacraments unnecessary. But Luther found no security in the mystic path, for similar questions about confidence in one's salvation emerged there in different forms. If mysticism appealed to a direct

18. Martin Luther, "Ninety-Five Theses," trans. C. M. Jacobs, *Luther's Works*, 31:28; see theses 30, 31, and 36.

experience of God, how could one be sure that one had really had such an experience, and not just some form of self-delusion? Of one mystic Luther complained, "He almost drove me mad because I desired to experience the union of God with my soul of which he babbles."[19] But how could one trust in having had such experience?

In his lectures on the Psalms in 1513, Luther occasionally praised Dionysius the Areopagite for grasping something of God's hiddenness. (The starting point for much of the mystical tradition, "Dionysius" was the author of texts modern scholars believe to have been written in the fifth or sixth century but which the Middle Ages and Luther attributed to a convert of Paul.) But by 1515 in his lectures on Romans, Luther suspected that such mystical contemplation offered but another way of trying to get to God by human efforts.[20] The only mystics Luther admired were those like Johannes Tauler and the anonymous author of the *German Theology* (which Luther edited as the first book he published), who precisely emphasized that mystical experience could not offer a path around the suffering and doubts of the Christian life.[21] Luther came to suspect even Tauler, however, of urging us to listen to an "uncreated Word" within ourselves rather than the incarnate Word.[22] The mystical theologians, Luther said, kept talking about "going into darkness" or "ascending above being and non-being." But, "Truly I do not know how they understand themselves, when they attribute this to elicited acts and do not rather believe that it signifies the sufferings of the cross, death, and hell. THE CROSS alone is our theology."[23] Even the most profound and painful interior mystical journey still seemed to depend too much on confidence in human efforts.

The *via moderna* theologians like Ockham and Biel offered another way "around the system" through their appeal to the "absolute power of God."[24] God has promised, they said, to operate according to certain rules, and the system thereby defined indeed represents God's normal course of action—

19. Martin Luther, *Table Talk, Luther's Works,* 54:112, no. 644. Luther is discussing Bonaventure.

20. See Brecht, *Martin Luther: The Road to Reformation,* 137.

21. Heiko A. Oberman, "Simul Gemitus et Raptus: Luther and Mysticism," in Steven E. Ozment, ed., *The Reformation in Medieval Perspective* (Chicago: Quandrangle Books, 1971), 223. "Whereas medieval mysticism understood the way of suffering and the *meditatio crucis* as a way to the divinization of man by means of the *via negationis,* Luther reverses this approach and sees in the cross God's descent to the level of our sinful nature and our death, not so that man is divinized, but so that he is dedivinized and given new humanity in the community of the crucified Christ." Jürgen Moltmann, *The Crucified God,* trans. R. A. Wilson and John Bowden (New York: Harper & Row, 1974), 213.

22. See Walther von Loewenich, *Luther's Theology of the Cross,* trans. Herbert J. A. Bouman (Minneapolis: Augsburg, 1976), 155–56.

23. Martin Luther, *Operationes in Psalmos* (on Psalm 5:12), *D. Martin Luthers Werke,* vol. 9 (Weimar: Harmann Böhlau, 1892), 176.

24. The distinction between "absolute" and "ordained" power of God had been around for a long time but became a major theme only in the theology of Scotus in the fourteenth century, and then even more important in the writings of the *via moderna.* See Oberman, *The Harvest of Medieval Theology,* 36.

what they called "the ordained power of God." But God remains absolutely free, and "the absolute power of God" can do anything. While it is true that, according to God's ordained power, we cannot receive grace without first doing all that is in us, with respect to God's absolute power there really are no rules.[25] After all, God had directly called Saul even when he was persecuting the church—who could say what God might do?[26]

But none of that did Luther any good. Perhaps God sometimes (occasionally? often? who knows?) breaks the normal rules and saves some folk who failed to make even moderately appropriate moral efforts. Perhaps—terrifying thought—God sometimes refuses to save those who *have* done their best. In practice, the appeal to God's absolute power became either a theoretical abstraction that left ordinary life just as it had been, or else, if one took it really seriously, a recipe for human despair in the face of an utterly arbitrary God. Either way, it offered no help in the quest for hope about salvation.

It seemed to Luther significant that neither speculative mysticism nor the *via moderna*'s appeal to God's absolute power centered on Christ. Indeed, from his point of view, both seemed ways of turning *away* from Christ—to the inner word within every heart, or to the unpredictability of God's freedom. What he had come to realize by the time he took that walk from Wittenberg to Heidelberg was that no human efforts, no institutional structures, no mystical experience or theological speculation could give Christians confidence of salvation. That confidence had to come from God's side, from grace, and Luther found confidence about such grace only in the cross of Christ.[27]

It was in a way a simple idea, but it touched a deep chord among many of Luther's contemporaries. To be sure, other factors played their part. Church corruption annoyed many Christians, and many Germans in particular resented the siphoning off of German money to church authorities in Italy. The newly invented printing press made possible the rapid circulation of Luther's ideas to a wide audience. But such factors cannot in themselves explain how Luther became an instant hero, how his ideas won such wide acceptance so quickly, and how many people were so soon willing to risk their fortunes and even their lives for this new theology. Germany in the generation or two before Luther had not witnessed strong movements in opposition to the church establishment; indeed, organized heresy, earlier prominent, had almost died out.

---

25. Guillelmi de Ockham, *In Librum Primum Sententiarum (Ordinatio)*, dist.14, q.2, *Opera Theologica*, vol. 3 (St. Bonaventure, N.Y.: St. Bonaventure University Press, 1977), 470. See Marilyn McCord Adams, *William Ockham* (Notre Dame, Ind.: University of Notre Dame Press, 1987), 2:1273.

26. Biel, *Collectorium crica quattuor libros Sententiarum*, book 1, dist.41, q.1, art.2, concl.3.

27. "We must beware, that neither the active life with its works nor the contemplative life with its speculations seduces us. Both are very alluring and peaceful, and therefore dangerous unless tempered by the cross and confounded by adversities. But the cross is the safest of all things. Blessed is the one who understands." Martin Luther, *Operationes in Psalmos* (on Ps. 3:4), *D. Martin Luthers Werke*, vol. 5 (Weimar: Hermann Böhlau, 1892), 85.

It *was* a time, if the evidence we can count provides an accurate measure, of increased concern about salvation—more money given to churches, more bequests for special prayers and masses for the deceased, more religious processions, prayer groups, church construction. The art of the time portrays death more terrifyingly, and the portraits of Christ, from artists like Cranach, Grünewald, Dürer, and Riemanschneider, focused with brutal vividness on his sufferings on the cross.[28] If Luther was obsessed, his obsessions were widely shared.

The Theology of the Cross

At the Heidelberg Disputation, therefore, Luther addressed a deeply felt issue of his time when he declared that the morally respectable may not be the prime candidates for receiving a divine grace that

> loves sinners, evil persons, fools and weaklings in order to make them righteous, good, wise and strong. Rather than seeking its own good, the love of God flows forth and bestows good. Therefore sinners are attractive because they are loved; they are not loved because they are attractive.[29]

There, in a phrase, Luther challenged a whole tradition of medieval theology. It is unclear how far back one should trace that tradition. Aquinas, for instance, insisted that God's love is the cause of all things, and therefore some persons or things are better than others because God loves them more, not the other way around.[30] Luther would have agreed. Ockham and Biel, though, had clearly fallen into what Luther considered disastrous error: however much they talked of grace, they still assumed that, if God was to love us, we had to be worthy of God's love. We had to cultivate our virtues on the model of Aristotle's ethics and *then* hope for grace. But no, Luther insisted, God loves us even in the midst of our sinfulness.

So, as Paul had long before imagined a critic asking, Should we sin the more, that grace may abound the more? "By no means!" (Romans 6:15). Indeed, Luther argued that it is a theology of grace that really frees us for a life of Christian virtue. If we are trying to earn our salvation, trying to be worthy of God's love, then we can never quite act simply for the good of our neighbors. We are always glancing back over our shoulders, as it were, to ask, How am I doing? But if we do not have to worry about that, then we stand a chance of living human analogues to what we can understand of God's love, trying to

28. See Bernd Moeller, "Piety in Germany around 1500," in Ozment, *The Reformation in Medieval Perspective*, 52–55.

29. Luther, "Heidelberg Disputation," *Luther's Works*, 31:57.

30. Aquinas, *Summa Theologiae* 1a.20.3, trans. English Dominican Fathers (London: Blackfriars, 1963–).

help people simply for their sake, indifferent to implications about our own score on some scale of moral virtue.[31]

"The article of justification," Luther once remarked, "is master and head, lord and governor and judge, over all the kinds of doctrine."[32] That principle may not hold true for all theologies, but it provides a good key to Luther's own. Once he realized that he could find salvation only by turning away from all his own efforts to faith in God's grace, then the other elements of his theology began to fall into place.

First, all those fears about his doubts and sins and inadequacies turned out to be quite misplaced. It would be self-confidence free of doubts, Luther insisted at Heidelberg, that would mark disaster:

> To trust in works, which one ought to do in fear, is equivalent to giving oneself the honor and taking it from God, to whom fear is due in connection with every work. But this is completely wrong, namely to please oneself, to enjoy oneself in one's works, and to adore oneself as a idol.[33]

Nothing can prepare us or move us toward grace, but moral or spiritual pride can get in its way, and those whom society judges successful, morally good, or holy are particularly susceptible to such pride. Thus,

> God is the God of the humble, the miserable, the afflicted, the oppressed, the desperate, and of those who have been brought down to nothing at all. And it is the nature of God to exalt the humble, to feed the hungry, to enlighten the blind, to comfort the miserable and afflicted, to justify sinners, to give life to the dead, and to save those who are desperate and damned.[34]

If God's grace cannot be a part of any system of moral virtues, then it stands most directly available to those brought to despair by any such system. This is the human side of what Luther, in the Heidelberg Disputation, called "the theology of the cross": the human path to salvation lies not in climbing virtuously upward but through suffering, the suffering of despair and the knowledge of one's sins. No self-congratulatory sense of our own accomplishment can survive in the presence of the cross.[35]

The other side of the theology of the cross—the side of our perception of God—is that when we, in the midst of *our* suffering, finally look to God, it is

---

31. See Eric W. Gritsch and Robert W. Jenson, *Lutheranism* (Philadelphia: Fortress Press, 1976), 146.

32. Martin Luther, "Die Promotionsdisputation von Palladius und Tilemann (1537), *D. Martin Luthers Werke* (Weimar: Hermann Böhlaus Nachfolger, 1926), 39/1:205.

33. Luther, "Heidelberg Disputation," *Luther's Works*, 31:46.

34. Luther, *Lectures on Galatians* (1535) (on Gal. 3:19), *Luther's Works*, 26:314.

35. "So tenacious is the lust for praise and glory, especially in spiritual things and gifts like knowledge and virtues." Martin Luther, *Lectures on Galatians* (1519) (on Gal. 6:14), trans. Richard Jungkuntz, *Luther's Works*, 27:404.

a suffering God that we see.[36] If we could see God powerful and majestic, then that, after all, would provide yet another way of getting to God by our own efforts: as thoughtful, prudent people confronted by this powerful God, we would figure out that we had better get to work at the task of appropriate worship and service.

> In order that there may be room for faith, it is necessary that everything which is believed should be hidden. It cannot, however, be more deeply hidden than under an object, perception or experience which is contrary to it.[37]

God therefore appears to us in Christ on the cross, so that all we can see is weakness and foolishness.[38]

> This is clear: He who does not know Christ does not know God hidden in suffering. Therefore he prefers works to suffering, glory to the cross, strength to weakness, wisdom to folly, and in general good to evil.[39]

Those who turn away from Christ inevitably get everything wrong. In contrast, Luther explained, faith proceeds in opposition to all appearances. There are no shortcuts by which reason can unambiguously see God in God's power.

Luther regularly delivered himself of passionate attacks on "the whore reason." His critics sometimes cite such passages to show that he was a blustering, irrational fool. Some of his defenders then protest that he is really protesting only against the particular ways in which late medieval theology made use of Aristotle. But such defenses overdomesticate him. With regard to ordinary human affairs, he had no doubt of reason's abilities:

> Plainly, three and two are five, are they not? Again, if a man makes a coat, is he not wise to make it of cloth, or foolish to make it of paper? . . . This is all true, but it is necessary to make a distinction between spiritual and temporal things. . . . in divine things, the things concerning God, and in which we must conduct ourselves acceptably with him . . . human nature is absolutely blind, staring stone-blind, unable to recognize in the slightest degree what these things are.[40]

The trouble is that reason cannot help thinking about justification in terms of fairness, and, with however many qualifications, in some sense getting what you deserve. Human reason cannot imagine the excess of divine love. There-

36. On the two sides of the theology of the cross, see Paul Althaus, *The Theology of Martin Luther,* trans. Robert C. Schultz (Philadelphia: Fortress Press, 1966), 28.

37. Martin Luther, *The Bondage of the Will,* trans. Philip S. Watson, *Luther's Works,* vol. 33 (Philadelphia: Fortress, 1972), 62.

38. Luther, "Heidelberg Disputation," *Luther's Works,* 31:52–53.

39. Ibid., 31:53.

40. Martin Luther, Sermon for Epiphany on Isaiah 60:1–6, *Sermons of Martin Luther,* ed. John Nicholas Lenker, vol. 6 (Grand Rapids: Baker Book House, 1988), 319.

fore, following reason in such matters leads either to utter despair about salvation or else to getting puffed up with the human confidence that maybe we can deserve grace after all.[41] Whether we fall into despair or into pride, either way, we have fallen into sin. "By my reason I cannot understand or declare for certain that I am accepted into grace for the sake of Christ, but I hear this announced through the gospel and take hold of it by faith."[42]

That God really would save us in spite of how little we deserve it is something reason could never figure out. But God's revelation does not come in a way that reason can recognize, so that human wisdom could organize all the appropriate activities, and salvation would come by human efforts.

> He who wants to ascend advantageously to the love and knowledge of God should abandon the human metaphysical rules concerning knowledge of the divinity and apply himself first to the humanity of Christ. For it is exceedingly godless temerity that, where God has humiliated Himself in order to become recognizable, man seeks for himself another way, by following the counsels of his own natural capacity.[43]

God is thus revealed in Christ on the cross, "hidden in suffering,"[44] and therefore simultaneously revealed and hidden.

The Hidden God

In the Heidelberg Disputation and other early works, Luther spoke of the way God is hidden *in* revelation. Later on, he developed a darker contrast between the hidden and revealed Gods.[45] In *The Bondage of the Will,* his 1525 polemic against Erasmus, he referred to the hidden God as an other God, or at least an other aspect of God, than that which is revealed in Christ. At one point, he was struggling with a passage in Ezekiel (33:11) where God says, "I have no pleasure in the death of the wicked, but that the wicked turn from their ways and live." How is it that some sinners do not turn and live, but

41. See Luther, *Lectures on Galatians* (1535) (on Gal. 4:8), *Luther's Works,* 26:396; Martin Luther, *Lectures on Romans* (on Rom. 8:19), trans. Hilton C. Oswald, *Luther's Works,* vol. 25 (St. Louis: Concordia Publishing House, 1972), 361.

42. Ibid., 238–39.

43. Martin Luther, *Lectures on Hebrews* (on Heb. 1:2), trans. Walter A. Hansen, *Luther's Works,* vol. 29 (St. Louis: Concordia Publishing House, 1968), 111.

44. Luther, "Heidelberg Disputation," *Luther's Works,* 31:52.

45. I am oversimplifying a complex story. Of the two accounts I am giving of the hidden God in Luther, some scholars see only one, some only the other, and some both. Sorting all this out "is the fundamental problem for the interpreter of Luther's doctrine of the hidden God." Hellmut Brandt, *Luthers Lehre vom verbergenen Gott, Theologische Arbeiten,* vol. 8 (Berlin: Evangelische Verlagsanstalt, 1958), 19. Assigning one account to 1518 and another to 1525 provides a way of introducing the issues, but I have to admit that there are passages that do not fit this way of dividing things. See Brian Gerrish, "To the Unknown God: Luther and Calvin on the Hiddenness of God," *Journal of Religion* 53 (1973): 263–92.

remain in their sin, Luther wondered, if this is contrary to the desire of God? He concluded that such a question misunderstands the text, for Ezekiel

> is here speaking of the preached and offered mercy of God, not of that hidden and awful will of God whereby he ordains by his own counsel which and what sort of persons he wills to be recipients and partakers of his preached and offered mercy. This will is not to be inquired into, but reverently adored, as by far the most awe-inspiring secret of the Divine majesty, reserved for himself alone.[46]

Behind the God who wills the salvation of all lies, it seems, a hidden God according to whose will some remain in their sin.

> The good God . . . deplores the death which he finds in his people and desires to remove from them. . . . But God hidden in his majesty neither deplores nor takes away death, but works life, death, and all in all. For there he has not bound himself by his word, but has kept himself free over all things.[47]

Reflecting on the Gospel passage where Jesus weeps over the fate of Jerusalem, Luther could even say,

> It is . . . the part of this incarnate God to weep, wail, and groan over the perdition of the ungodly, when the will of the Divine Majesty purposely abandons and reprobates some to perish. And it is not for us to ask why he does so, but to stand in awe of God who both can do and wills to do such things.[48]

The weeping incarnate God here seems radically distinct from the Divine Majesty who abandons some to perish.

These are difficult passages. Luther seems not only to be casting Christian confidence in Christ into doubt but almost to be talking about two different Gods. Brian Gerrish contrasts the God "hidden in" revelation described in the Heidelberg Disputation with this God "hidden outside" revelation and remarks that, "whereas the hiddenness of God in his revelation . . . has been found theologically fruitful in recent years, the hiddenness of God outside his revelation . . . has been found something of an embarrassment."[49] If there is a God hidden outside revelation, then can Christ really be God's *self*-revelation? Historians can point to the depressions Luther suffered in middle age, or find a reversion to the contrast between the absolute and ordained powers of God he learned in his early education in the *via moderna*, and no doubt such considerations and others like them contain an element of truth. Even in *The Bondage of the Will*, moreover, Luther was not consistent of these matters. At

46. Luther, *The Bondage of the Will, Luther's Works,* 33:139.
47. Ibid., 139–40.
48. Ibid., 146.
49. Gerrish, "To the Unknown God," 268.

one point he spoke of how God "hides his eternal goodness and mercy under eternal wrath, his righteousness under iniquity," and concluded that, if it were not so, "there would be no need of faith."[50] Here the hiddenness of God seems to function just as it did in earlier works—as the alien work by which God keeps us from trying to justify ourselves through reason and works.

Moreover, even those passages that point to a hidden God behind the revealed God promptly urge us to ignore this God:

> God must therefore be left to himself in his own majesty, for in this regard we have nothing to do with him, nor has he willed that we should have anything to do with him. But we have something to do with him insofar as he is clothed and set forth in his Word, through which he offers himself to us. . . . To the extent, therefore, that God hides himself and wills to be unknown to us, it is no business of ours.[51]

Luther was not, he insisted, urging us to turn to the hidden God, for we cannot. That God is not available to us. To confront the mystery of the hidden God is to see even more clearly the need to turn to the revealed God.

And yet, if there really is a darkly hidden God who wills to be unknown to us, then has the gospel of justification by faith left us any better off than was the young Luther, terrified that he had not confessed all his sins? As Karl Barth once remarked, surely Luther did not think "he could overcome this difficulty by his advice that we should worry as little as possible about" it.[52] Luther returned to the issue again in his lectures on Genesis, delivered in the last few years of his life, but neither there nor anywhere else did he offer an easy solution to the problem of the hidden God.[53] Perhaps part of the lesson he sought to teach was how to live without easy answers. He faced life's hard realities honestly: "Even after the promises which have been given, even after the

---

50. Luther, *The Bondage of the Will, Luther's Works,* 33:62–63.

51. Ibid., 139.

52. "As Luther clearly saw, and ultimately this was the issue of his controversy with medieval theology, it is obvious that if what the Nominalists understood by *potentia absoluta* was correct, there could be no assurance of salvation and therefore no stability and confidence in life and death. At bottom there could never be more than a restless seeking and asking for God's true capacity, and on high or in the depths it could actually be quite different from and even contradictory to the capacity with which we might assure ourselves on the basis of his work. What is not so obvious, however, is how far Luther really thought he could overcome this difficulty by his advice that we should worry as little as possible about the *Deus absconditus* and cling wholly to what he called God's *opus proprium,* to the *Deus revelatus,* and therefore to the God revealed in Jesus Christ. For how can we do this genuinely and seriously if all the time . . . there is not denied but asserted a very different existence of God as the *Deus absconditus,* a very real *potentia inordinata* in the background?" Karl Barth, *Church Dogmatics,* vol. 2, part 1, trans. T.H.L. Parker et al. (Edinburgh: T&T Clark, 1957), 542.

53. "In his old age Luther, as a rule, made no mention of this side of the matter. In the fragments of his preaching that have come down to us it is impossible to find any further trace of this background. The Christological reference became for Luther the one and only thing that mattered." Karl Barth, *Church Dogmatics,* vol. 2, part 2, trans. G. W. Bromiley et al. (Edinburgh: T&T Clark, 1957), 66.

covenant which has been most certainly concluded with us, [God] nevertheless allows us to perish as if He had forgotten His promise."[54] Children die in
agony in this world; people do not find God. A loving, merciful God sometimes just does not seem to be presiding over things, and Luther admitted it.
Yet still he had faith.

Aquinas had proposed one sort of theological dialectic: Christians believe,
as grace moves us to see Christ as God's self-revelation, that God is (for example) loving and wise—but we do not know what "loving" and "wise" mean
with respect to God. We accept the authority by which we are given this language and trust that, if we were to "see" God, then all our human forms of
love would seem but a pale reflection of what love is in God. At the same time,
divine love is so unlike human love that we can make only the most cautious
of inferences from our human experiences to what God would or would not
do. We have to live in trust of a God of whom we can know only what that
God is not—and we can do this only by grace.

Luther made analogous points in his dialectic between the hidden and revealed God. When we speak of God, he said, "our every assertion of anything
good is hidden under the denial of it, so that faith may have its place in God,
who . . . cannot be possessed or touched except by the negation of all our af-
firmatives."[55] "From an unrevealed God," Luther imagined God saying, "I will
become a revealed God. Nevertheless I will remain the same God."[56] Revelation does not dissolve the divine mystery, but confronts us with it. In Jesus on
the cross, Christians see God's love—yet humanly, what one sees is this poor,
dying, very human prophet. Only faith gets us from there to God, and for
Luther faith could never be a matter of feeling relaxed and secure. We cannot
imagine how the God of all the universe will turn out to have been revealed
in the crucified Jesus—in that sense God's revelation remains hidden—and yet
we believe that this is so. We therefore literally cannot help thinking of a "hidden" God apart from Christ—and yet we believe that this way of thinking is
only a sign of our failure to comprehend the mystery and love of God; for if
we did comprehend, we would see how this hidden God has been revealed
in Christ. When we think of the revelation of the hidden God, God hidden *outside* Christ is all that we can imagine, but we nevertheless have faith in God
hidden *in* Christ.[57] God thus remains hidden "for no other reason than that the
flesh, our own senses, understanding, and wisdom, may be mortified and that
we must accustom ourselves to trust His promises with simplicity and with eyes

---

54. Martin Luther, *Lectures on Genesis* (on Gen. 37:18–20), trans. Paul D. Paul, *Luther's Works*,
vol. 6 (St. Louis: Concordia Publishing House, 1970), 360.

55. Luther, *Lectures on Romans* (on Rom. 9:3), *Luther's Works*, 25:383.

56. Luther, *Lectures on Genesis* (on Gen. 26:9), trans. George V. Schick and Paul D. Paul, *Luther's
Works*, vol. 5 (St. Louis: Concordia Publishing House, 1968), 45.

57. I owe much of this way of stating the matter to Michael Root, whose views I hope I have
accurately presented.

shut even though He pretends to be exercising no care for us and appears to be quite indifferent."[58]

It can probably be a mistake to try to make all of Luther's rhetorical flourishes consistent, and the contrasts between hidden and revealed God in *The Bondage of the Will* in particular may sometimes go too far.[59] But Luther was struggling with a legitimate problem of perspective or standpoint. From God's perspective, the pieces *do* fit together, and one could see God at work even in the trials of our lives. But no human theologian can occupy that perspective, and so, even to make such confident claims is to try to reach beyond faith. By haunting us with the image of that unknown God, Luther reminds Christians of the insecurity with which we must be willing to live if we are to live in trust of a God who remains mystery even in revelation. It may be, he would have claimed, the most insecure among us—the doubters, those who struggle with despair, and those who have most reason to know themselves as sinners—who are in the best position to understand what living such a Christian life might mean.

58. Luther, *Lectures on Genesis* (on Gen. 37:18–20), *Luther's Works,* 6:359–60. "For the work of God must be hidden and never understood, even when it happens. But is is never hidden in any other way than under that which appears contrary to our conceptions and ideas." Luther, *Lectures on Romans* (on Rom. 8:26), *Luther's Works,* 25:366.

59. Though Luther never backed off them. See for instance Luther, *Lectures on Genesis* (on Gen. 26:9), *Luther's Works, 5:43.*

4   Calvin's Rhetoric of Faith

In 1528 or 1529, when John Calvin was nineteen or twenty, his father ordered him to withdraw from his philosophical studies in Paris and enroll in the law faculty at the University of Orleans. The elder Calvin, who oversaw the business interests of his local cathedral, found himself caught up in a dispute with his ecclesiastical employers and uncertain of the family's financial future. He was aware, his son wrote later, "that the legal profession commonly raised those who followed it to wealth,"[1] and so—like many a practical-minded father before and since—decided that his obviously brilliant second son ought to go to law school. Calvin received his law degree about three years later, shortly after his father's death. Only three or four years after that, however, he had abandoned the legal profession, converted to Protestantism, become an intellectual leader of the Protestant cause in France, and written the first edition of his greatest work, the *Institutes of the Christian Religion*.[2]

Calvin's critics sometimes blame his legal training for the "legalism" they deplore in his imposition of moral and ecclesiastical discipline on the city of Geneva. Such analyses, however, simply trade on the word "legal" and ignore the kind of education Calvin actually received. First, like the study of law today, it focused on persuading a particular audience.[3] It is not that lawyers necessarily care nothing for the truth, but they have little interest in truth for which they cannot argue, or for logically tight argument that leaves their audience unpersuaded. Second, Calvin's particular legal training was shaped by a Renaissance humanism that emphasized the study of classical texts as models of rhetoric or persuasive discourse. Aquinas subverted some of the logic of scholastic method from within; Luther rebelled against it. But Calvin never knew that world.

I do not want to overstate the point: Calvin had theological reasons for the way he did theology, and reference to his legal and humanistic training provides only a convenient starting point for thinking about the cast of his mind. But his training in texts, language, and rhetoric manifested itself on nearly every page he wrote and shaped the way he used the Bible and the way he

1. John Calvin, *Commentary on the Book of Psalms,* vol. 1, trans. James Anderson, *Calvin's Commentaries* (Grand Rapids: Baker Book House, 1989), 4:x1.
2. See François Wendel, *Calvin,* trans. Philip Mairet (London: Fontana, 1965), 21, 25–26.
3. E. David Willis, "Rhetoric and Responsibility in Calvin's Theology," in Alexander J. McKelway and E. David Willis, eds., *The Context of Contemporary Theology: Essays in Honor of Paul Lehmann* (Atlanta: John Knox Press, 1974), 48; William Bouwsma, "Lawyers in Early Modern Culture," *American Historical Review* 78 (1973): 318.

thought about truth and how language works.[4] To mention three prominent characteristics, Calvin's theology was *biblical, practically oriented,* and *consciously accommodated to human capacities.* For all those reasons, it was *anti-speculative.*[5]

Biblical

The bulk of Calvin's written work consists in sermons (always very much centered on biblical texts) and biblical commentaries. In the prefaces to a number of editions of his *Institutes,* he emphasized that even there his goal was not to produce a logically consistent systematic theology, but "to prepare and instruct candidates in sacred theology for the reading of the divine Word, in order that they may be able both to have easy access to it and to advance in it without stumbling."[6] He would therefore not engage in too much speculation beyond the texts before him. The seventeenth-century Calvinists who wrote the Westminster Confession announced that their theological conclusions were "either expressly set down in Scripture, or by good and necessary consequence may be deduced from Scripture."[7] Calvin would have been more cautious about "deducing." "Scripture," he wrote, "was not given to us to satisfy our foolish curiosity."[8] He was willing to leave questions unanswered, "necessary consequences" underived, and apparent inconsistencies suspended in tension. "We ought," he wrote, "to play the philosopher soberly and with great moderation; let us use great caution that neither our thoughts nor our speech go beyond the limits to which the Word of God itself extends. For how can the human mind measure off the measureless essence of God . . . ? Let us then willingly leave to God the knowledge of himself."[9] Calvin's way of interpreting what the Bible says is another story, and a complex one. My point here

---

4. "It is hardly an exaggeration to say that on almost every page of the *Institutes* Calvin engages in some sort of semantical analysis in which such problems as the definitional meanings or intentions of important terms, etymologies, common usage, ambiguity, metaphors or symbolic terms, and verbal disputes are considered." Robert H. Ayers, "Language, Logic and Reason in Calvin's *Institutes," Religious Studies* 16 (1980): 287.

5. I have modified the list in Edward A. Dowey, *The Knowledge of God in Calvin's Theology* (New York: Columbia University Press, 1952), 3–40. Dowey mentions that the knowledge of God in Calvin is (1) accommodated to our capacities; (2) correlative (knowledge of God and of ourselves are interrelated); (3) existential (practical rather than just speculative); and (4) clear and comprehensible, sufficient to our needs. In addition to Dowey's book, this chapter is particularly indebted to the work of B. A. Gerrish and William J. Bouwsma and to the opportunity to read in manuscript Serene Jones's book on Calvin's rhetoric.

6. John Calvin, *Institutes of the Christian Religion* 1.2.2, trans. Ford Lewis Battles (Philadelphia: Westminster, 1960). Unless otherwise indicated, citations of the *Institutes* will refer to this translation of the 1559 edition.

7. "Westminster Confession of Faith," chapter 1, *Book of Confessions,* Presbyterian Church (U.S.A.), 6.006.

8. John Calvin, "Préface des Anciennes Bibles Genevoises," *Opera,* vol. 9 (Brunsvigae: C. A. Schwetschke et filium, 1870), col. 825.

9. Calvin, *Institutes* 1.13.21.

is simply his willingness to respect the Bible's silences and ambiguities. Like Aquinas on the nature of our language about God, or Luther on the mysteries of the hidden God, Calvin counseled against claiming to know too much, or claiming to say what we know more clearly than we can.

Practically Oriented

If scripture does not satisfy all our curiosity, still, Calvin wrote, "it is useful . . . and how? To instruct us in good doctrine, to console us, and to exhort us to render ourselves perfect in all good works."[10] That emphasis on the "useful" takes us back to the practical character of Calvin's rhetorical and legal education. If "rhetoric" meant tricks and flashy gimmicks, then Calvin was against it. He rejoiced that Paul had "gloried" in a "rude, coarse, and unpolished style" in contrast to "mere disguise and lifeless show" that would have disfigured "the simplicity of the gospel."[11] But in a deeper sense, Calvin's own theology was thoroughly "rhetorical." He sought to help his readers, not to understand everything, but to acquire the right sensibility and attitudes and act in the right way.[12]

True knowledge of God, he wrote, is "not that knowledge which, content with empty speculation, merely flits in the brain, but that which will be sound and fruitful if we duly perceive it, and it takes root in the heart."[13] The Christian should try to be like the author of the Psalms, who "did not coldly philosophize about God's precepts but gave himself up to them with earnest affection."[14] "Indeed, we shall not say that, properly speaking, God is known where there is no religion or piety,"[15] and by piety Calvin meant "the reverence joined with love for God that the knowledge of his benefits induces."[16] Reverence and love are not extras to be added on to knowledge but at the center of the form that knowledge of God takes. Someone who says the right words without reverence and love does not really know God, and, since we cannot grasp God's nature, appropriate reverence and love rather than the ability to answer every possible question are here the signs of understanding.

---

10. Calvin, "Préface des Anciennes Bibles Genevoises," *Opera*, vol. 9, col. 825.

11. John Calvin, *Commentary on the Epistles of Paul the Apostle to the Corinthians* (on 1 Cor. 1:17), trans. John Pringle, *Calvin's Commentaries*, 20:73–74.

12. For parallel studies in how roughly contemporary texts were designed to develop the skills and virtues of their readers, see Victoria A. Kahn, *Rhetoric, Prudence and Skepticism in the Renaissance* (Ithaca, N.Y.: Cornell University Press, 1985); Nancy Streuver, "Lorenzo Valla," in *Renaissance Eloquence,* ed. James Murphey (Berkeley: University of California Press, 1983), 191–206.

13. Calvin, *Institutes* 1.5.9. Apprehension of God is thus, as in Aquinas, wisdom, *sapientia,* rather than knowledge, *scientia*—that is, practical rather than speculative. See Thomas F. Torrance, *The Hermeneutics of John Calvin* (Edinburgh: Scottish Academic Press, 1988), 75.

14. Calvin, *Commentary on the Book of Psalms* (on Ps. 119:98), vol. 4, *Calvin's Commentaries,* 6:476.

15. Calvin, *Institutes* 1.2.1.

16. Ibid. See B. A. Gerrish, *Grace and Gratitude: The Eucharistic Theology of John Calvin* (Minneapolis: Fortress Press, 1993), 25.

But rhetoric also wants to make us act. And so, alongside piety, Calvin added obedience: "All right knowledge of God is born from obedience."[17] To know God is also to try to live in a certain way. Someone who never repents or confesses sins, never kneels in awe before God, would not seem, after all, really to wonder and reverence God. Such reverence need not imply a life of consistent virtue or churchgoing. Indeed, those who never escape difficult struggles with doubt and sin may more easily come to that conviction of their "poverty and powerlessness" and therefore "true humility" that will lead them, as they ought, "to renounce all self-confidence, and . . . to ascribe . . . every good thing . . . to the kindness of God."[18] We become obedient to God when we throw ourselves on God's mercy.

Calvin's thought can be misleading because it *seems* so systematic. The table of contents of the *Institutes* suggests not a rhetorically shaped introduction to Scripture but a carefully ordered systematic theology. Indeed, Calvin himself sometimes lost track of what, I have been arguing, he most of the time understood himself to be doing. William Bouwsma contrasted a "philosophical side" of Calvin, which "craved desperately for intelligibility, order, certainty" with a rhetorical side "inclined to celebrate the paradoxes and mystery at the heart of existence." Both, Bouwsma argued, represented real aspects of Calvin's thought, for he was both "a philosopher, a rationalist . . . a man of fixed principles, and a conservative," *and* "a rhetorician and humanist . . . flexible to the point of opportunism, and a revolutionary in spite of himself."[19] To preserve such a tension, however, as Calvin did, rhetoric had to take the dominant place. If what Bouwsma called his philosophical side had dominated, the passion for order and certainty would finally have imposed itself on everything. Rhetoric can allow system and logic as one rhetorical strategy among others—indeed, it was a strategy Calvin used to great effect. As later chapters will indicate, however, many of Calvin's followers reversed the priorities and resolved the dialectic in favor of philosophy.

Accommodated to Our Capacities

Persuasive speakers have to know their audiences, and the need to "accommodate" oneself to what one's hearers know and believe was a commonplace of the rhetorical tradition Calvin studied. Good speakers do not make arguments, however valid, that their audience cannot understand, or argue from premises their audience would not accept. So, Calvin argued, "God cannot be comprehended by us except as far as he accommodates himself to our

17. Calvin, *Institutes* 1.6.2.
18. John Calvin, "The Necessity of Reforming the Church," trans. Henry Beveridge, *Tracts and Treatises* (Grand Rapids: Wm. B. Eerdmans Publishing Co., 1958), 1:160. See Gerrish, *Grace and Gratitude,* 157.
19. William J. Bouwsma, *John Calvin: A Sixteenth-Century Portrait* (New York: Oxford University Press, 1988), 230–31.

standard."[20] Even revelation has to use words and patterns of thought its intended audience can grasp.

> For who even of slight intelligence does not understand that, as nurses commonly do with infants, God is wont in a measure to "lisp" in speaking with us? Thus such forms of speaking do not so much express clearly what God is like as accommodate the knowledge of him to our slight capacity. To do this he must descend far beneath his loftiness.[21]

For example, Calvin spoke (faithfully, he would have said, to scripture) of the cross as "an astonishing display of the wrath of God that he did not spare even his only begotten Son, and was not appeased in any other way than by that price of expiation."[22] But he also conceded that that assertion is not quite right: God did not begin to love us "after we were reconciled to him by the blood of his Son. . . . Rather, he has loved us before the world was created."[23]

Some sort of contradiction arises here; God has to be won over to loving us, but God loved us all along. How to explain it? Well, Calvin said, "Expressions of this sort have been accommodated to our capacity." We need a dramatic image to convey to us the full power of the truth. If we were simply told that God has loved us all along, in spite of our sins, we would "experience and feel something" of what we owe to God's mercy. *But,* if we hear that we were "excluded from all hope of salvation, beyond every blessing of God, the slave of Satan, captive under the yoke of sin, destined finally for a dreadful destruction and already involved in it" until "Christ interceded," then we will be "even more moved by all these things which so vividly portray the greatness of the calamity" from which we have been rescued.[24]

Have we thereby been misled? No, Calvin would reply. We will have been given exactly the right sense of how remarkable it is that God could save sinners like us—a sense that, sinners as we are, we might not have grasped if we had simply been told that God loved us all along. The nurse who speaks baby talk, or the physics teacher who begins with a simplified model of a complex process, is giving a child or student a measure of truth in the form that the child or student can understand. "It is the part of a wise teacher to accommodate himself to the capacity of those whom he has undertaken to instruct, so that in dealing with the weak and ignorant, he drops in his instructions little by little, lest it should run over, if poured in more abundantly."[25] The language

---

20. John Calvin, *Commentaries on the Prophet Ezekiel* (on Ezek. 9:3–4), vol. 1, trans. Thomas Myers, *Calvin's Commentaries* 11:304.

21. Calvin, *Institutes* 1.13.1. See also 2.6.4, 2.10.6. John Calvin, *Commentaries on the Epistle of Paul the Apostle to the Romans* (on Rom. 1:19), trans. John Owen, *Calvin's Commentaries,* 19:69.

22. John Calvin, *Commentary on a Harmony of the Evangelists* (on Matt. 27:45), vol. 3, trans. William Pringle, *Calvin's Commentaries,* 17:316–17.

23. Calvin, *Institutes* 2.16.4.

24. Ibid., 2.16.2.

25. Calvin, *Commentary on the Epistles of Paul the Apostle to the Corinthians* (on 1 Cor. 3:2), *Calvin's Commentaries,* 20:122. "As our capacity cannot endure the fulness of that surpassing glory

gives its readers such understanding as they are capable of, but its real point is to produce in them the appropriate sensibility and action.[26]

Calvin used the principle of accommodation in a variety of contexts.[27] When the Old and New Testaments differ, it is because the ancient Israelites had a different level of potential for understanding things. When the Bible seems to assume that the earth is flat, or some other aspect of outmoded cosmology, it is just talking about things in a way that its original audience would have understood.[28] Genesis, for instance, speaks of the sun and moon as the two great lights in the sky, though of course the stars are really larger than the moon: "God speaks to us of these things according to how we perceive them, and not according to how they are."[29] When the Bible speaks of God as "repenting," it is speaking "figuratively."[30] "For had the prophets spoken without metaphors and simply narrated the things treated of by them," Calvin wrote, "their words would have been frigid and inefficient, and would not have penetrated into the hearts of men."[31] They appealed rhetorically, accommodating themselves to the attentiveness and intelligence of their audience.[32]

Sophisticated readers, however, can transcend such examples of accommodation, recognizing in an out-of-date cosmology or a potentially misleading metaphor how God is "lisping" for the common folk. But if *any*

---

which essentially belongs to God, whenever he appears to us, he must necessarily put on a form adopted to our comprehension." John Calvin, *Commentaries on the Prophet Daniel* (on Dan. 7:10), vol. 2, trans. Thomas Myers, *Calvin's Commentaries*, 13:34.

26. "If a householder instructs, rules, and guides his children one way in infancy, another way in youth, and still another in young manhood, we shall not on this account call him fickle and say that he abandons his purpose. Why, then, do we brand God with the mark of inconstancy because he has with apt and fitting marks distinguished a diversity of times? . . . He has accommodated himself to men's capacity, which is varied and changeable." Calvin, *Institutes* 2.11.13.

27. Like most of Calvin's interpreters, I am already trying to make him too much a philosopher, by giving him a "theory of accommodation." Calvin himself never uses the noun *accommodatio* but always the verbs *accommodare* or *attemperare*. Ford Lewis Battles, "God Was Accommodating Himself to Human Capacity," in Donald K. McKim, ed., *Readings in Calvin's Theology* (Grand Rapids: Baker Book House, 1984), 21.

28. The author of Genesis "did not treat scientifically of the stars, as a philosopher would; but he called them in a popular manner, according to their appearance to the uneducated, rather than according to the truth." John Calvin, *Commentaries on the First Book of Moses called Genesis* (on Gen. 6:14), vol. 1, trans. John King, *Calvin's Commentaries*, 1:256–57.

29. John Calvin, Sermon 34 on Job (on Job 9:7–15), *Opera*, vol. 33 (Brunsvigae: C. A. Schwetschke et filium, 1887), col. 423.

30. Calvin, *Institutes* 1.17.12. On divine anger, see *Institutes* 2.16.2–3; Calvin, *Commentaries on Romans* (on Rom. 1:18), *Calvin's Commentaries*, 19:68. On sorrow see Calvin, *Commentaries on Genesis* (on Gen. 6:6), vol. 1, *Calvin's Commentaries*, 1:249.

31. John Calvin, *Commentaries on the Book of the Prophet Jeremiah* (on Jer. 49:3), vol. 5, trans. John Owen, *Calvin's Commentaries*, 11:59.

32. Calvin celebrated in this context the egalitarian accessibility of scripture: "Moses everywhere spoke in a homely style, to suit the capacity of the people, and . . . he purposely abstained from acute disputations, which might savour of the schools and of deeper learning." Calvin, *Commentaries on Genesis* (on Gen. 6:14), vol. 1, *Calvin's Commentaries*, 1:256.

human being saw God in God's real glory, Calvin held, "that incomparable brightness would bring us to nothing."[33] We are *all* like children when it comes to understanding God. "For if he should speak his own language, should it be understood of mortal creatures? Alas, no. But how is it that he hath spoken to us in the holy scripture? As nurses do to their little babes . . . God made himself nurselike, who talketh not to her little babe as she would to a man, but hath a respect of the child's capacity."[34] No human beings ever get beyond the need for accommodation when it comes to hearing about God, and theologians therefore need to remember that all language about God bears the shape of accommodation.

That Calvin's theology is biblical, practically oriented, and accommodated to our capacities—all that means that it is *antispeculative,* and indeed a polemic against excessive speculation was one of the most prominent themes in Calvin's writing. He did not try to extract the truth *from* scripture but to provide us guides that direct us back *to* scripture as better readers. His primary goal was not to provide a set of propositions to believe, but to evoke feelings and behaviors. To the extent that he did set out propositions for belief, he kept insisting that they are adapted to our limited understandings. The function of images of God in Calvin, T. F. Torrance has written, is *ostensive* and *persuasive* but not *descriptive.* They point us toward God and help to move us toward lives of humility and obedience before God, but they do not purport to offer accounts of God's nature.[35]

At one point, for instance, Calvin considered three "epithets" of God's essence: immensity, spirituality, and simplicity. Like Aquinas, he argued that such attributes can give us only negative knowledge about God: God is not finite, not material, not divisible.[36] But in addition, the epithets invite us to certain attitudes toward God. Understood rhetorically, they seek to evoke reverent humility before God, not a confident sense of understanding the divine essence. "Recognition" of God thus "consists more in living experience than in vain and high-flown speculation."[37] "Of these things which it is neither given nor lawful to know, ignorance is learned; the craving to know, a kind of madness."[38]

Calvin did not, however, think that we can say nothing true about God. He vigorously attacked the Catholic idea of "implicit faith." As he understood it— probably too simply—defenders of implicit faith claimed that it sufficed for a

---

33. John Calvin, *Commentaries on the Four Last Books of Moses* (on Ex. 33:20), vol. 3, trans. Charles William Bingham, *Calvin's Commentaries,* 3:381.

34. John Calvin, Sermon 42 (on Deut. 5:22), *Sermons on Deuteronomy,* trans. Arthur Golding (Edinburgh: Banner of Truth Trust, 1987), 249, spelling modernized.

35. Torrance, *The Hermeneutics of John Calvin,* 92. See Calvin, *Institutes* 1.14.4.

36. "Surely, his infinity ought to make us afraid to try to measure him by our own senses. Indeed, his spiritual nature forbids our imagining him by our own senses." Calvin, *Institutes* 1.13.1.

37. Ibid., 1.10.2.

38. Ibid., 3.23.8. On "learned ignorance," see also 3.21.2.

Christian to think, "I believe whatever it is the church believes," without knowledge or understanding of what the church did in fact believe. This, Calvin said, would not do: "It would be the height of absurdity to label ignorance tempered by humility 'faith.' "[39] "Faith rests not on ignorance but on knowledge."[40]

He distinguished, however, two forms of faith: (1) "If someone believes that God is, [and] he thinks that the history related concerning Christ is true;" and (2) "the faith whereby we not only believe that God and Christ are, but also believe in God and Christ, truly acknowledging Him as our God and Christ as our Savior . . . and to be so strengthened by this thought, that we have no doubt about God's good will toward us."[41] Faith does require content. Some of that content takes the form of narratives of events. Such-and-such happened to the people of Israel. Jesus did such-and-such. The specificity of the historical claims Calvin wanted to make is a complex story, and he could treat the details of biblical narratives rather casually, but at least some historical claims were important to him.[42] Some of the content involves claims about God, and there, I have been arguing, much more caution is required, for we are often in the business of affirming claims we do not really understand. "So long as we dwell as strangers in the world there is such a thing as implicit faith, not only because many things are as yet hidden from us, but because surrounded by many clouds of errors we do not comprehend everything."[43] Moreover, this first kind of faith "is of no importance; thus it is unworthy to be called 'faith'."[44] We become Christian believers only when we appropriate it as a personal trust. As Calvin summarized his views:

> When we call faith "knowledge" we do not mean comprehension of the sort that is commonly concerned with those things which fall under human sense perception. For faith is so far above sense that man's mind has to go beyond and rise above itself in order to attain it. Even where the mind has attained, it does not comprehend what it feels. But while it is persuaded of what it does not grasp, by the very certainty

39. Ibid., 3.2.3.

40. Ibid. "When 'faith' is called 'knowledge,' it is distinguished not only from opinion but from that shapeless faith which the Papists have contrived; for they have forged an implicit faith destitute of all light of the understanding. But when Paul describes it to be a quality which essentially belongs to faith—to know the truth, he plainly shows that there is no faith without knowledge." John Calvin, *Commentaries on the Epistle to Titus* (on Titus 1:1), trans. William Pringle, *Calvin's Commentaries*, 21:282.

41. John Calvin, *Institutes of the Christian Religion* (1536 ed.), trans. Ford Lewis Battles (Grand Rapids: Wm. B. Eerdmans Publishing Co., 1975), 42. Hereafter referred to as *Institutes* (1536).

42. For some exemplary passages, see Bouwsma, *John Calvin*, 118–25.

43. Calvin, *Institutes* 3.2.4. "I do not deny that, in this sense, there may sometimes be a sort of implicit faith, that is, a faith which is not accompanied by a full and distinct knowledge of sound doctrine; provided we also hold that faith always springs from the word of God, and takes its origin from true principles, and therefore is always found in connection with some light of knowledge." John Calvin, *Commentary on a Harmony of the Evangelists* (on Matt. 15:22), vol. 2, *Calvin's Commentaries*, 16:263–64.

44. Calvin, *Institutes* (1536), 42.

of its persuasion it understands more than if it perceived anything human by its own capacity. . . . From this we conclude that the knowledge of faith consists in assurance rather than in comprehension.[45]

Just as for Aquinas we speak with confidence a language about God we do not understand, just as Luther urged turning aside from any effort to penetrate the mystery of the hidden God in favor of trust in God's promises, so for Calvin the words we speak of God can help us to a confident trust in God even as we recognize the inadequacies both of the words themselves and of our understandings of them.[46]

A Test Case: Predestination

Calvin's most famous—perhaps one should say *notorious*—doctrine, predestination, illustrates his approach at work. The conviction that predestination was somehow Calvin's "central" belief, which dominated many discussions of his theology in the late nineteenth and early twentieth centuries, has now largely dissipated.[47] He probably had no single "central" doctrine, but at any rate this was not it. If anyone "can produce a syllable in which I teach that we ought to begin with predestination in seeking assurance of salvation," he once wrote, "I am ready to remain dumb."[48] Indeed, the form of double predestination most distinctive to him stood at the periphery of his thought. As Edward Dowey has noted, Calvin drew "no ethical, ecclesiastical, or soteriological corollaries" from it and made "no harmonizing modifications in other doctrines" on its account.[49]

Calvin in fact did not know quite what to do with predestination. In various editions of the *Institutes* he placed it (in 1537) between a section on the Law and one on redemption, as an explanation of the different effects of preaching the word, then (from 1539 to 1554) together with providence in a chapter between his soteriology and his ecclesiology, and finally (in 1559) within his soteriology, after he had discussed sanctification and justification.[50] In contrast to many later Calvinists, however, Calvin *never* located it in the context of the doctrine of God. Predestination grows out of reflections on the manner of our salvation; it does not, for him, flow deductively out of an account of the divine nature.

Still, he concluded he could not omit either side of predestination. Christians

---

45. Calvin, *Institutes* 3.2.14.

46. See ibid., 3.2.16; 3.2.10; 3.6.4.

47. The key figures in picturing predestination as "central" seem to have been Alexander Schweizer and F. C. Baur. See François Wendel, "Justification and Predestination in Calvin," in McKim, *Readings in Calvin's Theology,* 160–61.

48. Calvin, "Second Defense of the Faith concerning the Sacraments," *Tracts and Treatises,* 2:343.

49. Dowey, *The Knowledge of God in Calvin's Theology,* 213. See also Wendel, *Calvin,* 263–65.

50. All this is usefully summarized in John S. Bray, *Theodore Beza's Doctrine of Predestination* (Nieuwkoop: De Graaf, 1975), 46–47.

who are ultimately saved stand among the elect without regard for their own merits, purely as a result of God's grace. Scripture teaches us, when we reflect on our salvation, "to turn aside from the contemplation of our own works, and look solely upon God's mercy and Christ's perfection."[51] That conviction was as central to Calvin as it had been to Luther, and it provided him the basis of a bold and liberating understanding of human freedom I will be discussing in chapter 6. But not all people, Calvin was convinced, are ultimately saved, and that poses a problem for a theology of pure grace. If there is a division between A and B, sheep and goat, and A's election is purely the result of God's choice, then B's reprobation must also be purely the result of God's choice: "Election itself could not stand except as set over against reprobation."[52] Yet Calvin's rhetoric as he entered the topic raised every possible warning flag. Within a single page in his first section on the topic he warned against "penetrating the sacred precincts of divine wisdom," entering "a labyrinth from which we can find no exit," "wandering in forbidden bypaths," and "rushing into this audacity and impudence." "Human curiosity," he wrote, "renders the discussion of predestination, already somewhat difficult of itself, very confusing and even dangerous."[53] If we have learned to attend to Calvin's rhetorical strategies, we will therefore be warned to note carefully how his language functions here. It turns out to manifest the characteristics of his theology I have already noted.

First, the discussion was resolutely biblical: "To seek any other knowledge of predestination than what the Word of God discloses is not less insane than if one should purpose to walk in a pathless waste, or to see in darkness."[54] He cited a long list of scriptural texts and examples in support of his position, and he tried to resist pursuing "implications" of the doctrine beyond what the biblical evidence warrants: "Within this limit then let every one remember to keep his own mind, lest he be carried beyond God's oracles in investigating predestination. . . . if we ought to follow the guidance of the Spirit, where he leaves us, there we ought to stop."[55]

Second, Calvin used the doctrine to obtain practical results in the affections and actions of believers. A proper understanding of predestination "builds up faith soundly, trains us to humility, elevates us to admiration of the immense goodness of God towards us, and excites us to praise this goodness."[56] Assured that their salvation rests on God's election and not their own uncertain efforts,

---

51. Calvin, *Institutes* 3.11.16.
52. Ibid., 3.23.1. "As Scripture, then, clearly shows, we say that God once established by his eternal and unchangeable plan those whom he long before determined once for all to receive into salvation, and those whom, on the other hand, he would devote to destruction. We assert that, with respect to the elect, this plan was founded upon his freely given mercy, without regard to human worth; but by his just and irreprehensible but incomprehensible judgment he has barred the door of life to those whom he has given over to damnation." Ibid., 3.21.7.
53. Ibid., 3.21.2.
54. Ibid.
55. Calvin, *Commentaries on Romans* (on Rom. 11:34), *Calvin's Commentaries*, 19:446.
56. John Calvin, *Concerning the Eternal Predestination of God*, trans. J.K.S. Reid (London: James Clarke, 1961), 56.

believers will be reassured. Recognizing that they have done nothing to earn their salvation, that nothing makes them somehow "better" than the reprobate, they will be humbled. Believing that a God who can with perfect justice abandon some to eternal reprobation nevertheless rescues others for eternal salvation, they will wonder at God's mercy: "We shall never be clearly persuaded, as we ought to be, that our salvation flows from the wellspring of God's free mercy until we come to know His eternal election, which illumines God's grace by this contrast: that He does not indiscriminately adopt all into the hope of salvation but gives to some what He denies to others."[57] The doctrine functions, when it functions properly, by leading to these results—to the right kind of gratitude, humility, and awe in Christian believers.

Third, in the consciousness that anything scripture says on this topic will be accommodated to our understanding, Calvin repeatedly warned against excessive speculation.

> If anyone with carefree assurance breaks into this place, he will not succeed in satisfying his curiosity and he will enter a labyrinth from which he can find no exit. For it is not right for man unrestrainedly to search out things that the Lord has willed to be hid in himself. . . . He has set forth by his Word the secrets of his will that he has decided to reveal to us. These he decided to reveal in so far as he foresaw that they would concern us and benefit us.[58]

And what does not concern or benefit us, we ought not to explore. For example, if God permitted Adam to sin, thereby beginning the whole tragedy that leads some to reprobation, we can assume that "the Lord had judged it to be expedient." But "why he so judged it is hidden from us. . . . Accordingly, we should contemplate the evident cause of condemnation in the corrupt nature of humanity—which is closer to us—rather than seek a hidden and utterly incomprehensible cause in God's predestination."[59] When we encounter really corrupt people, we should not "despair of them as if they were already lost. . . . For God, whenever it pleases him, changes the worst men into the best, engrafts the alien, and adopts the stranger into the church. And the Lord does this to frustrate men's opinion and restrain their rashness—which, unless it is checked, ventures to assume for itself a greater right of judgment than it deserves."[60] We human beings tend to think that we know who the respectable folk are, and that they must be the ones God would choose. In what he said about predestination, Calvin meant to shake that confidence down to its foundations.

The question of whether Christ died for all or only for the elect became a central issue in later debates among Calvinists. Calvin himself interpreted some

57. Calvin, *Institutes* 3.21.1.
58. Ibid.
59. Ibid., 3.23.8.
60. Ibid., 4.12.11.

scriptural passages as apparently implying that Christ did die for all.[61] But in setting out his critique of the Council of Trent, which had declared that Christ died for all and was being criticized on that count by some Protestants, he simply refused to comment.[62] When the context was not the interpretation of a particular text but ecumenical debate over issues of doctrine, Calvin apparently felt that the issue did not matter to our development as properly affected and acting Christians, and refused to draw a conclusion.

On other occasions, he dealt with the issue through a contrast between the two wills of God reminiscent of Luther's distinction between the hidden God and revealed God. The "revealed will," Calvin said, calls all to redemption, but the "secret will" intends to save only the elect.[63] In commenting on the phrase, "Thy will be done," in the Lord's Prayer, for instance, Calvin remarked, "Here, then, it is not a question of His secret will by which He governs all things and destines them to their end. . . . Rather here that other will is designated, namely, that to which voluntary obedience corresponds."[64] One will, it seems, calls us to respond, but another has already destined all things. Yet elsewhere Calvin firmly asserted that "nothing agrees less with God's nature than that He should be of double will."[65]

Two of Calvin's most vigorous adversaries, Jerome Bolsec and Sebastian Castellio, attacked him on just this issue: Did he believe in two divine wills? If so, how could he reconcile that with God's unity and simplicity?[66] Here too he followed his characteristic strategies: he reflected on particular biblical passages, living with apparent inconsistencies among them, drawing rhetorical conclusions about how we should relate to God and live our lives, and resisting the urge to excessive speculation. Beyond human comprehension, he said, God's will is unified and one.[67] Yet pious reflection on scripture leads us sometimes to speak of God's will to save all, sometimes to speak of God's election

61. See for instance John Calvin, *Commentary on the Book of the Prophet Isaiah* (on Isa. 53:12), vol. 4, trans. William Pringle, *Calvin's Commentaries*, 8:131; *Commentaries on the Epistle of Paul the Apostle to the Hebrews* (on Heb. 9:28), trans. John Owen, *Calvin's Commentaries*, 22:220; *Commentary on the Gospel according to John* (on John 1:29), trans. William Pringle, *Calvin's Commentaries*, 15:64.

62. John Calvin, "Antidote to the Sixth Session of the Council of Trent," *Tracts and Treatises*, 3:109.

63. "So wonderful is his love toward mankind, that he would have them all to be saved, and is of his own self prepared to bestow salvation on the lost. . . . But it may be asked, If God wishes none to perish, why is it that so many do perish? To this my answer is, that no mention is here made of the hidden purpose of God, according to which the reprobate are doomed to their own ruin, but only of his will as made known to us in the gospel." John Calvin, *Commentaries on the Second Epistle of Peter* (on 2 Peter 3:9), trans. John Owen, *Calvin's Commentaries*, 22:419.

64. Calvin, *Institutes* 3.20.43.

65. Ibid., 3.24.17. See also Calvin, *Concerning the Eternal Predestination of God*, 117.

66. See Brian G. Armstrong, *Calvinism and the Amyraut Heresy* (Madison: University of Wisconsin Press, 1969), 34; Philip C. Holtrup, *The Bolsec Controversy on Predestination from 1551 to 1555*, vol. 1, book 1 (Lewiston, N.Y.: Edwin Mellen Press, 1993), 59.

67. Calvin, *Institutes* 3.24.17.

of some. So be it. The divine will is an "abyss"; "while it is hidden from us, we ought reverently to adore it."[68] Yes, Calvin agreed, there are puzzles, but, "It is one thing to regard with modesty of faith this profound subject, quite another obstinately to reject it just because it overwhelms man's reason."[69] We have to acknowledge the limits of our understanding and seek to trust a God whose nature lies beyond even our imagining. We should extend our prayers, Calvin wrote, to "all . . . who dwell on earth" as brothers in Christ. "For what God has determined concerning them is beyond our knowing except that it is no less godly than humane to wish and hope the best for them."[70]

It would be unfaithful to Calvin's obsessive warnings about the dangers that surround discussions of predestination to insist that he—or any other theologian—never fell victim to those dangers. I mean to be defending Calvin's style of thought, not his every conclusion. That general way of thinking provides criteria, indeed, for evaluating his particular conclusions: Did he ever go beyond the biblical witness? or say something irrelevant to fostering the right affections and actions among Christian people? or engage in speculation that sought to reach beyond the language accommodated to our understanding?

Sometimes, I myself would answer, he did. For example, as noted above, Calvin thought that the principal rhetorical effect of believing that some are condemned to perdition is to amaze us all the more at God's mercy in saving others. I suspect it has often been rather to narrow the scope of Christians' sense of divine love and the generosity of their attitudes to their neighbors. If it has had the rhetorical effect I claim, then Calvin himself provided a warrant for rethinking what he said about it. Again, with Karl Barth, I believe that it is more faithful to the diversity of the biblical witness and to Calvin's own suspicion of speculation—as Calvin himself said, "no less godly than humane"— to hope, though we cannot know, that in the end all may be saved. But though Calvin could hint at such a view, his systematic account of predestination took another path.[71] These arguments are complex—Barth provided fifty pages of fine print on the Old Testament evidence just for a start—and my point is not to settle them but again to suggest how, faithful to Calvin's method, one might challenge his conclusions.

68. Ibid., 1.17.2.

69. John Calvin, *Brevis responsio ad diluendas Nebulonis cuiusdam calumnias,* in *Opera,* vol. 9 (Brunsvigae: C. A. Schwetschke et filium, 1870), col. 263; quoted in Armstrong, *Calvinism and the Amyraut Heresy,* 34. Armstrong's citation of volume 8 of the *Calvini Opera* is a misprint. Calvin "does speak of God's hidden, inscrutable will, but the function of his remarkable utterances on the terrifying abyss in God can only be, in a summary of piety, to drive the pious mind all the more eagerly to the fatherly goodwill of God disclosed in Scripture." Gerrish, *Grace and Gratitude,* 29.

70. Calvin, *Institutes* 3.20.38. I am grateful to George Hunsinger for calling this passage to my attention.

71. Karl Barth, *Church Dogmatics,* vol. 2, part 2, trans. G. W. Bromiley et al. (Edinburgh: T&T Clark, 1957), 417–18. See especially the astonishing review of Old Testament material, 354–409.

The Triune God

In one respect, this discussion of Calvin's God has so far remained inappropriately abstract; it has neglected to mention that that God is Triune. Calvin's nervousness about speculation concerning God's nature perhaps led him to say too little explicitly about the Trinity. Indeed, his discussions of that topic led Karl Barth to remark, in a famous line, that while he gave "indeed a thoroughly correct and respectful exposition of the doctrine of the Trinity . . . it is noteworthy that the author's interest in this matter is not exactly burning."[72] His refusal, in 1537, early in his time in Geneva, to sign an affirmation of the Apostles', Nicene, and Athanasian Creeds when he was charged with Arianism remains one of the puzzling episodes in Calvin's life.[73] Still, there is no real doubt of his Trinitarian orthodoxy, which moreover was not just a conventional acceptance of the tradition; his account of our knowledge and language about God was deeply, fundamentally Trinitarian.[74]

"Now we shall possess a right definition of faith," Calvin wrote, "if we call it a firm and certain knowledge of God's benevolence toward us, founded upon the truth of the freely given promise in Christ, both revealed to our minds and sealed upon our hearts through the Holy Spirit."[75] Christians have knowledge of God, in other words, because Christ reveals God, and because that revelation is sealed in our hearts by the Spirit.

Commenting on Paul's description of Christ as the "image of the invisible God," Calvin remarked,

> The term "image" is not made use of for reference to essence, but has a reference to us; for Christ is called the *image of God* on this ground— that he makes God in a manner visible to us. . . . God in himself, that is, in his naked majesty, is *invisible* and that not to the eyes of the body

---

72. Karl Barth, *Church Dogmatics,* vol. 1, part 1, trans. G. T. Thomson (Edinburgh: T&T Clark, 1936), 477.

73. He may have wanted to make clear the point that only scripture should be the final authority for Christian faith. He seems to have had reservations about the original historical context of the creeds—the fact, for instance, that the so-called Nicene Creed was not adopted at Nicaea. He was also a stubborn man who, on principle, did not yield easily to his opponents. See Wendel, *Calvin,* 54; B. A. Gerrish, *The Old Protestantism and the New* (Chicago: University of Chicago Press, 1982), 382.

74. I am largely avoiding the famous debate between followers of Barth and Brunner as to the possibility of "natural" knowledge of God. In general, Calvin—like Aquinas, interestingly enough —seems to have thought that we could have hints and glimmers of the knowledge of God apart from Christ, but that they would be so confused as not reliably to do us any good. See Nicholas Wolterstorff, "The Migration of the Theistic Arguments: From Natural Theology to Evidentialist Apologetics," in *Rationality, Religious Belief, and Moral Commitment,* ed. Robert Audi and William J. Wainwright (Ithaca, N.Y.: Cornell University Press, 1986), 58.

As Calvin himself put it, "An empty and confused knowledge of Christ must not be mistaken for Faith, but that knowledge which is directed to Christ, in order to seek God in Christ, and this can only be done when the power and offices of Christ are understood." Calvin, *Commentaries on the Epistle of Paul to the Ephesians* (on Eph. 3:12), *Calvin's Commentaries,* 21:257.

75. Calvin, *Institutes* 3.2.7.

merely, but also to the understandings of men. . . . he is revealed to us
in Christ alone, that we may behold him as in a mirror.[76]

As sinners, we can know God only through Christ: "After the fall of the first
man no knowledge of God apart from the Mediator has had power unto salvation."[77] But even apart from sin, God's nature lies beyond the capacity of
human understanding, and thus we would have needed God's self-revelation:
"The Father, himself infinite, becomes finite in the Son, for he has accommodated himself to our little measure lest our minds be overwhelmed by the immensity of his glory."[78] Thus Calvin thought that even God's appearances in
the Old Testament were really appearances of Christ, for the Son *is* the self-
revelation of the Father.[79] In sum, "It is not necessary for us to mount up on
high to inquire about what must be hidden from us at this moment. For God
lowers himself to us. He shows us only in his Son—as though he says, 'Here
I am. Contemplate me.' "[80]

But how do we know that what we encounter in Christ is the self-revelation of God? Why do we believe the biblical claims to that effect? The Holy
Spirit, Calvin said, is "the inner teacher by whose effort the promise of salvation penetrates into our minds, a promise that would otherwise only strike the
air or beat upon our ears."[81] There are, he conceded, human arguments that
can refute some criticisms of scripture and provide modest evidence for its authority. But none of them, or even all of them together, adds up to a persuasive case.[82] "The word itself is not quite certain for us unless it be confirmed

76. John Calvin, *Commentary on the Epistle to the Colossians* (on Col. 1:15), trans. William
Pringle, *Calvin's Commentaries*, 21:149–50. "The Father himself is represented as *invisible,* because he is in himself not apprehended by the human understanding. He exhibits himself, however, to us by his Son, and makes himself in a manner visible." Calvin, *Commentary on the Epistles of Paul to the Corinthians* (on 2 Cor. 4:4), *Calvin's Commentaries*, 20:197.
    77. Calvin, *Institutes* 2.6.1.
    78. Ibid., 2.6.4, "God is not to be *sought out* in His unsearchable height . . . but is to be known
by us, in so far as He manifests himself in Christ." Calvin, *Commentary on the Epistles of Paul the
Apostle to the Corinthians* (on 2 Cor. 4:6), *Calvin's Commentaries*, 20:200.
    79. "The holy men of old knew God only by beholding him in his Son as in a mirror. . . . From
this fountain Adam, Noah, Abraham, Isaac, Jacob and others drank all that they had of heavenly
teaching." Calvin, *Institutes* 4.8.5.
    80. John Calvin, *Congregation on Eternal Election*, in Holtrup, *The Bolsec Controversy on Pre-
destination from 1551 to 1555*, vol. 1, book 2, 717. In the famous "extra-Calvinisticum," Calvin insisted, against Luther, that something of God's infinity remained uncapturable in God's finite self-
revelation in Christ. As with the theory of accommodation, this did not, I think, imply that what
we know of God is false, but only that, while true as far as it goes, it is necessarily limited to our
finite capacities. Calvin's real concern here seems to have been to preserve the reality of the incarnation, which appeared to him threatened by a view in which even Christ's humanity took on
divine infinity and thereby ceased to be really human. See Calvin, *Institutes* 2.13.4 and 4.17.30, as
well as Heiko A. Oberman, "The 'Extra' Dimension in the Theology of Calvin," in idem, *The Dawn
of the Reformation* (Edinburgh: T&T Clark, 1986), especially 248; and E. David Willis, *Calvin's
Catholic Christology: The Function of the So-called Extra Calvinisticum in Calvin's Theology* (Leiden: E. J. Brill, 1966).
    81. Calvin, *Institutes* 3.1.4.
    82. Ibid., 1.8.13.

by the testimony of the Spirit."[83] "The same Spirit, therefore, who has spoken through the mouths of the prophets must penetrate into our hearts to persuade us that they faithfully proclaimed what had been divinely commanded."[84]

This aspect of the Spirit's work involves two parts. First, it "enlightens" the mind; it produces "knowledge" and enables us to understand what the Bible means. Second, it "establishes the mind"; it brings our minds (and our hearts) into "a firm and steady conviction" regarding the claims embodied in the text.[85] Amid feelings of humility and gratitude, in a life lived in obedience, Christians find that the stories the Bible tells of Christ as the revelation of God's identity have a compelling force. They sense that that force does not result from their own efforts, and Calvin, again on scriptural grounds, attributed it to the work of the Holy Spirit. "To sum up, the Holy Spirit is the bond by which Christ effectually unites us to himself."[86]

What do we know of God? For Calvin, we know what is revealed in Jesus Christ. How do we know that Christ as encountered in the scriptures is in fact God's self-revelation? We know by the inner testimony of the Holy Spirit. Thus we do not have a knowledge of God in the abstract, to which we could then append a doctrine of the Trinity. Our knowledge of God *is* Trinitarian. It is, moreover, a knowledge rhetorically presented, practically oriented to transform our lives under trust in God's grace rather than to satisfy our curiosity about God's nature, accommodated to our capacities, and based on scripture in a way that will be distorted if we engage overmuch in speculation.

Calvin's theology was not the same as that of Aquinas or of Luther. Not only did they differ on particular doctrines, but Calvin's education in Renaissance humanism produced a style of thought different from that of either Luther or Aquinas. Still, I hope I have indicated some common patterns in how they thought about God. In their different ways, all three emphasized how little we can understand about God, and how inadequate our language is for talk about God: Aquinas's emphasis on the impossibility of positive claims about God, and his contrast between our trust that our language speaks truly of God and our inability to understand how it does so; Luther's attacks on the confidence of theologies of glory and insistence on the need to return to trust in the God revealed to us in the crucified Christ; Calvin's self-conscious use of rhetorical strategies, cautions against speculation, and theory of accommodation.

All three agreed that human reason and human efforts cannot make it to God, that thus whatever relation we have with God depends on God's gracious initiative, to which we must be related in a faith that never fully under-

---

83. Ibid., 1.9.3.
84. Ibid., 1.7.4.
85. Calvin, *Commentaries on the Epistle of Paul to the Ephesians* (on Eph. 1:13), *Calvin's Commentaries*, 20:208. See also John Calvin, "Catechism of the Church of Geneva," *Theological Treatises*, trans. J.K.S. Reid (Philadelphia: Westminster Press, 1954), 102; *Institutes* 1.7.5, 1.9.3.
86. Calvin, *Institutes* 3.1.1.

stands, a faith which, in Calvin's phrase, "consists in assurance rather than in comprehension." Given that radical dependence on God's gracious initiative, it follows that the wise, the humanly virtuous, and the socially respectable have no advantage when it comes to knowing and loving God. All three writers, finally, understood this divine initiative, and therefore the basis of all our knowledge of God, in Trinitarian terms.

On all these points, many Christian thinkers in the seventeenth century took a different path. They were more confident of human capacities to understand God and human efforts to participate in our salvation. They narrowed the field of what counted as reasonable or acceptable argument. Putting less emphasis on the initiatives in the revelation and grace of the Triune God, they tended to see God more as a unitary, powerful creator of the cosmos and a guarantor of moral law and social order.

Part 2

The Modern Turn: God

5 The Domestication of God

Analogy Revisited

A good place to start considering new patterns of thought among seventeenth-century philosophers and theologians is with the ways they understood language about God.[1] The reticence represented by Aquinas's emphasis on God's unknowability, Luther's attacks on theologies of glory, and Calvin's rhetorical strategies for a language of faith got lost, to be replaced by claims for more univocal language and tighter arguments. The most natural beginning for the story is with analogy, and not in the seventeenth century but back in the summer of 1498. In that year Thomas de Vio, an Italian Dominican, thirty years old, was enjoying the summer vacation after his first year of teaching at the University of Pavia. "Motivated both by the obscurity of the subject itself and by the deplorable scarcity of profound studies in our age," he decided, he wrote, "to publish during this vacation a treatise on the analogy of names."[2] De Vio stood at the beginning of a remarkable career. He would become Master General of the Dominican Order and a cardinal (taking on, in honor of his hometown, the name Cardinal Cajetan). In the key years of 1518 and 1519, as papal

1. I am trying, as I noted in chapter 1, to discuss what happened without offering a systematic account of why it happened. Hans Blumenberg has developed one powerful explanation of the causes of changes in how people understood language about God in the early modern period. He sees the emphasis on God's absolute power, and thereby away from "the rationality and human intelligibility of creation," in late medieval Nominalism as driving its opponents to a renewed emphasis on reason's power to understand God. See Hans Blumenberg, *The Legitimacy of the Modern Age,* trans. Robert M. Wallace (Cambridge: MIT Press, 1983), 160, 173.

I suspect that is only a part of the story. Cajetan, for instance, was dealing with Renaissance Platonists like Pomponazzi, who argued that a doctrine can be true in philosophy and false in theology, and was anxious to refute them by showing a kind of continuity between philosophical and theological discourse. Suárez was conscious of the need of Jesuit missionaries to find some way of making intellectual contact with non-Christian cultures. (See Charles H. Lohr, "Metaphysics," in *The Cambridge History of Renaissance Philosophy,* ed. Quentin Skinner and Eckhard Kessler [Cambridge: Cambridge University Press, 1988], 604, 616.) Many seventeenth-century thinkers were suspicious of ordinary language—scientists were moving to mathematical language, and a number of philosophers tried to invent artificial languages for the sake of greater clarity and precision. (See Margreta de Grazia, "The Secularization of Language in the Seventeenth Century," *Journal of the History of Ideas* 41 [1980]: 319.) The battles among Protestants and Catholics also pressed both sides to offer clearer statements of their positions.

In short, many factors were pressing for more univocal language and tighter argumentation in theology. I am not sure of the relative importance of these various causes, but I am convinced that most historians of the period have too much tended to trace the story of philosophy from Aquinas and Scotus through the Nominalists to the modern period, unfairly neglecting Cajetan and, even more, Suárez.

2. Thomas de Vio, Cardinal Cajetan, *The Analogy of Names* 1.1, trans. Edward A. Bushinski (Pittsburgh: Duquesne University Press, 1953).

legate to Germany, he tried, none too successfully, to deal with Luther. He remains one of the most famous of all commentators on Aquinas, and the short treatise on analogy he wrote that summer has, in David Burrell's words, "furnished the very mode in which all subsequent Thomistic discussion was cast."[3]

Burrell's comment, cited in chapter 2, is worth recalling: though Aquinas "is perhaps best known for his theory of analogy . . . it turns out that he never had one." Aquinas talked about analogy quite unsystematically, and in a number of different ways, by way of making the point that our language about God is not purely equivocal (it is not just arbitrary and random that we speak of God as "wise" or "good"), but neither is it univocal. Even words we use nonmetaphorically do not mean, when applied to God, what they mean when applied to creatures, and in fact we do not really know what they mean. We believe that, knowing God, we would see how their use was somehow appropriate, but, situated as we are, we are unable to know how they apply to God. This is not so much a theory, then, as an account of why we should not have a theory.

More than anyone else, Thomas de Vio, Cardinal Cajetan, systematized Aquinas's varied references into a "theory of analogy." He distinguished three basic types:

1. In analogy of inequality the same term is applied to two subjects with exactly the same meaning, but it is "unequally participated in." Thus "fire" and "the heaven" are both "bodies" in just the same sense—both three-dimensional substances—but they are different sorts of bodies.[4]

2. In analogy of attribution the same term is applied to two subjects, and the meaning of the term "is *the same* with respect to the *term* but *different* as regards" the subjects' "*relationship* to this term." As in Aquinas, health provided the classic example: "health" means the same thing as applied to animal or diet or urine, but each is related to health in a quite different way: as subject of health, cause of health, or sign of health.[5]

3. In analogy of proportionality the term itself is used with different meanings, but in a way "proportional" to the things to which it is applied. Cajetan gave "seeing" as an example. We talk about seeing in both a corporeal and an intellectual sense—seeing a stop sign or seeing how to solve a problem in physics. In each case the subject is engaged in the kind of seeing appropriate ("proportional") to the corporeal or intellectual context, but (in contrast to the other kinds of analogy) the term means something quite different. Intellectual "seeing" is different from the sort we do with our eyes.[6]

3. David B. Burrell, *Analogy and Philosophical Language* (New Haven: Yale University Press, 1973), 120.

4. Cajetan, *The Analogy of Names* 1.4. The crucial text in Aquinas for this and what follows is *Scriptum super Libros Sententiarum* 1.19.5.2 ad 1 (Paris: P. Lethielleux, 1929).

5. Cajetan, *The Analogy of Names* 2.8, *emphases added*.

6. Ibid., 3.23.

Having worked out this classification, Cajetan then said that only analogy of proportionality really counts as analogy.[7] Analogy of inequality is not really analogy at all, but a kind of univocity: different physical objects are "bodies" in the same sense. Analogy of attribution, on the other hand, did not seem to him even a form of analogy, but just equivocation. Diet may cause health, and urine may signify health, but neither is really itself "healthy"—"health" applies to them only "in a confused manner and by way of reduction to the primary relationship."[8] If we cannot specify exactly how different uses of a word are related, Cajetan did not want to count the uses as analogous. The possibility that we could meaningfully use a term without really understanding how it applies, which lay at the center of Aquinas's account of analogical talk about God, seemed to Cajetan unacceptably "confused."

He took his battle against confusion one step further by distinguishing, in the case of analogy of proportionality, between metaphorical and proper cases. In a metaphorical case—a friend smiles at me; good fortune smiles on me—it is only by a metaphor that the same term is used in both cases. But in analogy of *proper* proportionality, "the common name is predicated of both analogates without the use of metaphors." The heart, for instance, is the "principle" of an animal, and the foundation is the "principle" of a house—neither in a metaphorical sense.[9]

For Cajetan analogy of proper proportionality defined the analogical relation between talk of creatures and talk of God, but a reader fresh from Aquinas might wonder whether it is really an instance of analogy at all. Perhaps the heart as principle of an animal is less like the foundation as principle of a house than, say, the tallness of a person is like the tallness of a building (a case of univocal predication), but still, are we not basically using *principle* in the same way in both cases? Cajetan would not exactly disagree. Analogy of proper proportionality, he said at one point, is midway between analogy of attribution and univocity.[10] At another point he even classified it along with univocity.[11] Moreover, he pushed the mathematical connotations of the idea of "proportionality" in a way that Aquinas never did. For instance, in one argument he noted that the human soul is immaterial and intellectual but God is even more radically immaterial than a human being. Therefore, "one could very well conclude that God is proportionally intellectual, i.e., to the degree that His immateriality exceeds that of man, His intellectuality exceeds that of man."[12]

7. Ibid., 5.53.
8. Ibid., 2.10, 2.15. See Ralph McInerny, *Studies in Analogy* (The Hague: Martinus Nijhoff, 1968), 101.
9. Ibid., 3.25–26.
10. Ibid., 7.77.
11. Thome de Vio Caietani, *Doctoris angelici diui Thome Aquinatis summe theologie prima pars* 1am.16.6 (Venice: Luceantonij junte Florentini, 1533). See McInerny, *Studies in Analogy*, 73.
12. Cajetan, *The Analogy of Names* 10.107.

By this point, Cajetan had moved a long way from Aquinas. Unsystematic references have become a systematic theory. Whereas, push come to shove, Aquinas was prepared to classify analogy as a form of equivocation, Cajetan classified analogy of proper proportionality, the only kind of real interest to him, with univocity. The mathematical connotations of "proportion" invite us to think that we can measure how much God differs from us, and thereby understand just how terms applied to God differ from the same terms applied to us. Far from offering a series of reminders concerning how we cannot understand what we mean when we speak of God, analogy now functioned as a way of explaining just what we do mean.[13]

The Spanish Jesuit Francisco Suárez, born eighty years after Cajetan (he lived from 1548 to 1617), is probably the only commentator on Aquinas more famous than Cajetan himself. Although Suárez has been rather neglected—there is neither a complete translation of his key work, the *Metaphysical Disputations,* nor a major study of his metaphysics available in English[14]—his writing shaped the teaching of philosophy and theology in both Catholic and Protestant institutions for centuries.[15] Descartes studied and quoted him, and the young Leibniz, finding the *Metaphysical Disputations* in his father's library, read them, he said, like a novel.[16] Suárez thought Cajetan had gone wrong, and that it is analogy of attribution rather than analogy of proper proportionality that provides the key for understanding our language about God. But he shared the same dangerous determination to systematize and clarify.

Suárez rejected analogy of proportionality because, he said, "all true analogy of proportionality includes something metaphorical and inappropriate."[17] Cajetan had not gone far enough for him. After all, the way in which the heart is the principle of an animal is not really the same as the way in which the foundation is the principle of a house, and we cannot specify the difference with precision. Suárez found a source of greater precision in analogy of attribution. Cajetan, he said, had dismissed it too quickly because he had considered only analogies of *external* attribution, where the cause or sign lacks the

---

13. See ibid., 6.69.

14. Though see a variety of essays and translations by Jorge E. Gracia, and the helpful translation of some key sections in Francis Suárez, *On the Essence of Finite Being as Such, On the Existence of That Essence, and Their Distinction,* trans. Norman J. Wells (Milwaukee: Marquette University Press, 1983). Much more has been written about Suárez as a legal thinker. For a brilliant analysis much more detailed than what follows, see Jean-Luc Marion, *Sur la Theologie Blanche de Descartes* (Paris: Presses Universitaires de France, 1981), 96–135.

15. "Suárez was, certainly, the dominant metaphysician of the age." Richard A. Muller, "Arminius and the Scholastic Tradition," *Calvin Theological Journal* 24 (1989): 274. See also José Ferrater Mora, "Suárez and Modern Philosophy," *Journal of the History of Ideas* 14 (1952): 528–47.

16. Clare C. Riedl, "Suárez and the Organization of Learning," in *Jesuit Thinkers of the Renaissance,* ed. Gerard Smith (Milwaukee: Marquette University Press, 1939), 2–5.

17. Francisco Suárez, *Disputationes Metaphysicae* 28.3.11, *Opera Omnia,* vol. 26 (Paris: Ludovicus Vives, 1878), 16. In what follows I am drawing on Frederick Copleston, *A History of Philosophy,* vol. 3 (London: Burns, Oates & Washbourne, 1953), 353–79, which remains the best introduction to Suárez in English.

characteristic of the thing of which it is the cause or sign. The diet and the urine are not themselves, in the primary sense of the word, healthy. But sometimes a cause *does* have the property it causes in its effect. A fire, for instance, not only *causes* heat in a pan; the fire itself is hot. Indeed, it is as hot or hotter than the pan it heats. Suárez called the language we use in such a case "analogy of *internal* attribution." I feel the hot pan, and I know what heat is. I see the fire heating the pan and, without feeling the fire, I can talk about the "hot fire" and know what "heat" means here too, because I know the cause contains, in at least the same degree, the property it produces in the effect.[18]

Suárez centered much of his career on commenting on Aquinas, and yet, on the crucial issue of language about God, he appealed to Aquinas's greatest rival among medieval philosophers, John Duns Scotus. Aquinas had written of God as "sheer existence subsisting of his very nature."[19] Creatures *have* being, a being they derive from God, but God just *is* being. The definition of "king of France" does not include whether there actually is a king of France or not, but, Aquinas taught, one aspect of God's simplicity is that there is no distinction between God's essence and God's existence. One does not define God's essence and then add existence later. As a result, God's relation to being is just totally different from anything else's relation to being,[20] and we cannot imagine what "being" means as applied to God.[21]

Scotus and Suárez took a different tack. Created things, they said, are something and not nothing, and so is God, and so they share the property of "being."[22] Scotus even said that one can attribute "being" univocally to both God and creatures. Suárez backed off at that point—we can use the term, he said, only analogically.[23] Still, since he had redefined analogy to put it closer to univocity, he remained substantively on Scotus's side against Aquinas. Both God and creatures have being and therefore, understanding what "being" means in reference to creatures, we can extend the usage to God by analogy of internal attribution.[24] Creatures are, and God causes them to be. So, just as we can say that the fire must be at least as hot as the pan, so we can say that God must have at least as much being—and in the same sense of "being"—as the things God creates.[25]

As with being, so with substance: created substance, Suárez said, is different from God, the uncreated substance, but "it is possible to abstract the

18. Surárez, *Disputationes* 28.3.13.
19. Thomas Aquinas, *Summa Theologiae* 1a.44.1, trans. English Dominican Fathers (London: Blackfriars, 1963–).
20. Ibid., 1a.3.5.
21. Ibid., 1a.12.13 ad 1.
22. John Duns Scotus, *Opus oxoniense* 1.1.3, *Philosophical Writings,* trans. Allan Wolter (Edinburgh: Nelson, 1962).
23. Suárez, *Disputationes Metaphysicae* 28.3.2.
24. Ibid., 32.2.12.
25. Ibid., 28.3.10. See also Lohr, "Metaphysics," 616.

common concept of substance from created and uncreated alike."[26] We can talk about substance as applied to God and creatures "not univocally, but [only] analogously," but "substance" means the same thing in both cases, since we can "abstract" the concept itself from the different ways it applies to God and to creatures. Similar arguments follow about goodness or wisdom or any number of other properties that are not somehow tied to the nature of finite beings. Only a finite being can have properties like shape or temperature, so it makes no sense to ask what shape or how hot God is. But, since wisdom or goodness can apply independently of whether something is finite or infinite, such terms apply to God. They are, moreover, not metaphors, and certainly not Aquinas's reminders that we really do not know what we are saying. To say that the terms apply analogously to God is simply to say that God has them in greater degree—such was the teaching of Suárez. And when most Catholic teachers taught Thomism, the philosophy of Thomas Aquinas, for several centuries, what they taught on these matters was probably Suárez, or, failing that, Cajetan.[27] Jean-Luc Marion speaks of the "univocist drift that analogy undergoes with Suárez and others";[28] it was the first stage of what I am calling the domestication of God's transcendence.

Among the Protestants

Suárez died shortly after the beginning of the seventeenth century. As the century continued, that domestication of talk about God extended into the Protestant world as well. Some of the pressures at work are obvious. In a time of intense religious conflict, it would have been hard to admit that one's ideas were less clear, one's arguments less tight, than those of one's opponents. But the resulting concern for clear ideas and tight arguments, when applied to talk about God, moved Protestant theology away from some of the insights of the Reformation.

Among Lutherans, Jacob Martini's *Partitiones et Questiones Metaphysicae,* a sort of basic philosophical textbook published in Wittenberg in 1615, provided the standard categories for analyzing language about God, and Martini pretty much took over Cajetan's and Suárez's classifications. Lutheran theologians followed. Take for instance Johannes Andreas Quenstedt's monumental *Theologia Didactico-Polemica,* published in Wittenberg in 1685, of which Robert Preus, referring to its "unexcelled quality," says that it is "so big, so complete, so concise

---

26. Ibid., 32.1.6. See Jean-Luc Marion, "The Essential Incoherence of Descartes' Definition of Divinity," in Amelie Oksenberg Rorty, ed., *Essays in Descartes' Meditations* (Berkeley: University of California Press, 1986), 306.

27. See Lohr, "Metaphysics," 619; Etienne Gilson, *Being and Some Philosophers* (Toronto: Pontifical Institute of Medieval Studies, 1949), 112; Emerich Coreth, *Metaphysics,* trans. Joseph Donceel (New York: Herder & Herder, 1968), 81.

28. Marion, "The Essential Incoherence," 306.

and systematic, and so excellent that no later Lutheran ever came close to equaling it."[29] Quenstedt has often been called "the bookkeeper of orthodox Lutheranism,"[30] a sobriquet which, if it does not exactly honor his imagination, at least pays tribute to his orthodoxy and his influence. He made almost exactly Suárez's moves: created beings are not nothing, they have being, and God has being too. So we can use the word "being" (like any number of other predicates) of both creatures and God in an intrisinic analogy of attribution. "And although Being, as it is in God, is infinite, it is nevertheless possible to prescind the principle of that infinity. God differs from creatures in every way, not, however, in that He has Being, but in the sort of Being He has, i.e., infinite."[31] Again, the analogy seems only a matter of degree: God's being is infinite; creatures' finite. But if we can "prescind" the idea of being from that infinity, then we are really using being (or goodness, or wisdom) of God and creatures in the same way. Terms apply, Quenstedt said, *proprie,* properly, to both God and creatures.[32]

When he came to the doctrine of justification, Quenstedt followed Luther. All the initiatives come from God, in ways that no human rules can specify. Human reason finds divine grace utterly mysterious. But, as Karl Barth argued, in Quenstedt's discussion of our language about God he had already betrayed such principles, for he claimed that our human categories of wisdom and goodness and justice, and therefore the rules according to which we understand them to operate, precisely *are* transferable to God.[33] Other Lutheran theologians of the seventeenth century followed in the same path.[34] For them, we could understand the reasons for God's grace; it sounds like what Luther would have called a theology of glory.

The picture seems more complex on the Reformed side. By the seventeenth century the influence of Cajetan and Suárez had also widely spread among

---

29. Robert D. Preus, *The Theology of Post-Reformation Lutheranism,* vol. 1 (St. Louis: Concordia Publishing House, 1970), 62. Preus is a reliable guide to traditional reputations.

30. A. C. Ahlen, "The Seventeenth-Century Dogmaticians as Philosophers," *Concordia Theological Monthly* 30 (1959): 164.

31. J. A. Quenstedt, *Theologia didactico-polemica* 1.8.2.1 (Lipsiae: Thomas Fritsch, 1715). See also Robert D. Preus, *The Theology of Post-Reformation Lutheranism,* vol. 2 (St. Louis: Concordia, 1972), 41; Battista Mondin, *The Principle of Analogy in Protestant and Catholic Theology* (The Hague: Martinus Nijhoff, 1968), 111–12; Karl Barth, *Church Dogmatics,* vol. 2, part 1, trans. T.H.L. Parker et al. (Edinburgh: T. & T. Clark, 1957), 238. Barth says that Quenstedt is following Cajetan. I think the closer parallel is in fact with Suárez.

32. Barth, *Church Dogmatics,* vol. 2, part 1, 237.

33. Ibid., 241.

34. Take for instance David Hollaz, whom Preus calls the author of "the last great orthodox dogmatics" (the *Examen Theologicum Acroamaticum,* published in 1741; Preus adds, "No later dogmatics ever rivaled it in popularity," Preus, *The Theology of Post-Reformation Lutheranism,* 1:62). Hollaz wrote that "since God is one who shares His goodness and perfection, He has imparted many streams of His goodness and many rays of His perfection to His creatures with the result that they possess a certain, though limited, degree of perfection." We lack the infinity and necessity of God's being, goodness, or wisdom, but we do *have* being, goodness, and wisdom. Again, the issue becomes a matter of degree, Preus, *The Theology of Post-Reformation Lutheranism,* 2:41.

Reformed theologians.[35] As a result, they came to have surprising things to say (surprising at least to anyone has read Calvin) about human reason's ability to understand and speak clearly about God. To take one example, Girolamo Zanchi, whose time at Heidelberg established him as one of the most influential teachers of Reformed theology at the end of the sixteenth century, once wrote,

> Holy Scripture clearly teaches that God lives, and that God is living, and that that life is eternal. . . . On the other hand, what "life" means when applied to God and how to understand that God lives is not clearly explained there. From what God teaches, however, it is clear enough that we must first grasp the kind of thing that life and "to live" are. This is to be learned from philosophy.[36]

The Bible, in other words, tells us what terms can be applied to God, but we learn what those terms *mean* from philosophy—and therefore reason must be able to derive that meaning from their use with respect to creatures.

On the other hand, in their christological and eucharistic debates with the Lutherans, Reformed theologians preserved the "extra-Calvinisticum." Lutherans believed that, in the union of human and divine natures in Christ, all the divine attributes are communicated to Christ's human nature. Thus we can even say that Christ's humanity is "omnipresent" (a divine attribute) and therefore present (among all other places) in the bread and wine of the Eucharist. But the Calvinists replied that humanity lacks the capacity to take on all of divinity; there remains always something "extra." Omnipresence, in fact, they thought a good example of the sort of thing that just makes no sense when applied to a human nature.[37]

Though the extra-Calvinisticum emerged mainly out of christological concerns, it did offer a way of emphasizing the radical gap between human and divine, and therefore the inadequacy of human language as applied to God. But many Reformed theologians then controverted that emphasis by distinguishing between "incommunicable" and "communicable" attributes. The author of the most popular textbook of Reformed theology, Francis Turretin—his *Institutes* was the textbook at Princeton Seminary well into the nineteenth century—even identified this as *the* most important "among the various dis-

35. See John S. Bray, *Theodore Beza's Doctrine of Predestination* (Nieuwkoop: De Graff, 1975), 132; Paul Dibon, *La Philosophie néerlandaien au siècle d'or* (Paris: Elsevier, 1954), 257.

36. Hieronymus Zanchius, *De natura Dei seu de divinis attributis* 2.5.1, *Operum Theologicorum* (Geneva: Stephanus Gamonetus, 1613). Zanchius earlier discussed analogy, even using the classic Scholastic example of different meanings of "healthy," ibid., 1.10.8.

37. See E. David Willis, *Calvin's Catholic Christology: The Function of the So-called Extra Calvinisticum in Calvin's Theology* (Leiden: E. J. Brill, 1966), 8–25, and Heinrich Heppe, *Reformed Dogmatics*, trans. G. T. Thomson (London: George Allen & Unwin, 1950), 62. Heppe's volume cites Petrus van Mastricht, *Theoretico-practica Theologia* (Utrecht and Amsterdam: n.p., 1725), 2.4.12, but in the edition available to me (Trajecti ad Rhenum: W. van de Water, 1724) the most relevant discussion appears at 2.10.13. The key passages in Calvin are in the *Institutes* 2.13.4 and 4.17.30.

tinctions of the divine attributes."[38] Incommunicable attributes, like omnipresence, lie beyond the reach of any creature. But with communicable attributes, like goodness, justice, and wisdom, Turretin explained, we have to make a distinction. "Essentially" God's own goodness or wisdom remains part of God, and not something God can share—we could never possess God's own wisdom. But "formally" God can share communicable attributes, "since God produces . . . in creatures (especially in rational creatures) effects analogous to his own properties."[39]

And at this point, Turretin started to sound like Suárez. Communicable attributes are predicated of God and creatures neither univocally nor equivocally, he explained, but analogically in two senses: analogy of attribution and analogy of similarity. God is "good," for instance, in that God causes goodness in creatures (attribution) but also that goodness in God has "a certain similarity" to goodness in creatures (similarity).[40] Turretin has thus arrived by a different route at exactly what Suárez called analogy of internal attribution—A causes a property in B and also itself possesses the property it causes.[41] Thus the "shift to univocity"—the growing confidence that our language about God makes roughly the same sort of sense as our language about creatures—was nearly as common among both Lutheran and Reformed theologians as among Catholics in the seventeenth century. Historians often blame this development on the Protestant side on "scholasticism" and sometimes claim that these theologians turned back to Aquinas. If only they had! What they turned to was Suárez, and ways of thinking about God as different from Aquinas's as from Luther's or Calvin's.

Among the Philosophers

The standard ways of writing about and teaching the intellectual history of the seventeenth century tend to put theologians and philosophers in separate compartments. It is hard to imagine a course that would move chronologically from Descartes to Quenstedt, and Turretin to Leibniz. Yet theologians and philosophers at the time were wrestling with the same issues and often in conversation with each other. It is surprising how often Suárez lies in the background for all of them. Some of the philosophers, however, may illustrate the changes this chapter has been describing most clearly of all. Catholic theologians often balanced the sharp rigor of their theological systems with reflections on

---

38. Francis Turretin, *Institutes of Elenctic Theology* 3.6, trans. George Musgrave Giger (Phillipsburg, N.J.: Presbyterian and Reformed, 1992), 1:189.
39. Ibid., 3.6.
40. Ibid.
41. On Suárez's impact on Reformed theology, see John Platt, *Reformed Thought and Scholasticism: The Arguments for the Existence of God in Dutch Theology, 1575–1650* (Leiden: E. J. Brill, 1982), 229.

the spiritual life that preserved a sense of divine mystery. Protestants, even as they moved toward an un-Reformation optimism about human reason's ability to understand what we say about God, still preserved a doctrine of grace that reminded them that everything had to begin with divine initiatives. With philosophers, often nothing counterbalanced the push toward tighter arguments and more precise ideas.

No one so championed "clear and distinct ideas" as René Descartes, that symbol of the beginning of modern philosophy. Descartes had been educated by Suárez's order, the Jesuits, at La Flèche, their school in Paris. Well into middle life, he still remembered his textbooks there and praised the education he had received.[42] Challenged on a technical point of terminology, he admitted the issue "might . . . have worried me" had he not found the term used in just the same way "in the first philosophical author I came across, namely Suárez, in the *Metaphysical Disputations*."[43] In the almost ostentatiously casual reference, he may be showing off a bit, but it is hardly an accident that he turned to Suárez. As Gilson put it, "To Descartes, Scholastic philosophy was Suárez."[44]

Descartes was engaged, however, in an un-Scholastic project. In the midst of the social and intellectual chaos of his time, he was looking for some absolute certainty he could grasp and use as a foundation for a new system of scientific knowledge. Even with a good education, he said, we all acquire, one way or another, false beliefs. Some of them we hold with considerable conviction, and we base any number of other beliefs on them, so that we end up led badly astray. As he put it in the famous opening of his *Meditations on First Philosophy,*

> Some years ago I was struck by the large number of falsehoods that I had accepted as true in my childhood, and by the highly doubtful nature of the whole edifice I had subsequently based on them. I realized that it was necessary, once in the course of my life, to demolish everything completely and start again right from the foundations if I wanted to establish anything at all in the sciences that was stable and likely to last.[45]

As he challenged all his beliefs with the acid of methodological doubt, he discovered one that survived: his own existence as a thinking thing. Even if I am in error, still *I* am in error; even if someone is deceiving me, still *I* am being deceived. "I must finally conclude that this proposition, *I am, I exist,* is neces-

---

42. "Nowhere on earth is philosophy better taught than at La Flèche." René Descartes, Letter to Debaune, 12 September 1638, *The Philosophical Writings of Descartes,* vol. 3, trans. John Cottingham et al. (Cambridge: Cambridge University Press, 1991), 124. See also Letter to Mersenne, 30 September 1640, ibid., 154.

43. René Descartes, "Fourth Set of Replies," *Philosophical Writings,* vol. 2, trans. John Cottingham, Robert Stoothoff, and Dugald Murdoch (Cambridge: Cambridge University Press, 1984), 164.

44. Gilson, *Being and Some Philosophers,* 109.

45. Descartes, "Meditations on First Philosophy," *Philosophical Writings,* 2:12.

sarily true whenever it is put forward by me or conceived in my mind."[46] But the world is still a lonely place if the only reality of which I can be certain is my own existence.

From this starting point, however, Descartes derived a general principle: "So I now seem to be able to lay it down as a general truth that whatever I perceive very clearly and distinctly is true."[47] That is, reflecting on his own existence as a thinking thing, analyzing the idea, he had realized that it made no sense to doubt it. If he could find other truths of the same sort, then they too would be trustworthy. Inspecting the ideas that cluttered his mind, however, he found many of them far from clear and distinct, easily liable to illusion. But from some of them Descartes thought he could derive an argument for the existence of God and thereby get his project properly begun.[48]

He discovered that he had an idea "of a supreme God, eternal, infinite, immutable, omniscient, omnipotent, and the creator of all things that exist apart from him."[49] Whether there existed any external reality corresponding to such an idea remained for the moment an open question, but the idea existed, there in Descartes's understanding. "Now it is manifest by the natural light that there must be at least as much reality in the efficient and total cause as in the effect of that cause."[50] Descartes could be quoting from Suárez on the analogy of proper proportionality (in *proper* proportionality, it will be recalled, the cause as well as the effect has the attribute in question—the fire has to be as hot or hotter than the pan it is heating), but he is making a simple enough point. If I find myself lost in the woods and needing to start a fire, I cannot start a real fire with an imagined match, because an imagined match would not have "as much reality" as a real fire, and therefore would not suffice as its "total and efficient cause." Taking the argument one step further, Descartes added,

> But it is also true that the *idea* of heat, or a stone, cannot exist in me unless it is put there by some cause which contains at least as much reality as I conceive to be in the heat or in the stone. . . . in order for a given idea to contain such and such objective reality, it must surely derive it from some cause which contains at least as much formal reality as there is objective reality in the idea.[51]

In other words, if I have an idea of something, then the cause of that idea must have at least as much "reality" as the object of which it is an idea.

So what about the ideas I discover within myself? I have an idea of myself, but I could myself be the cause of that. Indeed, with all my ideas of finite

46. Ibid., 2:17.
47. Ibid., 2:24.
48. I am oversimplifying the story. In fact he offered, by the standard count, three arguments for the existence of God; I am focusing on the first.
49. Ibid., 2:28.
50. Ibid.
51. Ibid., 2:28–29.

things, I have as much reality as their objects, and therefore I could be their cause. But I do have one idea of an object with more reality than I possess:

> By the word "God" I understand a substance that is infinite, eternal, immutable, independent, supremely intelligent, supremely powerful, and which created both myself and everything else (if anything else there be) that exists. All these attributes are such that, the more carefully I concentrate on them, the less possible it seems that they could have originated from me alone. So from what has been said it must be concluded that God necessarily exists.[52]

Analyzing the idea I find I have of God, I conclude that nothing has enough reality to cause that idea but, in fact, God. And therefore God exists. Then it turns out that this God made me: since I contain an idea of infinite perfection, only an infinite and perfect cause would suffice to produce me. Further, this God is perfect—a fact I derive just by reflecting on my idea of God—and therefore would not engage in deception, "For in every case of trickery or deception some imperfection is to be found; and although the ability to deceive appears to be an indication of cleverness or power, the will to deceive is undoubtedly evidence of malice or weakness, and so cannot apply to God."[53] Therefore, if I use the faculties God gave me as they were designed to be used, I will not be deceived. In remarkably short order, Descartes then recovered most of the world, its reality now established on a secure foundation. "This is a revolutionary moment in Western philosophy," Michael Buckley has written. "It is not the sensible universe that is the evidence for god, but the nature of god that is the warrant for the sensible universe."[54]

That reversal forced Descartes to make stronger claims concerning his knowledge of God. For Aquinas, James Collins once wrote, God was outside any metaphysical system, but "in the deductive enterprise of Descartes, God had work to do and was thus included among the principles and subject matter of metaphysics precisely because of his functional contribution to the whole system."[55] Suárez (and behind him Scotus) had already claimed that "being" had essentially the same meaning with respect to God and creatures and thus set the stage for Descartes's argument that God has more being (but "being" in the same sense) than we do. But, if Suárez had to admit that he did not understand this idea of God's being clearly and distinctly, his whole system did not collapse. In contrast, "if I do not know this," Descartes admitted, "it seems that I can never be quite certain about anything else."[56]

52. Ibid., 2:31.
53. Ibid., 2:37.
54. Michael J. Buckley, *At the Origins of Modern Atheism* (New Haven: Yale University Press, 1987), 92.
55. James Collins, *God in Modern Philosophy* (Chicago: Henry Regnery Co., 1959), 59.
56. Descartes, "Meditations on First Philosophy," *Philosophical Writings,* 2:25.

That need to understand God, however, trapped Descartes in a dilemma, for one of the properties of this God is infinity, and Descartes believed that the infinite is beyond our comprehension: "The idea of the infinite, if it is to be a true idea, cannot be grasped at all, since the impossibility of being grasped is contained in the formal definition of the infinite."[57] Thus as Jean-Marie Beyssade has written, "There is a paradox at the heart of Cartesian metaphysics. On the one hand, Descartes's whole system of scientific knowledge depends on our assured knowledge of God; but on the other hand, the idea of God is explicitly stated by Descartes to be beyond our comprehension."[58] Nor is this a problem identified only by modern commentators. Descartes had his *Meditations* circulated among a number of his contemporaries for their critical comments, and they rather consistently accused him of claiming to have a clear idea of something that, by definition, he could not clearly understand.[59]

Given Descartes's project, however, he could not retreat to a vague idea of something-or-other greater than himself.[60] To make his argument work, he needed a clear and distinct idea, such that he could draw the relevant inferences from it, and that idea had to include perfection, since only perfection permits the inference that this creator God, as perfect, cannot deceive us. A merely very powerful but mysterious being might, after all, be a trickster.[61] But Descartes argued for God's perfection on the grounds that God was infinite, and infinity implied perfection—even though he had admitted he could not really understand infinity.[62]

To make matters worse, that infinitely perfect being would have to combine every kind of perfection, and to an infinite degree.[63] After all, this God must be infinitely powerful, must be my creator, must have such moral perfection as to be incapable of deception. But is it obvious that possessing any one perfection infinitely is compatible with possessing every other perfection infinitely?[64] Many kinds of excellence, after all, are incompatible with each other. The most beautiful mountain scenery is not the most productive cropland. The

57. Descartes, "Fifth Replies," *Philosophical Writings*, 2:253. See also 2:100 and 2:133. See also Descartes, Letter to Mersenne, 15 April 1630, *Philosophical Writings*, 3:23.

58. Jean-Marie Beyssade, "The Idea of God and the Proofs of His Existence," in John Cottingham, *The Cambridge Companion to Descartes* (Cambridge: Cambridge University Press, 1992), 174.

59. See Johannes Caterus, "First Set of Objections," in Descartes, *Philosophical Writings*, 2:69–70; Marin Mersenne, "Second Set of Objections," ibid., 2:91; Thomas Hobbes, "Third Set of Objections," ibid., 2:131; Pierre Gassendi, "Fifth Set of Objections," ibid., 2:206.

60. Jean-Luc Marion suspects him of occasional retreats. See Marion, "The Essential Incoherence of Descartes' Definition of Divinity," 300–301. To cite one worrisome passage: "Is there not a God, or whatever I may call him?" Descartes, "Meditations on First Philosophy," *Philosophical Writings*, 2:16.

61. ". . . some malicious demon of the utmost power and cunning," ibid., 2:15.

62. Descartes, "Discourse on Method," *Philosophical Writings*, vol. 1, trans. John Cottingham, Robert Stoothoff, and Dugald Murdoch (Cambridge: Cambridge University Press, 1985), 128.

63. Descartes, "Meditations on First Philosophy," ibid., 2:32.

64. See Edwin Curley, *Descartes against the Skeptics* (Oxford: Basil Blackwell, 1978), 130, 168.

best sumo wrestler will not be the best marathon runner. It may be that the kinds of perfections God possesses *are* all mutually compatible, but one would have to lay them out, understand them, and make the argument. And Descartes even admitted that God has an infinite number of perfections we do not know, and that we cannot fully comprehend the ones we do know.[65]

Descartes was himself aware of the problems he faced. On several occasions, he distinguished between "grasping," which we can do only of something finite, and "understanding" or "seeing" or "perceiving," which we can manage even of God:

> A finite mind cannot grasp God, who is infinite. But that does not prevent him from having a perception of God, just as one can touch a mountain without being able to put one's arms round it.[66]

Or again, in a quite remarkable passage:

> When we look at the sea, our vision does not encompass its entirety, nor do we measure out its enormous vastness; but we are still said to "see" it. . . . if we fix our gaze on some part of the sea at close quarters, then our view can be clear and distinct. . . . In the same way, God can be taken in by the human mind. . . . But those who try to attend to God's individual perfections and try not so much to take hold of them as to surrender to them, using all the strength of their intellect to contemplate them, will certainly find that God provides much more ample and straightforward subject matter for clear and distinct knowledge than does any created thing.[67]

In that brief phrase, "not so much to take hold of them as to surrender to them," there is a hint of a radically different way of thinking about God, one that might have had much more in common with Aquinas, or with Descartes's contemporary Blaise Pascal, but it is a hint Descartes did not pursue. He needed clarity—an idea of the existence of divine perfection, he once wrote, "at least as certain as any geometrical proof."[68] In Jean-Luc Marion's elegant phrase, "The paradox of ontological equivocity coupled with epistemological univocity results from the complete absence of analogy."[69] Without an appeal to faith that makes possible speaking confidently even as we confess that we do not

---

65. Descartes, "Meditations on First Philosophy," *Philosophical Writings*, 2:32, 35.
66. Descartes, "Appendix to the Fifth Set of Objections and Replies," *Philosophical Writings*, 2:273–74. See also Descartes, Letter to Mersenne, 27 May 1630, *Philosophical Writings*, 3:25.
67. Descartes, "First Set of Replies," *Philosophical Writings*, 2:81–82.
68. Descartes, "Discourse on Method," *Philosophical Writings*, 1:129.
69. Marion, *Sur la Theologie Blanche de Descartes*, 439. "The *Replies* use analogy only to reduce the essence of God to the general rule which governs finite beings—causality. This is why, far from reducing the tendency to univocity, this *analogy* augments it. . . . Descartes takes this decision for univocity very consciously since, to establish it, he has to modify two concepts—that of cause (efficient) and that of aseity (divine), opposing himself to St. Thomas in both cases." Ibid., 428, 432.

understand what our words mean, the contrast between divine mystery and the need for clear and distinct ideas produces an intellectual crisis.

A few lonely voices—Pascal's for instance—proposed admitting the problems in Descartes's project and giving up the whole idea of placing God within a rational system of clear and distinct ideas. But the dominant response was damage control: if there were flaws in what Descartes had done, fix them. Most philosophers in the seventeenth century wanted to drive back mystery by the clear application of reason. No one, for instance, ever sought to extend the field of human reason with greater energy than the German philosopher-mathematician-historian-diplomat Gottfried Wilhelm Leibniz. Mathematicians, Leibniz reflected, do not go to war when they come up with different results. They sit down and review their calculations to find who made the mistake. His dream was that political and religious differences might be settled in a similar way; he once even attempted a geometric proof of who should be elected the next king of Poland. But if God had a place in the way we understand the world—as was the case for Leibniz—then the realization of that dream required clear reasoning about God.

In 1676, thirty-five years after Descartes had published the *Meditations,* Leibniz, on his way to take a new job in Hanover, stopped off in Holland to visit Baruch Spinoza.[70] He had, before his visit, been reading Descartes, and he had drafted a brief memorandum—just a page—he wanted to show Spinoza about how to repair a flaw in Descartes's philosophy. He had titled it, "That a Most Perfect Being Exists."[71] According to Leibniz, Descartes had shown that, if God's existence is possible, then God exists. That is, if we can formulate a clear and logically coherent idea of God, then Descartes's arguments do in fact establish God's existence. But, Leibniz said, Descartes had left the task incomplete, since he had not in fact established that we can formulate a logically coherent idea of God.[72] If God is like a round square, the sort of idea that, on closer examination, proves to be internally contradictory, then the question of God's existence cannot even arise.[73]

For Leibniz, the central problem was that God is supposed to possess all perfections. As already noted, it is not clear that all perfections are mutually compatible, and therefore the idea of God might break down. In his memorandum to Spinoza, Leibniz explained that, "By a *perfection* I mean every

70. Stuart Brown, *Leibniz* (Brighton: Harvester, 1984), 61.

71. Gottfried Wilhelm Leibniz, *Philosophical Papers and Letters,* trans. Leroy E. Loemker (Chicago: University of Chicago Press, 1956), 259–61.

72. Leibniz returned to this issue again and again. For a range of references, see Robert Merrihew Adams, *Leibniz: Determinist, Theist, Idealist* (Oxford: Oxford University Press, 1994), 135. Leibniz's focus was on Descartes's version of the ontological argument, presented in the Fifth Meditation, rather than the argument I traced earlier in this chapter, but similar issues arise in either case.

73. See Leibniz's letter to Countess Elizabeth (1678), *Philosophical Essays,* trans. Roger Ariew and Daniel Garber (Indianapolis: Hackett Publishing Co., 1989), 238.

simple quality which is positive and absolute or which expresses whatever it expresses without any limits."[74] But simple qualities are logically independent of each other, and therefore they can never be in contradiction. If for instance (Leibniz himself did not at this point offer examples) we think of goodness and indivisibility as simple qualities, then they just represent different realms, so that no characteristics of God's goodness could be inconsistent with God's indivisibility. By contrast, the idea of a round square does embody a contradiction, since "round" and "square" are not really simple qualities. Both describe patterns of lines, they thus have to do with the same sort of thing, and they can therefore be incompatible.[75]

Find simple qualities that are positive and absolute, and that admit of a highest degree, then, and your idea of God can have as many of them as you like without fear of inconsistency. By thinking through the nature of simple qualities, Leibniz thought he had shown that the idea of God, consisting as it did only of such qualities, is consistent. Thus he had repaired the flaw in Descartes's argument, and the existence of God could be established as a foundation for a system of knowledge after all.

Only two years after his meeting with Spinoza, however, Leibniz himself was already having doubts. He thought that one step of his argument involved claiming that a most perfect being would have to be a necessary being, and he now was unsure that that would follow. Moreover, as he and his critics considered the matter, the definition of "simplicity" proved steadily more complex.[76] From some points of view, there is something comic about thinking that one has nearly established definitively that the world makes sense and human knowledge is basically trustworthy, but there are one or two weak points in the argument that need attention. Yet Leibniz, like many of his contemporaries, was engaged in roughly such a project, and that points to an important change in seventeenth-century thought.

Reflection about God had moved a long way from the intellectual world of Aquinas, Luther, and Calvin. For Aquinas, "simplicity" marked the ways we cannot understand God—we cannot divide God into component parts, we cannot distinguish potentiality and actuality in God, and so on. For Leibniz, "simplicity," as applied to God's perfections, guaranteed that we have clear and logically consistent ideas of God's properties. For Aquinas (and Luther and Calvin as well) the words appropriately used about God apply best of all to God, but in a way that none of us can understand. If we were to see God, we would understand that God is wise or good in a way that dwarfs all human wisdom or goodness. But we cannot see God, and therefore we cannot imagine what wisdom or goodness is like in God. But for Leibniz, as for Descartes,

74. Leibniz, "That a Most Perfect Being Exists," *Philosophical Papers and Letters,* 259.
75. See Leibniz, "Discourse on Metaphysics" (1686), *Philosophical Essays,* 35.
76. Adams, *Leibniz,* 172.

we can recognize the finitude and imperfection of the created world only because we even now have clear and distinct ideas of God's infinity and perfection, so that we can recognize failures to measure up to them.[77]

We can understand God, many seventeenth-century philosophers and theologians believed, because God is not utterly different from us. God's omniscience, omnipotence, and infinite goodness are the same sorts of qualities we have, differing only in degree—otherwise we would not be able to analyze them well enough to see their mutual coherence.[78] God acts according to reasons we can understand, Leibniz said, to create a world that combines the greatest variety together with the greatest order.[79] Obviously, none of us can grasp the details, but we can understand the principles at work. We cannot prove that this is the best of all possible worlds, but we can understand what "best" means, for God's standards have to be, in the new strong sense, analogous with ours. The God of Aquinas, Luther's hidden God, the object of Calvin's faith—those haunting reminders of the limits of our understanding when we turn to God—were not the sort of thing for which most seventeenth-century thinkers had much patience.

77. Gottfried Wilhelm Leibniz, *New Essays on Human Understanding*, trans. Peter Remnant and Jonathan Bennett (Cambridge: Cambridge University Press, 1982), 157–58.
78. Leibniz, "Principles of Nature and Grace," *Philosophical Essays*, 210.
79. Ibid.

6   The Domestication of Grace

"Sin boldly," Luther once famously advised his cautious young friend
Philipp Melanchthon. It is a dangerous phrase to quote out of context, but it
does capture something about the daring ethical freedom implied by the account of grace the Reformation drew from deep in the Christian tradition. Confident of one's salvation in Christ, one can live out one's gratitude to God in
joy, even occasionally with a certain recklessness, in the service of this God
who, Luther said, "loves sinners, evil persons, fools and weaklings."[1] "The
knowledge of this freedom," Calvin wrote in characteristically more measured
tones, "is very necessary for us, for if it is lacking, our consciences will have
no repose and there will be no end to superstitions."[2]

In the seventeenth century, much of that spirit got lost, as both Protestants
and Catholics turned to worrying about the state of their souls and the criteria
by which they could measure it. Chapter 5 discussed how seventeenth-century
philosophers and theologians claimed to grasp what they said about God with
greater precision. This chapter will trace parallel developments away from accepting the mystery of divine grace toward attempts to discern its presence by
human standards. It would be too simple to say that one sort of change caused
the other, but the search for clarity in language about God certainly could lead
to a search for rules in the operation of grace. Such attempts led some in the
seventeenth century to *limit* the role of grace so as to "leave more room" for
human freedom—more about them in chapter 9. This chapter considers those
who championed a *strong* understanding of grace—specifically Pietists,
Jansenists, and Puritans, the three movements with which, Jaroslav Pelikan has
asserted, the modern period of Christian thought began.[3] In practice, even they
often limited grace's role.

All three groups were near their height in the 1640s, at the same time
Descartes was trying to lay foundations for modern philosophy. All three emphasized that we are saved by grace alone. But all were also haunted by the
question of whether individuals can know for certain that they themselves have
been saved. Moreover, in the face of corruption in the churches, social disorder, and a rising secularism that did not seem to take sin very seriously, all
three groups wanted to call Christians back to strong moral values. Many of

---

1. Martin Luther, "Heidelberg Disputation," trans. Harold J. Grimm, *Luther's Works*, vol. 31
(Philadelphia: Muhlenberg Press, 1957), 57.
2. John Calvin, *Institutes of the Christian Religion* 3.19.7, trans. Ford Lewis Battles (Philadelphia:
Westminster Press, 1960).
3. Jaroslav Pelikan, *Reformation of Church and Doctrine* (Chicago: University of Chicago Press,
1983), viii. Pelikan adds to his list developments in Eastern Orthodoxy I will not be discussing.

them doubted that gratitude to God by itself would turn the trick, and they sought to encourage moral rigor by inviting Christians to take a long, hard look at themselves to see if they were worthy of grace. The Reformers would have judged that a bad question, believing that none of us are worthy. "We shall not find assurance of our election in ourselves," Calvin had written. Rather, Christ "is the mirror wherein we must, and without self-deception may, contemplate our own election."[4] In different ways, however, Pietists, Jansenists, and Puritans, like Descartes, all sought certainty by looking inward. Such rigorous self-examination seemed to them not only the road to Christian self-confidence but a foundation for moral seriousness and social order. It put such emphasis on looking at ourselves, however, that the fact that everything depended on God's grace kept risking getting lost. And it just didn't work: honest Christians with a serious understanding of sin found it hard to discover assurance of their salvation by looking within themselves. Calvin had been right: their consciences found no repose, and there was no end of superstitions.

From Luther to the Pietists

Hiding out in Wartburg Castle in 1521, under sentence for heresy, Luther had to watch with frustration as Melanchthon and others cautiously tried to manage the new movement of Reformation back in Wittenberg. Impatiently, he wrote Melanchthon:

> If you are a preacher of grace, then preach a true and not a fictitious grace; if grace is true, you must bear a true and not a fictitious sin. God does not save people who are only fictitious sinners. Be a sinner and sin boldly, but believe and rejoice in Christ even more boldly, for he is victorious over sin, death, and the world. As long as we are here, we have to sin. This life is not the dwelling place of righteousness, but, as Peter says, we look for new heavens and a new earth in which righteousness dwells. It is enough that by the riches of God's glory we have come to know that Lamb that takes away the sins of the world.[5]

If we are justified by grace alone through faith alone, he said, then we can take risks in our faith. After all, a Christian should not think "he is pleasing to God on account of what he does, but rather by a confident trust in his favor he does such tasks for a gracious and loving God and to his honor and praise alone. And in so doing he serves and benefits his neighbor."[6] The person trying to earn salvation can never fully concentrate on either the glory of God or the

---

4. Calvin, *Institutes* 3.24.5.

5. Luther To Melanchthon, 1 August 1521, *Luther's Works*, vol. 48, trans. Gottfried G. Krodel (Philadelphia: Fortress Press, 1963), 281–82. For much of what follows, see Paul Althaus, *The Ethics of Martin Luther*, trans. Robert C. Schulz (Philadelphia: Fortress Press, 1972).

6. Martin Luther, *Treatise on Good Works*, trans. W. A. Lambert, *Luther's Works*, vol. 44 (Philadelphia: Fortress Press, 1966), 97. See also "Preface to the Epistle of St. Paul to the Romans," trans. Charles M. Jacob, *Luther's Works*, vol. 35 (Philadelphia: Muhlenberg Press, 1960), 370.

good of a needy neighbor; one will always be thinking about how much credit a morally good act will build up in one's own account. If we realize that we need not worry about our salvation, by contrast, that "for ourselves we need nothing to make us pious," then we act out of "pleasure and love." "If someone desires from me a service I can render him, I will gladly do it out of good will, whether it is commanded or not. I will do so for the sake of brotherly love and because service to my neighbor is pleasing to God."[7] I can glorify God because God deserves the glory, and I can help my neighbors because they need the help; my own fate already rests secure in God's grace.

Such confidence ought to free Christians from worrying overmuch about moral rules. Luther even proposed that, to make sure we do not take our own virtues too solemnly, we should from time to time consciously exercise our Christian freedom in a harmless way: sleep too late, eat or drink more than usual, take part in a practical joke.[8] A faithful relation to God, he proposed, is like a good marriage. "When a husband and wife really love one another, have pleasure in each other, and thoroughly believe in their love, who teaches them how they are to behave one to another . . . ?" They do not need checklists of instructions—indeed, if they are resorting to such checklists, then something has already gone wrong with the marriage—but they spontaneously do "even more than is necessary," and freely, "with a glad, peaceful, and confident heart."[9]

In the seventeenth century, however, even among Lutherans most committed to Luther's principles, things changed. About a century after Luther's death, a twelve-year-old Lutheran boy named Philipp Jakob Spener was persuaded to join in some dancing. "Indeed, I was bad," he wrote years later. "Hardly had I begun, however, when I was overladen by such fear that I ran away from the dance and never since that time tried it again."[10] Given Luther's impatience with Melanchthon, it is hard to imagine what he might have made of Spener. As an adult, Spener became the leading figure in the Lutheran Pietist movement. The Pietists encouraged lay Bible study, prayer groups, and moral improvement as well as sermons that appealed more to the heart than the arid intellectualism of much Lutheran scholastic preaching. They did *not* challenge traditional Lutheran views on faith and grace. "We gladly acknowledge," Spener wrote, "that we must be saved only and alone through faith and that

---

7. Martin Luther, *Sermons on the First Epistle of St. Peter* (on 1 Peter 2:13–17), trans. Martin H. Bertram, *Luther's Works*, vol. 30 (St. Louis: Concordia Publishing House, 1967), 79.

8. Karl Holl, *The Reconstruction of Morality*, trans. Fred W. Meuser and Walter R. Wietzke (Minneapolis: Augsburg Press, 1979), 96–97.

9. Luther, *Treatise on Good Works, Luther's Works*, 44:26–27.

10. Quoted in Carl Hildebrand von Constein, *Ausführliche Beeschreibung der Lebenz-Geschichte . . . des seligen Herrn D. Philipp Jakob Spener*, in *Speners Kleine Geistliche Schriften* (Magdeburg: Christoph Seidels und Ernst Scheidhauer, 1741), 1:16; cited in Theodore G. Tappert, "Introduction," to Philipp Jakob Spener, *Pia Desideria*, trans. Theodore G. Tappert (Philadelphia: Fortress Press, 1964), 10.

our works or godly life contribute neither much nor little to our salvation. . . . Far be it from us to depart even a finger's breadth from this teaching."[11]

Their concern for moral and spiritual life, however, encouraged them to much greater reflection on the state of their souls. Christians, Spener said, not only "must become accustomed not to lose sight of any opportunity in which they can render their neighbor a service of love," but also "while performing it they must diligently search their hearts to discover whether they are acting in true love or out of other motives."[12] If self-examination disclosed the wrong motives, one was in trouble as a Christian. Pietist manuals discussed such matters with the scrupulous detail of the most legalistic Catholic texts. August Hermann Francke, Spener's most noted successor as a Pietist leader, even published as his first work a translation of the Spanish Jesuit Miguel de Molinos's *Spiritual Guide,* with implied approval of most of its contents.[13]

If anything, these Lutherans pushed beyond their Catholic models. Not only were "games and other pastimes such as dancing, jumping, and so forth" condemned because they "arise from an improper and empty manner of life," but the good Pietist was even told to "guard yourself from unnecessary laughter. All laughter is forbidden. . . . Joking does not please God; why then should it please you? If it does not please you, why do you laugh over it?"[14] Students, according to Spener, should be given "concrete suggestions" on "how to know themselves better through self-examination,"[15] and only those who "lead a godly life" should be allowed to graduate, "even if they are behind the others in their studies."[16] Each person, Francke agreed, "must consider what he has done with himself . . . and if he has banned all evil intentions from his heart."[17] Today the word *pious* often evokes the image of a pale, nervous, unimaginative young person—an image unfair to the Christian gospel, unfair to the Reformation, but perhaps not completely unfair to these seventeenth- and eighteenth-century Pietists. Many of their contemporaries talked about them as "zealots," "hypocrites," "long-noses," "double-reformers," and "misanthropes."[18]

Most significantly, the Pietists began to change the way they told the

11. Spener, *Pia Desideria,* 63.

12. Ibid., 96.

13. Gary R. Sattler, *Nobler than the Angels, Lower than a Worm* (Lanham, Md.: University Press of America, 1989), 11.

14. August Hermann Francke, "Rules for the Protection of Conscience and for Good Order in Conversation or in Society" (1689), in *Pietists,* ed. and trans. Peter C. Erb (New York: Paulist Press, 1983), 111–12. Already at age eleven, Francke began to resist "the bad example of other children," in aid of which his family gave him "a room to myself" that he might "daily cultivate my heartfelt devotions and prayers to God."August Hermann Francke, "August Hermann Franckes Lebenslauf," *Werke in Auswahl* (Berlin: Luther Verlag, 1969), 7.

15. Spener, *Pia Desideria,* 112.

16. Ibid., 107–08.

17. August Hermann Francke, "Following Christ," *Pietists,* 142.

18. Gisbert Voetius, "Concerning 'Precision' in Interpretation of Questions 94, 113, and 115 of the Catechism," *Reformed Dogmatics,* ed. and trans. John Beardslee III (New York: Oxford University Press, 1965), 325.

Christian story. Calvin never directly mentioned his own conversion; Luther talked often of his own spiritual development, but almost always as passing illustration. For the Reformation, as for most earlier Christians, what was central was the story of God's gracious acts from creation through covenant through incarnation on to final judgment. The believer's life had meaning and significance only as it fit into that framework.[19] No Pietist would have denied any of that, and yet in practice the stories they most often told were the stories of their own lives. The greatest documents of the Reformation are its biblical commentaries; the greatest documents of seventeenth-century Christianity are its diaries and spiritual biographies. Theologically considered, this is not an improvement. At worst, "Christ" risks becoming the name of an event in *their* lives.

In its efforts to systematize and clarify its account of faith, Protestant orthodoxy had already developed a detailed account of the stages of salvation: each believer is, according to one list, in sequence elected, called, illumined, converted, regenerated, justified, mystically united with Christ, sanctified, preserved to the end, and finally glorified with the Son. The Pietists explored each stage in greater detail and emphasized illumination, conversion, and sanctification, arguably the three most "psychological" of them. As Peter Erb remarks of Spener, the Pietists generally "focused more on the subjective appropriation of the believer's redemption than on God's objective saving act in history."[20] For assurance of salvation, they looked within themselves, and they looked systematically.

From Trent to the Jansenists

Jansenism became important in France about the time of Spener, and it has intriguing parallels with Pietism. While the Jansenists were Catholics, their Catholic opponents regularly accused them of crypto-Protestantism, precisely because they so emphasized grace at the expense of any element of free will.[21] Yet, like the Pietists, they gave new attention to believers' internal states, worrying about right human attitudes in a way that potentially moved away from trusting all to God's grace.

In a Catholic context, to be sure, the Jansenists were the champions of a strong doctrine of grace. In the middle of the sixteenth century, the Council of

19. See Hans W. Frei, "Eberhard Busch's Biography of Karl Barth," in idem, *Types of Christian Theology* (New Haven: Yale University Press, 1992), 161.

20. Peter C. Erb, "Introduction," *Pietists,* 6. See also Eric Lund, "Lutheran and Reformed Spirituality," in *Christian Spirituality: Post-Reformation and Modern,* ed. Louis Dupré and Don E. Saliers (New York: Crossroad, 1989), 221.

21. The Jansenist Antoine Arnauld indeed once denounced Protestantism as "a completely sensual heresy . . . which makes people fodder for their passions . . . [and] completely ruins the penitence of sinners, the virginity of virgins, the vows of members of religious orders, the celibacy of priests, the fasts of the faithful, and the good works of all the church." Antoine Arnauld, "De la fréquente communion," *Oeuvres,* vol. 27 (Paris: Sigismond d'Arnay, 1779), 103.

Trent, systematizing the Catholic response to the Reformation, had declared that, while grace is necessary for salvation, Christians must help in the process "by freely assenting to and cooperating with . . . grace."[22] Ignatius Loyola, the founder of the Jesuits, expanded on the point:

> We ought not to emphasize the doctrine that would destroy free will. We may therefore speak of faith and grace to the extent that God enables us to do so, for the greater praise of His Divine Majesty. But, in these dangerous times of ours, it must not be done in such a way that good works or free will suffer any detriment.[23]

At about the same time, however, a professor at the University of Louvain named Michael Baius was defending a more Augustinian view of grace: we are saved by grace alone, without the need of human "cooperation." In 1567 Pope Pius V condemned his efforts as too close to Protestant views, but they remained in circulation at Louvain, where two friends, Cornelius Jansen and Du Vergier de Hauranne, were students at the beginning of the seventeenth century. Jansen became a faculty member at Louvain and spent much of his life working on a massive book on Augustine, published in 1640, two years after his death. His friend returned to France and became the abbot of Saint Cyran and spiritual advisor to, among many others, Angélique Arnauld, the young abbess of a convent at Port-Royal.

Mother Angélique's wealthy family had installed her as abbess at the age of ten. While still in her teens, she began a radical reform of the convent, turning what had been a rather comfortable home for unmarriageable daughters of the wealthy into an austere religious community. Port-Royal became the center of "Jansenism" and soon attracted the support of two polemicists of genius, Mother Angélique's younger brother Antoine Arnauld, and Blaise Pascal, mathematician, philosopher, and brother of one of her nuns.[24]

The Jansenists attacked an ethical leniency they saw pervading the church and which they identified particularly with the Jesuits. Some Jesuit confessors would let sinners off the hook if they could find any "probable" account of why their act had not been a sin—any authority in the history of the church who would make such an argument[25]—and French aristocrats sought out

---

22. "Decree on Justification," chap. 5, *Canons and Decrees of the Council of Trent,* trans. H. J. Schroeder (St. Louis: B. Herder, 1941), 32.

23. Ignatius Loyola, "Rules for Thinking with the Church," in *The Spiritual Exercises of St. Ignatius,* trans. Anthony Mottola (Garden City, N.Y.: Doubleday & Co., 1964), 141.

24. Antoine Arnauld was one of the initial critics of Descartes's *Meditations* mentioned in the last chapter.

For the liveliest, if not always fairest, account of Jansenism, see Ronald Knox, *Enthusiasm* (New York: Oxford University Press, 1980), 176–230.

25. Bartolomaeo a Medina, *Expositio in primam secundae angelici doctoris D. Thomae Aquinatis* (Venice: Petrus Dehuchinus, 1580), 178. On the pre–seventeenth-century understanding of "probability" as "supported by some authority," see Jeffrey Stout, *The Flight from Authority* (Notre Dame, Ind.: University of Notre Dame Press, 1981), 7.

accommodating confessors with the eagerness of defendants today seeking high-priced lawyers. The Jansenists in contrast insisted that true repentance had to involve "contrition," authentic regret for one's sin simply because it had been a sin against God, while the Jesuits said that "attrition," regretting the sin just out of fear of hell or because it would involve an inconvenient penance, sufficed.[26] In Pascal's withering phrase, the Jansenists thus accused their Jesuit opponents of freeing people "from the *irksome* obligation of actually loving God."[27] For a combination of political and theological reasons, papal declarations repeatedly condemned Jansenism, and in 1709 the last fifteen nuns were forcibly removed from Port-Royal and the convent torn down.

The reform of the Catholic church that began at Trent had tightened moral standards, acknowledging the justification of many Protestant attacks on late medieval corruption. But Trent's focus was on *external* corruption, on practices in the church that had led to scandal or inefficiency—priests with concubines, church officials who took their salaries but never did their jobs, priests too badly educated to teach their people, and so on. The members of the council explicitly rejected the idea that one should or could look inward to establish certainty about one's salvation, "since no one can know with the certainty of faith, which cannot be subject to error, that he has obtained the grace of God."[28]

Christians should be sustained, in the midst of the "fear and apprehension" consequent on considering their own "weakness and indisposition," by reflecting on God's grace and the sacraments of the church:[29]

> For though during this mortal life, men, however holy and just, fall at times into at least light and daily sins . . . they do not on that account cease to be just, for that petition of the just, *forgive us our trespasses,* is both humble and true . . . For God does not forsake those who have been once justified by His grace, unless He be first forsaken by them.[30]

Even "those who through sin have forfeited the received grace of justification can again be justified when, moved by God, they exert themselves to obtain through the sacrament of penance the recovery, by the merits of Christ, of the grace lost."[31] These passages mark all sorts of differences with Luther and Calvin, but they share a conviction that we look for our salvation to trust in divine grace, and not within ourselves.

It was different among the Jansenists. Mother Angélique once explained, "In order to discover whether we are among the happy number of his elect, we have

---

26. Blaise Pascal, *The Provincial Letters,* trans. A. J. Krailsheimer (Harmondsworth, Middlesex: Penguin Books, 1967), 156–58.
27. Ibid., 160.
28. "Decree of Justification," chapter 9, *Canons and Decrees of the Council of Trent.*
29. Ibid.
30. Ibid., chapter 11.
31. Ibid., chapter 14.

only to examine our consciences to see whether we have the necessary resolve to commit ourselves to pious practices and to continue them until death."[32] And the right resolve would generate the right practices. To be sure, those who were saved would be saved because they were among the elect, but one could determine election through self-examination—not only of consciences but of deeds. In the end, as Saint Cyran put it, "It is not necessary to have regard for anything but good works, which ought to be our principal concern."[33]

Jansenist piety had a grim scrupulousness that reminds one of the Lutheran Pietists. Mother Angélique once said she would rather live in a corrupt convent, since "there will be more merit in it; I shall meet with strong opposition, and have few good examples."[34] Each day she picked some nuns at random not to receive communion, that they might be "taught that they can be deprived of Holy Communion just as holily as they can receive it."[35] When the Christian community becomes a testing ground and the sacraments a reward for the righteous, can either function as grace for sinners? The debate over attrition and contrition exacerbated these tendencies. One can sympathize with the Jansenists' concerns: someone who repents out of fear of hell (attrition) is hardly manifesting the joy and freedom that ought to flow from living under grace. But the demand for authentic contrition led to scrupulous examination of one's motives. Mother Angélique for a time, for instance, refused all gifts to the convent at Port-Royal unless they were motivated purely by the love of God. Anything that might possibly have been given out of, for instance, personal affection for one of the nuns was firmly returned. The ethical ideal is heroic, but the kind of internal probing it requires risks both legalism and a kind of self-absorption thoroughly opposed to earlier visions of Christian freedom. "There is not one of them," Ronald Knox remarked of the Jansenists, "that knows how to say, with a shrug of the shoulders, 'Well, after all, God is merciful.'"[36]

From Calvin to the Puritans

Neither Pietists nor Jansenists, however, could match the Puritans in passion for introspection. "From the seventeenth century onwards," Lawrence Stone has written of them, "there bursts onto paper a torrent of words about intimate thoughts and feelings set down by large numbers of quite ordinary

---

32. Angélique Arnauld, *Lettres de la Mère Angélique Arnauld,* vol. 1 (Utrecht: Aux depends de la compagnie, 1742), 214; quoted in Alexander Sedgwick, *Jansenism in Seventeenth-Century France* (Charlottesville: University Press of Virginia, 1977), 103. I am following Sedgwick and Knox in much of this section.

33. Jean Duvergier de Hauranne, Abbé de Saint Cyran, Letter 78, to Pelletier des Touches, October 1642, *Lettres Inédites* (Paris: Librairie Philosophique J. Vrin, 1962), 192.

34. Quoted in Knox, *Enthusiasm,* 190.

35. Angélique Arnauld, *Lettres,* 1:70; quoted in F. Ellen Weaver, *The Evolution of the Reform of Port-Royal* (Paris: Editions Beauchesne, 1978), 69.

36. Knox, *Enthusiasm,* 217.

English men and women."[37] And in New England, Perry Miller and T. H. Johnson remark, if with some exaggeration, "almost every literate Puritan kept some sort of journal."[38] James Janeway, an English Puritan writing the biography of his brother John published in 1673, captured a characteristic Puritan attitude. "He was," he wrote of his brother,

> one that kept an exact watch over his thoughts, words and actions . . . at least once a day, in a solemn manner. . . . He took notice what incomes and profit he received in his spiritual traffique; what returns from that far country. . . . he every night made even his accounts; and if his sheets should prove his winding sheet, it had been all one; for he could say, his work was done; so that death could not surprize him.[39]

Janeway presented his brother as the ideal Reformed saint, daily noting his moral and spiritual account. But the ideal he portrayed had not come from Calvin.

In contrast to Luther, to be sure, Calvin did talk about an important positive role for biblical law in a Christian's life. Where Luther held that, in the light of the gospel, the law functions (1) to condemn all humanity for unrighteousness, so that we might understand that salvation comes by grace alone, and (2) to restrain sinful people at least by fear of punishment, so as to preserve minimal social order among sinners,[40] Calvin added a "third use of the law"—that it will (3) also help believers "learn more thoroughly each day the nature of the Lord's will to which they aspire."[41] Freed by grace from the impossible task of trying to earn their own salvation, Christians should live out lives of gratitude, Calvin said—but biblical law provides a helpful guide as to how to express that gratitude in practice.

Still, he insisted that such use of the law should not conflict with "Christian freedom," in which he distinguished three elements: (1) Christians "in seeking assurance of their justification before God, should rise above and advance beyond the law, forgetting all law righteousness."[42] We obey the law out of gratitude, not in hope of winning a salvation God has already given us. (2) Chris-

---

37. Lawrence Stone, *The Family, Sex and Marriage in England 1500–1800* (London: Weidenfeld, 1977), 228.

38. Perry Miller and T. H. Johnson, *The Puritans* (Cambridge: Harvard University Press, 1924), 461.

39. James Janeway, *Invisibles, Realities, demonstrated in the Holy Life and Triumphant Death of Mr. John Janeway* (London: Th. Parkhurst, 1673), 58. The first edition was printed with an admiring preface by Richard Baxter, and the book was regularly reprinted into the nineteenth century.

40. Calvin, *Institutes* 2.7.10.

41. Ibid., 2.7.12. It may be oversimple to say even of Luther that he thought the law could never function in this third way, and both Melanchthon and the Lutheran Formula of Concord explicitly made room for the "third use." See Philip Melanchthon, *Loci Communes,* trans. Charles Leander Hill (Boston: Meador Publishing Co., 1944), 229; *Book of Concord,* ed. Theodore G. Tappert (Philadelphia: Fortress Press, 1959), 479.

42. Calvin, *Institutes,* 3.19.2.

tians should not feel the law to be a "yoke," but obey it willingly and gladly.[43]
(3) "Regarding outward things that are of themselves 'indifferent,' we are not bound before God by any religious obligation."[44] Worrying about trivial details destroys the joy of Christian freedom:

> For when consciences once ensnare themselves, they enter a long and inextricable maze, not easy to get out of. If a man begins to doubt whether he may use linen for sheets, shirts, handkerchiefs, and napkins, he will afterward be uncertain also about hemp; finally, doubt will even arise over tow. For he will turn over in his mind whether he can sup without napkins, or go without a handkerchief. If any man should consider daintier food unlawful, in the end he will not be at peace before God, when he eats either black bread or common victuals, while it occurs to him that he could sustain his body on even coarser foods. If he boggles at sweet wine, he will not with a clear conscience drink even flat wine, and finally he will not dare touch water if sweeter and cleaner than other water.[45]

Calvin rejected such a trajectory not only as a fastidious Frenchman but also as a theologian of grace.

His discussion of the Sabbath provides a good example of how he put Christian freedom into practice. Christ, he said, has abolished the ceremonial significance of the Sabbath. "Christians ought therefore to shun completely the superstitious observance of days." Indeed, the church sets apart the first day of the week rather than the seventh, among other things, precisely to signal that we are not tied to Old Testament sabbatarian laws. If some Christian community wanted to replace Sunday with some other day of the week, Calvin had no objection, in principle. But we do need to set apart some day for church services, for particular reflection on God, and "to give a day of rest for servants and those who are under the authority of others, in order that they should have some respite from toil," and having a different day in each congregation or town would create no end of confusion, so the Lord's Day observance on Sunday may offer the best solution.[46] Still, Calvin kept everything matter-of-fact and practical—one was not, for instance, to throw dice or play cards in the taverns on Sunday until after the church service was over.[47] Details are not of crucial importance and certainly not part of how we earn salvation.

To be sure, under Calvin's leadership the consistory of Geneva, made up of pastors and elders, met regularly to cross-examine drunkards, fornicators, quarrelers, and wife-beaters, to hand out punishments, and to decide when offenders could be readmitted to communion. Two-thirds of those who

43. Ibid., 3.19.4.
44. Ibid., 3.19.7.
45. Ibid.
46. Ibid., 2.8.31–34.
47. Ross W. Collins, *Calvin and the Libertines* (Toronto: Claude, Irwin, 1968), 99.

appeared got off with a lecture or a reprimand; the rest were excommunicated until they seemed to have amended their ways—which nearly always happened before the next communion.[48] One senses that consistory meetings often involved more cajoling of quarrelsome neighbors than assigning of punishments, and in treating spousal abuse as a serious issue, they may have been ahead of their time. Still, one should not paint too positive a picture—some of their moral judgments were, by our standards, brutal and narrow-minded, and it was a system that even at its best encouraged busybodies.

The rules, however, were not unusual for Calvin's time. Two things did stand out. First, as many of their contemporaries noted with surprise, in Geneva the rules were generally enforced consistently, and on rich and poor alike.[49] Second, theologically, such discipline was *never*, for Calvin, a matter of making people ethically better so that they could be saved, and neither the consistory nor Calvin himself tried to regulate Genevans' inner lives. Calvin insisted on the right of excommunication (1) "that they who lead a filthy and infamous life may not be called Christians, to the dishonor of God"; (2) "that the good be not corrupted by the constant company of the wicked"; and (3) "that those overcome by shame for their baseness begin to repent."[50] The goal was public order and decency, not verifying inward states. It is impossible, Calvin insisted, to distinguish the elect from the damned with certainty in this life.[51] Our conspicuously sinful neighbor might be in secret the repentant object of divine election; the local pillar of virtue might prove a hypocrite. Even when we look within ourselves, a haunted sense of our own unworthiness might in some ways be a better sign of grace than spiritual confidence. But it would be absurd to try to measure the depth of self-abnegation as a sign of grace. Our trust must lie in Christ.

If anything, Calvin discouraged too much introspection, which "does not so much strengthen the spirit in secure tranquillity as trouble it with uneasy doubting."[52] After all,

> the godly heart feels in itself a division because it is partly imbued with sweetness from its recognition of the divine goodness, partly grieves in bitterness from an awareness of its calamity; partly rests upon the promise of the gospel, partly trembles at the evidence of its own iniquity; partly rejoices at the expectation of life, partly shudders at death.[53]

Christians should seek comfort, not in trying to sort out these tensions, but in turning our attention from ourselves to Christ. To quote a key passage again,

---

48. See E. William Monter, "The Consistory of Geneva, 1559–1569," *Bibliothèque d'Humanisme et Renaissance* 38 (1976): 471–77.

49. E. William Monter, *Calvin's Geneva* (New York: Wiley, 1967), 152.

50. Calvin, *Institutes* 4.12.5.

51. Ibid., 3.24.5.

52. Ibid., 3.2.15.

53. Ibid., 3.2.18.

"We shall not find assurance of our election in ourselves," but only in Christ, "the mirror wherein we must, and without self-deception may, contemplate our own election."[54] A Christian society will seek to avoid public violence and disorder and scandal in the church, and Christians, in gratitude to God, will strive to live morally good lives. But in their good works they will find neither the preparation for salvation nor the assurance of having achieved it. "Farewell, then, to the dream of those who think up a righteousness flowing together out of faith and works."[55]

By the seventeenth century, among Reformed Christians as well as Lutherans and Catholics, the picture had changed. That change was a vast phenomenon, and I will concentrate in the rest of this chapter on English Puritans, with a final look at Massachusetts. (Chapter 9 will give at least some attention to Scotland and the Continent.) The Puritans would in principle have agreed with Calvin that salvation comes through grace alone and on the importance of Christian freedom, but, looking within themselves for assurance that they had received it, many of them became concerned about their works. In times of social disorder, some also worried about the destabilizing effects of utterly unpredictable grace.

"Puritan," to be sure, is a term of many meanings. In the words of an anonymous pamphlet published in 1641,

> In the mouth of a drunkard, he is a Puritan which refuseth his cups; in the mouth of a swearer, he which feares an oath; in the mouth of a libertine, he which makes any scruple of common sin; in the mouth of a rude souldier, he which wisheth the Scottish War to an end without blood.[56]

Puritans tended to represent particular political and economic interests, they opposed many of the liturgical rituals that had developed in the Church of England, and they shared other characteristics as well. But theologically, two traits they shared with Pietists and Jansenists were central to Puritan identity. First, in a time when many in England were proposing that human efforts contribute to salvation or that free human choice can accept or reject grace, the Puritans emphasized election and irresistible grace.[57] Second, however, they worried intensely about people's moral and spiritual lives, and they urged

---

54. Ibid., 3.24.5.
55. Ibid., 3.11.13.
56. "A Discourse concerning Puritans," quoted in John T. McNeill, *Modern Christian Movements* (New York: Harper & Row, 1968), 15.
57. "There was a rough correlation between Puritan Nonconformity and enthusiasm for the doctrine of predestination. . . . The preaching of the gospel of God's grace in Christ has with some justice been regarded as the central motif of the Puritan movement." Dewey D. Wallace, *Puritans and Predestination* (Chapel Hill: University of North Carolina Press, 1982), 37, 44. After surveying the sermons of Puritan preachers before the Long Parliament, Ethyn Kirby concludes, "To them church reform meant the substitution of Calvinism for Arminianism." Ethyn W. Kirby, "Sermons before the Commons 1640–1642," *American Historical Review* 44 (1939): 547.

careful introspection in such matters, warning that one's eternal salvation might well be at stake. As with Pietists and Jansenists, this second concern tended to undercut the first.

Thus William Perkins, perhaps the greatest of the Puritan theologians, distinguished two ways of seeking knowledge of one's election: one could either ascend up "into heaven, there to search the counsell of God" or one could descend "into our owne hearts." "The first way," he concluded, "is dangerous, and not to be attempted. For the waies of God are unsearchable and past finding out. The second way alone is to be followed."[58] Calvin, in other words, had been wrong to urge turning from ourselves to Christ for assurance; we ought to look to ourselves. A collection of Puritan wisdom that included passages from Perkins explained that true conversion could be distinguished by two sorts of marks: it produced clear awareness of one's sins, true grief for them, and a hungering after grace, and it led to the performance of good works.[59] If the first of these left matters unclear, Perkins elsewhere explained, "the other testimony, the sanctification of the heart, will suffice to assure us."[60]

What really matters, Puritans would have agreed, is justification, and justification comes by grace without regard to merit. Yet as one Puritan preacher put it, "If thou are chosen, then shalt thou in time feele of the fruite of thy election in Christ, by holinesse and sanctimonie."[61] Since those fruits, whether of inward holiness or of outward good works, were thought to be in some degree measurable, they increasingly drew most of the Puritans' attention. One Puritan writer put the matter bluntly: "Our sanctification is more manifest to us than our justification. It is easier discerned."[62]

What about the worldly success of those discernibly successful folk? Calvin's reading of the Bible had persuaded him that, if anything as to their material fate identified the elect, it would be that they were subject in this world to suffering and persecution. Prominent Puritans never quite said, as they are often accused of saying, that worldly prosperity was a sign of election, but they came far too close. Richard Baxter, for instance, identified poverty as often a consequence of the sin of sloth and idleness—it was only a step to thinking that wealth was a sign of hard work, thus of sanctification, and thus of election.[63] "Industry and diligence in a lawful and warrantable vocation and calling, in

---

58. William Perkins, "An Exposition of the Symbole or Creed of the Apostles," in *Works*, vol. 1 (Cambridge: John Legatt, 1608), 284.

59. Richard Rogers, ed., *A Garden of Spirituall Flowers* (London: John Wright, 1643), 217–18. See also John Jewel, *An Exposition upon the Two Epistles of St. Paul to the Thessalonians* (on 2 Thess. 2:13–14), in *Works*, vol. 2 (Cambridge: Cambridge University Press, 1847), 934.

60. William Perkins, *Cases of Conscience*, in *Works*, vol. 2 (London: John Legatt, 1613), 19.

61. Bartimaeus Andrewes, *Certaine verie worthie, godly and profitable Sermons, upon the fifth Chapter of the Song of Solomon* (London: Robert Waldegra, 1583). See Wallace, *Puritans and Predestination*, 51.

62. Peter Bulkeley, *The Gospel-Covenant* (London: M. Simmons, 1651), 263.

63. Richard Baxter, "A Christian Directory," in *The Practical Works of Richard Baxter*, vol. 1 (Ligonier, Pa.: Soli Deo Gloria Publications, 1990), 380.

order to gain a competent provision of earthly things for our children and re-lations, is not condemned in sacred Writ, but commended," one Puritan preacher declared. "Grace in a poor man is grace and 'tis beautiful; but grace in a rich man is more conspicuous, more useful."[64] Thus in one satirical play of the period, a Puritan character advises,

> First then,
> I charge thee, lend no money; next, serve God;
> If ever thou hast children, teach them thrift;
> They'll learn religion fast enough themselves.[65]

Like any good satire, this no doubt exaggerates, but it exaggerates a trait its original audience would have recognized.

Many of their contemporaries already worried about what this emphasis on discernible inward transformation and good works implied for the Puritans' understanding of grace. A non-Puritan member of the Church of England ac-cused them of teaching justification by works, "the very justification of Ro-manists."[66] John Saltmarsh, a Parliamentary army chaplain more radical than the mainstream of Puritans, said that their preaching contained "usually but a Grain or Dram of Gospel, to a Pound of Law."[67] John Owen, himself a Puritan particularly devoted to Calvin, in a preface to William Eyre's *Justification with-out Conditions*, published in 1653, recommended it as a valuable corrective to the rising tide of belief in justification by works.[68] One evidence of a loss of their distinctive Reformed identity is that one of the Puritans' most popular guides to a moral life—Edmund Bunny's *The Christian Directory, or Book of Resolution*, first published in 1584 but going through many editions—turns out to have been an unacknowledged translation of a Catholic manual of casuistry by the Jesuit Robert Parsons.[69]

The Puritan emphasis on cultivating Christian virtue grew even greater in response to the chaos of the English Civil War in the middle of the seventeenth century. In the Parliamentary armies identified with the Puritan cause, folks from a range of social classes, most of them young, found themselves thrown together, broken loose of fidelity to traditional loyalties to king, nobles, and bishops, and with time away from home to talk to each other at great length. Everything came up for debate: Why were some people wealthier than others?

---

64. "The Vanity and Mischief of Making Earthly Treasures Our Chief Treasure," anonymous ser-mon preached in 1655; quoted in Christopher Hill, *The World Turned Upside Down* (New York: Viking Press, 1972), 265.

65. William Cartwright, *The Ordinary*, act 5, scene 1, in *The Plays and Poems of William Cartwright*, (Madison: University of Wisconsin Press, 1951), 338.

66. Henoch Clapham, *A Manuell of the Bibles Doctrine* (London: Nathaniell Butter, 1606), 139; quoted in Wallace, *Puritans and Predestination*, 36–37.

67. John Saltmarsh, *Free-Grace: or, The Flowing of Christ's Blood freely to Sinners* (London: John Marshall, 1700), 38. "Luther I could quote," Saltmarsh ironically observed, "but he is now lookt on by some as one that is both over-quoted, and over-writ Free-grace." Ibid., 162.

68. Quoted in Wallace, *Puritans and Predestination*, 120.

69. F. Ernest Stoeffler, *The Rise of Evangelical Pietism* (Leiden: E. J. Brill, 1965), 60.

Why was there private property at all? Why should one have sex only within marriage? Do moral laws constrain us at all? Is God a being separate from us, or just within each of us? A whole country seemed to turn into a radical, late-night college bull session. Moderate Puritan leaders grew terrified that a movement they had helped begin had gotten completely out of their control. As Christopher Hill, one of the best historians of the period, has written:

> One of the fascinating problems in the intellectual history of seventeenth-century England is the collapse of Calvinism. . . . So long as the elect were respectable bourgeois Puritans, their sense of freedom through cooperation with God brought no fundamental danger to the social order. But it was impossible, once discipline broke down, to decide who the elect were. . . . Failure to agree on who the elect were drove the men of property back to works.[70]

Could one imagine an ordered society based on Christian freedom, whose order rested on a shared gratitude for God's grace? Perhaps—but works righteousness surely provided an easier way to keep people in line.

Every detail of Christians' lives drew attention. Where Calvin had specified that one should not play at dice in the taverns on Sunday until after church, Nicholas Bound's *The Doctrine of the Sabbath* had in 1595 already warned against even "honest recreations" and "lawful pleasures," indeed against any talk of "worldly matters," anytime on the Sabbath.[71] In the aftermath of the Civil War, Cromwell's Parliament passed a law against "idle sitting, openly, at gates or doors or elsewhere" on Sundays.[72] Later, the great Puritan writer Richard Baxter warned, "that when judgment comes God will call you to account, both for every hour of your misspent time, and for all the good which you should have done in all that time, and did it not."[73] Think of all that the Christian ought to be doing:

> Thou hast a pardon to procure through Jesus Christ, for all the sins that ever thou didst commit, and all the duties which ever thou didst omit; thou hast an offended God to be reconciled to. . . . What abundance of Scripture truths hast thou to learn which thou art ignorant of! How many holy duties, as prayer, meditation, holy conference, &c, to learn which thou are ignorant of! and to perform when thou hast learned them! How many works of justice and charity to men's souls and bodies hast thou to do! How many needy ones to relieve as thou art able![74]

Take an hour of leisure when all these duties are completed, if you like, but,

---

70. Hill, *The World Turned Upside Down*, 276.
71. Nicholas Bownd, *The Doctrine of the Sabbath* (London: John Porter and Thomas Man, 1606), 263, 274; quoted in ibid., 66.
72. Quoted in Hill, *The World Turned Upside Down*, 67.
73. Baxter, *Christian Directory*, 234.
74. Ibid., 233. On the relation of anxiety to clocks, see William J. Bouwsma, "Anxiety and the Formation of Early Modern Culture," in *After the Reformation*, ed. Barbara C. Malament (Philadelphia: University of Pennsylvania Press, 1980), 219.

"For my own part, I must tell thee, if thou have time to spare, thy case is very much different from mine."[75]

"I was never tempted," Baxter once remarked, "so much to grudge at God's natural ordering of man, in any thing, as that we are fair to waste so much of our little time in sleep . . . that it deprived me of so much precious time, which else might have been used in some profitable work."[76] He is in this confessing a fault, to be sure, but he seems very nearly proud of it. Rather than trusting God's providence to give us the time we need to do what we are called to do, he wanted extra time for more work. "Christ is so far from redeeming us from a necessity of good works," Baxter warned, "that he died to restore us to a capacity and ability to perform them, and hath new-made us for that end."[77] So we had best be getting on with it. In the order for public worship he drew up, the prayer of confession was followed by an assurance of pardon but *then* by a reminder of "what you must be and do . . . if you would be saved."[78] Even liturgically, grace did not get the last word.

I have been painting, to be sure, too bleak a picture. Most Puritans were good people, serious about their faith, serious about trying to lead Christian lives. They trusted in God's grace for their salvation. Historians of the period continue to debate whether the trends I have been tracing dominated or merely constituted one strand among others.[79] Perhaps the greatest of all Puritan writers, John Bunyan, once wrote

> I am for going on, and venturing my eternal state with Christ, whether I have comfort here or no; if God doth not come in, thought I, I will leap off the ladder even blindfold into Eternitie, sink or swim, come heaven, come hell; Lord Jesus, if thou wilt catch me, do; if not, I will venture for thy Name.[80]

Luther could not have said it better. But amid worries about assurance and morally good lives, that message of trust in grace too often got lost.

The Case of Anne Hutchinson

If in England Puritan concern for the evidence of justification in good works came to be closely and clearly connected with a desire for social order only

---

75. Baxter, *Christian Directory,* 236.

76. Ibid., 339.

77. Ibid., 111.

78. Ibid., 925.

79. Janice Knight usefully distinguishes the "Intellectual Fathers" of Puritanism—men like Perkins, Ames, Hooker, Shepard, Bulkeley, and Winthrop—for whom human cooperation in preparing the heart for grace was important and works were evidence of salvation, from the "Spiritual Brethren," such as Sibbes, Preston, Cotton, and Davenport, for whom human effort was neither preparation nor sign of grace. See Janice Knight, *Orthodoxies in Massachusetts: Rereading American Puritanism* (Cambridge: Harvard University Press, 1994), 2–3.

80. John Bunyan, *Grace Abounding to the Chief of Sinners* (London: SCM Press, 1955), 145–46.

after the Civil War of the 1640s, it was present in Massachusetts Bay Colony almost from the start. Here Puritans had a clearer shot at establishing a community according to their own ideals—their famous "city on a hill." As Increase Mather later wrote,

> The Lord intended some great thing when he . . . said unto New-England (as sometimes to Sion) *Thou art my People;* And what should that be, if not so a Scripture Pattern of Reformation, as to Civil, but especially in Ecclesiastical respects, might be here erected, as a First Fruits of that which shall in due time be accomplished the whole world throughout.[81]

A good moral order would be crucial for this community of God's chosen, and its leaders found that order threatened in the first decade of the colony's existence.

The catalyst for the explosion was Anne Hutchinson, "a woman," Governor John Winthrop, who did not like her at all, wrote in his official history of the episode, "of a haughty and fierce carriage, of a nimble wit and active spirit and a very voluble tongue, more bold than a man."[82] Born in England in 1591, in the early 1630s she was regularly traveling from her home in the village of Alford to Boston, twenty miles away, to hear the preaching of John Cotton, a Puritan preacher who preached with a strong emphasis on grace. Cotton fled to New England in 1633, and Hutchinson followed, with her husband William and twelve children, a year later. The Hutchinsons met at first with great success in the new colony. William was elected a deputy to the Massachusetts General Court in November 1634, and Anne began to attract local women to discussion groups she led in her home. Soon she was drawing as many as sixty people to her seminars, and using them to criticize nearly all the colony's ministers—except John Cotton—for waffling on the subject of grace.[83]

Against those who urged that people prepare their hearts for grace, Cotton insisted that the initiative comes from God, and without preconditions:

> If wee bee active in laying hold on Christ, before he hath given us his Spirit: then wee apprehend him, before he apprehend us: then wee

81. Increase Mather, "To the Reader," in Samuel Tarey, *An Exhortation unto Reformation* (Cambridge, Mass., 1674), sig. A2; quoted in Charles E. Hambrick-Stowe, *The Practice of Piety* (Chapel Hill: University of North Carolina Press, 1982), 248.

82. John Winthrop, "A Short Story of the Rise, reign and ruine of the Antinomians, Familists & Libertines," in *The Antinomian Controversy, 1636–1638: A Documentary History,* ed. David D. Hall (Durham, N.C.: Duke University Press, 1990), 263.

83. "Deputy Governor: . . . About three years ago we were all in peace. Mrs. Hutchinson from that time she came hath made a disturbance. . . . she in particular hath disparaged all our ministers in the land that they have preached a covenant of works, and only Mr. Cotton a covenant of grace." "The Examination of Mrs. Ann Hutchinson at the court of Newton, November 1637," Appendix 2 to Thomas Hutchinson, *The History of the Colony and Province of Massachusetts Bay* (Cambridge: Harvard University Press, 1936), 2:374.

should doe a good act, and so bring forth good fruites, before wee become good trees; yea, and bee good trees before we be in Christ.
But these are all contrary to the Gospell.[84]

Good works or godly life, moreover, cannot provide decisive evidence of one's
justification—if we know ourselves justified in Christ, we need no other assurance, and, if we do not, no purely human accomplishments would do us
much good.[85] Indeed, to base assurance of justification on evidences of sanctification is "to clothe unwholesome and Popish doctrine with Protestant
and wholesome words."[86] For that matter, the observably "holy" are "apt to
live . . . in the strength of their gifts and not in the strength of Christ," and
therefore "it pleaseth the Lord sometimes to leave them to greater falls, than
other weaker Christians."[87] "Hence observe: God doth sometime poure out the
Spirit of grace upon the most bloody, and most haynous, and most desperate,
and most prophane, and most abominable sinners."[88]

This would not do. Take Cotton seriously, and the local drunk might be as
likely to receive divine grace as the pious governor of the colony. To leaders
of a colony striving to create a city on a hill to inspire all the world with its
virtues, Cotton seemed to be opening up, as one of them put it, "such a faire
and easie way to Heaven, that men may passe without difficulty."[89] Would
ethical efforts not even matter?

Most of Cotton's opponents believed that human efforts played a part in salvation, and that, as Peter Bulkeley put it, "it is a warrantable and safe way for
a man by and from his sanctification to take evidence of his justification and

84. John Cotton, *Gospel Conversion* (London: F. Dawson, 1646), 39. "There is nothing . . . that
can establish or assure faith, but the liberal Embassaye whereby God in Christ reconcileth the
world unto himself, which promise neither requireth faith nor works to go before it, though it doth
require and will produce both to follow it." John Cotton, "Mr. Cottons Rejoynder," *The Antinomian Controversy*, 93, citing Calvin, *Institutes* 1.3.2.

85. "I conceive our faith depending on Christ is as soon discerned, and sooner than our Sanctification by Christ. . . . If my Justification lyeth prostrate (that is, altogether dark and hidden from
me) I cannot prove my selfe in a state of Grace by my Sanctification: For whilst I cannot beleeve
that my Person is accepted in Justification, I cannot beleeve that my Works are accepted of God,
as any true Sanctification." John Cotton, "Sixteene Questions of Serious and Necessary Consequence," Hall, *The Antinomian Controversy*, 52.

86. Cotton, "Mr. Cottons Rejoynder," *The Antinomian Controversy*, 134.

87. Ibid., 88–89. Cotton later (ibid., 105–06) cited a crucial passage from Calvin's commentary
on 1 John: "If we, in truth, love our neighbors, we have an evidence that we are born of God,
who is truth, or that the truth of God dwells in us. But we must ever remember, that we have not
from love the knowledge which the Apostle mentions, as though we were to seek from it the certainty of salvation. And doubtless we know not otherwise that we are the children of God, than
as he seals his free adoption on our hearts by his own Spirit, and as we receive by faith the sure
pledge of it offered in Christ. Then love is accessory or an inferior aid, a prop to our faith, not a
foundation on which it rests." Calvin, *Commentaries on the First Epistle of John* (on 1 John 3:19),
trans. John Owen, *Calvin's Commentaries* (Grand Rapids: Baker, 1989), 22:221–22.

88. John Cotton, *The Way of Life* (London: L. Fawne and S. Gellibrand, 1641), 109.

89. Thomas Weld, preface to Winthrop, "A Short Story . . .," in Hall, *The Antinomian Controversy*, 203.

of his estate in grace before God."[90] In the words of Thomas Shepard to his congregation just across the river from Boston, "The saving knowledge of Christ is dependent upon the sensible knowledge of a man's self."[91] Cotton could not persuade any of his colleagues to take seriously Calvin's notion that we might turn from ourselves to Christ for assurance of salvation, and that ordered Christian life might be based on gratitude rather than the effort to deserve salvation.

The other ministers of the colony angrily demanded whether he really thought that Christians could be confident of salvation even if their "course is grown much degenerate." They conceded that, in principle, we must "leave an unlimited liberty to the Spirit of God," and yet, God's "usual course with his people" is to carry out "all parts of his work both of Faith and holiness in some nearer Symmetry and proportion." To say that God *may* give grace to the conspicuous sinner or lead the holy to a fall, after all, "usually implyeth a possibility out of ordinary way."[92] The Massachusetts Bay ministers, in short, had reinvented late-medieval theology, in which the ordained power of God rewards those who do their best, and a theoretical acknowledgment of the absolute power of God ("a possibility out of the ordinary way") preserves, in principle, divine freedom.

Cotton, however, was clever, thoroughly trained, and cautious. He defended his position or retreated into ambiguities. "Mr. Cotton," Shepard noted in his journal, "repents not, but is hid only."[93] Hutchinson was another matter. She had equal intelligence but little caution, and questions about her right as a woman to teach made her all the more vulnerable. Arrested, ill, exhausted, and isolated, she fended off her adversaries until, pushed as to how she could know the truth about justification, she finally blurted out that, just as Abraham had known he must kill Isaac, she knew it "by an immediate voice."[94] Cotton tried to warn her but also to distance himself from any claim to direct, miraculous revelation.[95] One of the ironies of the story is that her claim to find absolute assurance by looking inward to a direct testimony of the Spirit helped to secure Hutchinson's condemnation—in a different form, the inward search for certainty had been the fault she and Cotton had seen in their opponents.

If the classic (male) diagnosis might be that Hutchinson became hysterical,

---

90. Peter Bulkeley, *The Gospel Covenant* (London: Benjamin Allen, 1646), 183. On Governor Winthrop's view that grace and works are inextricably intertwined in the process of salvation, see John Winthrop, 12 November 1636/7, *The Winthrop Papers,* vol. 3 (Boston: Massachusetts Historical Society, 1943), 342.

91. Thomas Shepard, *The Parable of the Ten Virgins opened and applied* (London: John Rothwell and Samuel Thomson, 1660), 1:78.

92. "The Elders Reply," *The Antinomian Controversy,* 65–66.

93. Thomas Shepard, *Journal,* in Michael McGiffert, *God's Plot* (Amherst: University of Massachusetts Press, 1972), 74.

94. "The Examination of Mrs. Ann Hutchinson . . .," Hutchinson, *The History of the Colony and Province of Massachusetts Bay,* 2:383–84.

95. Ibid., 2:386.

her opponents more than matched her. Thomas Weld, writing a preface to Winthrop's narrative of the events six years later, could still barely contain himself. Hutchinson's pregnancy had ended in a spontaneous abortion, of what modern medical authorities diagnose as a hydatiform mole.[96] She "brought forth," Weld wrote, "not one . . . but . . . thirty monstrous births . . . none at all of them (as farre as I could ever learne) of humane shape. . . . And see how the wisdom of God fitted this judgment to her sinne every way, for looke as she had vented mishapen opinions, so she must bring forth deformed monsters."[97] She was driven out of the colony, first to Rhode Island, and then to New York, where she and most of her family were killed by the local native inhabitants. Noting that he had never heard of Indians engaging in such an unprovoked massacre, he happily reports the death of virtually the whole Hutchinson family and concludes that "God's hand is the more apparently seene herein, to pick out this wofull woman, to make her and those belonging to her, an unheard of heavie example."[98]

It is a story with many morals about the relations between religion and political power, and about relations between the genders.[99] For the purposes of this book, however, it bears a lesson about grace, and about how even the most self-consciously orthodox of Reformed Protestants, analogously to the most pious of Lutherans and the most devout Jansenists, decided against the risk of the Reformation doctrine of grace as too disruptive of moral striving and political order. "I know there is wilde love and joy enough in the world," wrote Thomas Hooker, one of Hutchinson's principal opponents, "as there is wilde thyme and other herbes, but we would have garden-love and garden-joy, of God's own planting."[100] But grace, many theologians before the seventeenth century would have said, does not entirely admit of careful cultivation.

96. Emery J. Battis, *Saints and Sectaries* (Chapel Hill: University of North Carolina Press, 1962), 346.

97. Weld, preface to Winthrop, "A Short Story . . .," in Hall, *The Antinomian Controversy*, 214.

98. Ibid., 218.

99. See Patricia Caldwell, "The Antinomian Language Controversy," *Harvard Theological Review* 69 (1976): 345–67.

100. Thomas Hooker, *The Soules Implantation into the Natural Olive* (London: R. Young, 1640), 180. I am grateful to Christopher Coble for helping me track down this passage.

Part 3

The Modern Turn: God and the World

7   Nearer Than We Are to Ourselves

Chapters 2 through 6 have contrasted some ways of thinking about God and God's grace before and during the seventeenth century. In Aquinas, Luther, and Calvin—three representative figures from earlier centuries—God remained radically transcendent, wholly other, a mystery whose being and love lay utterly beyond our understanding. In the seventeenth century, a good many Christian theologians sought to understand God, language about God, and the workings of God's grace with a rigor that, I have argued, regrettably domesticated both God and grace. The next three chapters turn to implications of that change for how seventeenth-century folk understood the relation of God and the world—though like most thematic distinctions in the study of history, this one is a bit arbitrary in practice, and there are issues and writers that could have been discussed in either context. This chapter will review Aquinas, Luther, and Calvin on God's relation to the world (though Luther, who discussed these issues less systematically, will get less attention). The following two chapters will look at some contrasting seventeenth-century views.

Increasingly, Christian writers in the seventeenth century, since they did not want to think of God as utterly beyond their comprehension, thought of God's otherness in terms of distance and remoteness from the world. Though they did not use the terms, they were in effect contrasting *transcendence* with *immanence*. Such a "contrastive" account of transcendence—I am using Kathryn Tanner's terminology—makes divine transcendence and involvement in the world into a zero-sum game: the more involved or immanent, the less transcendent, and vice versa.[1]

Aquinas, Luther, and Calvin, however, had had a more radical understanding of transcendence. God was not one of the things or agents among others in the world, to be located either closer or farther away, more involved in interactions or less. Rather, God transcended all our ways of classifying, locating, and relating the things in the world—transcendence in that sense, indeed, is what makes God God. To quote Tanner,

---

1. "God's transcendence and involvement with the world vary inversely . . . only when God's transcendence is defined contrastively. . . . God becomes one being among others within a single order. . . . a non-contrastive transcendence of God suggested an extreme of divine involvement with the world in the form of a productive agency extending to everything that is in an equally direct manner. . . . Such an extreme of divine involvement requires, one could say, an extreme of divine transcendence. A constrastive definition is not radical enough to allow a direct creative involvement of God with the world in its entirety." Kathryn Tanner, *God and Creation in Christian Theology: Tyranny or Empowerment?* (Oxford: Basil Blackwell, 1988), 89.

[such] a radical transcendence does not exclude God's positive fellowship with the world or presence within it. Only created beings, which
remain themselves over and against others, risk the distinctness of their
own natures by entering into intimate relations with another. God's
transcendence alone is one that may be properly exercised in the radical immanence by which God is said to be nearer to us than we are
to ourselves.[2]

If God were one of the things in the world—as implied by a contrastive model
of transcendence—then it would be natural to ask where God is located—in
the world or outside it? Concerning anything that occurs, it would be natural
to ask, Who did it? Was it the result of some natural force? Or did it happen
by chance? Or did some human being do it? Or did God do it? As chapters 8
and 9 will indicate, such questions indeed often preoccupied theologians beginning in the seventeenth century, whether they were talking about God's relation to the natural world or the relation between divine grace and human
freedom.

But if we ask Aquinas or Luther or Calvin, Where is God? or, concerning the
tornado or the rain that broke the drought, the airplane crash or our neighbor's act of kindness, Who did it? God or some other agent? they refuse to answer the question posed in those terms. They say that God is present in the
world but not contained in it. They sort out actions in terms of those done by
human agents, those that follow necessarily from natural causes, the results of
chance, and some actions that occur by direct divine intervention. But they
also say, with only limited qualifications, that God causes *all* these events.
Their accounts do not even permit us to say that God and some other agent
collaborated in bringing about events, assigning a percentage of responsibility
to each. Yes, they say, X was the result of human decision, or natural force, or
accident—but also, X was fully the result of God's will. As Tanner says, prior
to the modern age,

> The theologian talks of an ordered nexus of created causes and effects
> in a relation of total and immediate dependence upon divine agency.
> Two different orders of efficacy become evident: along a "horizontal"
> plane, an order of created causes and effects; along a "vertical" plane,
> the order whereby God founds the former.[3]

God is not one agent among others, but what we say about what God "does"
functions in an entirely different way, in a different "order of efficacy," than
our talk about creatures. Given the conclusions of the preceding chapters, this
is hardly surprising. Indeed, if God is not one of the beings we can include
within any metaphysical system, not the someone whose grace to us follows

2. Ibid., 79.
3. Ibid., 89.

the rules of human interaction, not anything about which we can speak in language whose meaning we really understand, then it *would* be surprising if God functioned after the model of other agents.[4]

God and the World of Nature

The Aristotelian tradition thought of God as an external cause producing motion in the things of the world; neo-Platonism considered God as the ultimate form in which all finite things participate, and who is thus internal to them. Aquinas combined elements of both traditions into something new that made God more radically different from any other agent. Several of the "five ways" illustrate his Aristotelian side: God is the first mover, or the first efficient cause. Aquinas's neo-Platonism appears in the fourth of the five ways (where God is the highest in various degrees of perfection), or when he says that "all things other than God are not their own existence but share (*participant*) in existence" which they derive from God.[5] If we read only Aquinas's Aristotelian side, we might think of a God external to the world, acting on it as one agent among others. Since, however, God gives everything that is, the whole system of the world, whole and in its parts, its "to be," its *esse,* "God is uniquely intimate [to each thing], as the very *esse* of a thing is intimate to the thing itself."[6]

To make the point more precisely, Aquinas distinguished the sense in which God is "in" all things in terms of *power, presence,* and *essence.* He considered the analogy of a king. A king is present in *power* in every part of his kingdom (wherever his royal power extends), present by *presence* in everything within his range of vision (everywhere, we might say, that is visually present to him), and present by *essence* "in those things in which his substance is" (in the space of his own physical body). God's power extends to all things, and God sees all things, so God is obviously present everywhere in the first two senses. But also, Aquinas asserted, "He is present everywhere by his essence, because his

---

4. "The paradox of divine transcendence is that it can be consistently maintained only as long as God is conceived as fully immanent. . . . Mystics and spiritual men of all ages have known that God becomes more transcendent to us as he becomes more immanent to us. . . . Precisely where man is most autonomous, he is most intrinsically dependent. For the only dependence compatible with full autonomy consists in God's immanent presence, and that presence grows more intensive as man partakes more directly in God's own autonomy. Not the exercise of freedom limits man's dependence, but the restrictions of his freedom. Only the latter can be called exclusively his own." Louis Dupré, "Transcendence and Immanence as Theological Categories," *Proceedings of the Catholic Theological Society* 31 (1976): 9.

5. Aquinas, *Summa Theologiae* 1a.44.1, trans. English Dominican Fathers (London: Blackfriars, 1963–).

6. Aquinas, *Scriptum super Libros Sententiarum* 1.41.1.3 (Paris: P. Lethielleux, 1929). "During the whole period of a thing's existence, therefore, God must be present to it, and present in a way in keeping with the way in which the thing possesses its existence. Now existence is more intimately and profoundly interior to things than anything else. . . . So God must exist and exist intimately in everything." Aquinas, *Summa Theologiae* 1a.8.1.

essence is innermost in all things. . . . God is the maker and preserver of all things, with respect to the *esse* of each. Hence, since the *esse* of a thing is innermost in that thing, it is plain that God by his essence, through which he creates all things, is in all things."[7] On the other hand, God is not "in the world" in the sense that God is contained in the world, or is a part of some larger whole. "Indeed, if we can speak this way, the entire universe is in a certain sense a part, since it participates in a partial way in his goodness."[8] As is often the case, at least a large part of Aquinas's point can be captured by stating a negative rule: it would be equally wrong to try to place God either within the world or at a distance from it. Such categories, like all others, break down when applied to God.

True, Aquinas did speak of God as sustaining and directing created things. He asserted that, since "to be" does not belong to the essence of created things, God must sustain them at every moment, or they "would at once cease to be, and their nature would collapse."[9] Further, God directs things, as well as sustains them: "The causality of God . . . covers all existing things. Hence everything that is real in any way whatsoever is bound to be directed by God to an end. . . . Since his Providence is naught else than the idea whereby all things are planned to an end . . . we conclude quite strictly that all things in so far as they are real come under divine Providence."[10] God does not "intervene" in the world, as if God had for the most part been watching from the sidelines. To say such things, however, is not to define reactions of "sustaining" or "directing" that God has to creatures but to remind ourselves that no created thing can give another its very "to be," and thus the relation of words like "making" or "sustaining" or "directing" as applied to God and creatures is not even analogical but only equivocal.[11] We cannot understand what these words mean as applied to God.

Moreover, although God in some sense directs all things, the "secondary causes" we see at work in the world really do have the effects they appear to cause. If God simply did everything, and no other agents performed real actions, this would imply two problems. First, God would apparently lack the power to make anything that itself had any active power, and a God who can make only purely passive entities would have only limited power. Second, "if the active powers that are observed in creatures accomplished nothing, there would be no point in their having received such powers." What would be the

7. Aquinas, *Commentary on the Gospel of St. John* (1:9–10), no. 134, trans. James A. Weisheipl and Fabian R. Larcher (Albany, N.Y.: Magi Books, 1980).

8. Ibid., no. 133, 73.

9. Aquinas, *Summa Theologiae* 1a.104.1.

10. Ibid., 1a.22.2. See David B. Burrell, *Knowing the Unknowable God* (Notre Dame, Ind.: University of Notre Dame Press, 1986), 95.

11. Aquinas, *Commentary on Aristotle's "Physics"* 8.2.974, trans. Richard J. Blackwell, Richard Spath, and W. Edmund Thirlkel (New Haven: Yale University Press, 1963).

point of designing such a charade? But God does not act without a point. "God, acting in creatures, therefore, must be understood in such a way that they themselves still exercise their own operations."[12] Thus the potter makes the pot, the sun warms the meadow, and the lion kills the antelope—but God does all these things as well. Moreover, "the same effect is not attributed to a natural cause and to divine power in such a way that it is partly done by God, and partly by the natural agent; rather, it is wholly done by both, according to a different way."[13]

Still, even if we think of language about God primarily as specifying rules for how not to think about the divine, and acknowledge the real agency of secondary causes, to say that "all things . . . come under divine providence" is to raise questions about apparently evil things. Should we say, even acknowledging how little we can understand, that God sustains and directs the flood and the plague? (I will address the question of human sins in the second half of this chapter.) Aquinas offered three partial explanations, but he ended by warning about their inadequacy.

First, in line with a long tradition, he insisted that evil is not a positive thing, but "a certain absence of a good."[14] If the unchained tiger is about to pounce on me, the tiger itself remains a beautiful creature. If the rain falls on already-flooded land, the rain itself is nevertheless not evil. Indeed, nothing that God has made is an evil thing—evil comes in the lack of what might have been, or the inadequate arrangement of what is.[15]

Still, why allow lacks and inadequacies? Aquinas's second point is that the world is richer for its diversity of imperfect things.[16] No one could have said that God is unreasonable had God chosen simply to dwell alone in divine perfection. But if God chooses to make limited creatures, whose goods will be imperfect and will conflict with the goods of other creatures, this seems a sign of God's overflowing love, not some flaw in God.

Specifically, and third, sometimes one sort of good produces another sort of evil. A wonderful, roaring fire reduces timber to ashes. It was a good fire, but its goodness was not compatible with the continuing good of the timber.[17] To generalize:

---

12. Aquinas, *Summa Theologiae* 1a.105.5. The governing of something, Aquinas explained, involves both design and execution. As to design, perfection involves attending to every detail. But as to execution, "there is more excellence in a thing's being both good in itself and a cause of good in others, than in its simply being good in itself. Consequently, God governs things in such a way that he establishes some beings as causes over the governing of others. An example is a teacher who not only causes his students themselves to learn but also to be teachers of others." Ibid., 1a.103.6. See also *Summa contra Gentiles: On the Truth of the Catholic Faith* 3.65 and 3.69, trans. Vernon J. Bourke (Garden City, N.Y.: Image Books, 1956).

13. Aquinas, *Summa contra Gentiles* 3.70.8.

14. Aquinas, *Summa Theologiae* 1a.48.1.

15. Ibid., 1a.49.1.

16. Ibid., 1a.47.2.

17. Ibid.

> Defects and death are said to be against the nature of the particular na-
> ture concerned, yet in accordance with the purpose of Nature as a
> whole, in that loss to one yields gain to another. . . . since God is the
> universal guardian of all that is real, a quality of his Providence is to
> allow defects in some particular things so that the complete good of
> the universe be disentangled. Were all evils to be denied entrance,
> many good things would be lacking in the world: there would be no
> life for the lion were there no animals for its prey, and no patience of
> martyrs were there no persecution by tyrants.[18]

Sometimes doing away with what is, in itself, truly horrible would cause the
loss of an even greater good.

Aquinas surrounded all such suggestions, however, with caution. He did
not say that, looking over the world, we can determine how each of the world's
evils contributes to some greater good. Quite apart from the limitations of our
perspective, "good," like any word we apply to God, has a meaning we cannot understand, and God "acts" and "makes" in a way unlike any acting or
making we know. When we say that God creates and sustains the world as it
is, and that that has evil consequences, we can note, negatively, that it is inappropriate to speak of God making mistakes or bearing grudges. We can recognize that sometimes our impatience with creaturely imperfection indicates
how far we fall short of God's overflowing love. Beyond that, we can only trust
that, if we could see all the things that God has created as God sees them, then,
in a way we cannot imagine, we would consent that they should be. We would
see them, moreover—and this is the point for the argument of this chapter—
not as independent or operating outside the Providence of God, albeit as in
some relation to God we cannot now imagine.

On these issues, turning from Aquinas to Calvin yields a different terminology, and a different rhetorical style, but little difference in substance. Calvin
would probably have regarded Aquinas's analysis of God as giving all created
things their "to be" with the suspicion that he often brought to metaphysical
analysis, but he agreed that God is not only the world's creator but "also ever-
lasting Governor and Preserver—not only in that he drives the celestial frame
as well as its several parts by a universal motion, but also in that he sustains,
nourishes and cares for everything he has made, even the least sparrow."[19] "If
God should but withdraw His hand a little, all things would immediately perish and dissolve into nothing."[20] Calvin applied this belief to concrete cases.
He thought for instance that the earth could not remain suspended in mid-air
among all the rapid motions of the heavens "were it not upheld by God's

18. Ibid., 1a.22.2 ad 2.
19. John Calvin, *Institutes of the Christian Religion* 1.16.1, trans. Ford Lewis Battles (Philadelphia: Westminster Press, 1960).
20. John Calvin, *Commentaries on the First Book of Moses called Genesis,* vol. 1 (on Gen. 2:2),
trans. John King, *Calvin's Commentaries* (Grand Rapids: Baker Book House, 1989), 1:103.

hand."[21] He often remarked that water would flood the whole earth, as it had in the time of Noah, if God were not holding it back.[22] Calvin's God does not "intervene" in the world, as if generally elsewhere but entering the picture from time to time. God is always present and thoroughly engaged.

Most importantly for Calvin, God directs all of creation according to a providential plan. God is not "idle," he said repeatedly.[23] We should think of the events in the world around us as manifestations of God's purposes. Christians "differ from profane men especially in that we see the presence of divine power shining as much in the continuing state of the universe as in its inception."[24] Like Aquinas, Calvin did not mean to dismiss the role of secondary causes.[25] If critics would protest that such a doctrine of providence implies that there is no point in taking precautions or that the prayers of believers are useless, given that God has already planned everything, Calvin responded that God has given us charge to exercise care over our lives, and to pray for others, and our precautions and prayers are also part of God's plan.[26] In 1545 Calvin found himself in debate with a party of "spiritual libertines" who apparently believed, among other things, that everything is the action of a single Spirit, so that no one person had individual responsibility for his or her actions. No, Calvin insisted, God is responsible for everything, but human beings also are responsible for their actions: "This universal operation of God's does not prevent each creature . . . from having and retaining its own quality and from following its own inclination."[27] Suppose one person is shipwrecked or killed by a falling tree while another reaches harbor safely or escapes death by an inch. Calvin would not deny the role of the tree or of human precautions or negligence. Still, where "carnal reason ascribes all such happenings to chance," Christians "will look further afield for a cause and will consider that all events are governed by God's secret plan."[28]

This might seem unfair if you happened to be the person hit by the falling tree! Here, as chapter 4 suggested was characteristic of Calvin, he was willing

21. John Calvin, *Commentary on the Book of Psalms* (on Ps. 93:1), trans. James Anderson, *Calvin's Commentaries,* 6:7.

22. See, for instance, ibid. (on Ps. 33:7), 4:544; John Calvin, *Commentaries on the Book of the Prophet Jeremiah* (on Jer. 5:22), vol. 1, trans. John Owen, in *Calvin's Commentaries,* 9:296. Thus, "The power of nature is not sufficient to sustain and preserve the world," and "the world stands through no other power than that of God's word, and . . . inferior or secondary causes derive from him their power." John Calvin, *Commentaries on the Second Epistle of Peter* (on 2 Peter 3:5), trans. John Owen, in *Calvin's Commentaries,* 22:416.

23. For instance, Calvin, *Institutes* 1.16.3, 1.16.4.

24. Ibid., 1.16.1.

25. Ibid., 1.17.9.

26. Ibid., 1.17.5.

27. John Calvin, "Against the Fantastic and Furious Sect of the Libertines," *Treatises against the Anabaptists and against the Libertines,* trans. Benjamin Wirt Farley (Grand Rapids: Baker Book House, 1982), 243.

28. Calvin, *Institutes* 1.16.2.

to admit that he could not answer some questions and determined to consider the practical impact, the rhetorical effect of what he did say. Thus to say that the goods of nature come to us from God, but not the evils, "is too weak and profane a fiction." If people say of a hailstorm that destroys the crops or some other sudden calamity, "this will not be God's work," then "no place is left for God's fatherly favor."[29] If we are to be properly grateful for the good things that happen to us, we must therefore be persuaded that "whatever happens to us, happy or said, prosperous or adverse . . . comes to us from him"[30]

Since we have faith in God's goodness, we will further believe "that God always has the best reason for his plan."[31] If we did not realize that we "owe everything to God" and "should seek nothing beyond him," then we would "never yield him willing service." But we will not claim to understand how this is so. "We do not try to make God render account to us."[32] "His wonderful method of governing the universe is rightly called an abyss."[33] We use the language scripture gives us concerning God's sovereignty and providence, and only the frame of mind it induces will make us properly grateful to God and enable us to live in the trusting confidence that the world is not a mad chaos. What we say is not false; indeed, if we understood things as God does, then we would recognize that words like "love" and "wisdom" apply to God's relation to creation in a way that makes all human love and wisdom look trivial by comparison. But we do not understand things as God does, and therefore fundamental questions about the relation of God and world remain incomprehensible to us.

Luther's language about the relation of God and world was even more dramatic: "The course of world events and especially the activities of His saints," he wrote, "are God's mummery, behind which He hides Himself and reigns and bestirs Himself in the world."[34] The "mummery" is, on its own level, real enough. Though God determines the outcome of the battle, "he uses man and the horse, the sword and bow: but not because of the strength and power of man and of the horse, but under the veil and covering of man and the horse he fights and does all."[35] God can be thus at work in all things since God "ex-

---

29. Ibid., 1.16.5.

30. John Calvin, *Institutes of the Christian Religion* (1536), trans. Ford Lewis Battles (Atlanta: John Knox Press, 1975), 66. Hereafter cited as *Institutes* (1536).

31. Calvin, *Institutes* 1.17.1.

32. Ibid.

33. Ibid., 1.17.2.

34. Martin Luther, "Der 127 Psalm ausgelegt an die Christen zu Riga in Liefland" (1524), *D. Martin Luthers Werke*, vol. 15 (Weimar: Hermann Böhlaus Nachfolger, 1899), 373, quoted in Heinrich Bornkamm, *Luther's World of Thought* (St. Louis: Concordia Publishing House, 1958), 203.

35. Martin Luther, Sermon for the First Sunday in Lent (on Matt. 4:1–11), in *Sermons of Martin Luther*, trans. John Nicholas Lenker et al. (Grand Rapids: Baker Book House, 1988), 2:141. "For Luther, the world is not a ship constructed to sail by itself. The 'nothing' of the world, from which it has come, therefore does not lie somewhere in the past but is that from which every new creature, every new person appears at their birth; indeed, every moment and every hour are constantly newly created by God." David Löfgren, *Die Theologie der Schöpfung bei Luther* (Göttingen: Vandenhoeck & Ruprecht, 1960), 25.

ists at the same time in every little seed whole and entire, and yet also in all and above all and outside all created things."[36] Even heathen poets and quite ordinary folk, Luther noted, recognize guidance behind all events: Virgil said that "in the destruction of Troy and the rise of the Roman Empire, Fate counts for more than all the endeavors of men, and therefore it imposes a necessity on both things and men," and the common people speak casually and often of something happening "God willing."[37] All the more should Christians see God's universal activity, since it is crucial to our faith. Faith, after all, trusts that God will do what God has promised, and thus it "is the one supreme consolation of Christians in all adversities to know that God does not lie but does all things immutably, and that his will can neither be resisted nor changed nor hindered."[38] Still, this does not imply that human beings and other forces are completely passive; the picture involves two quite different orders of causal efficacy, and, for Luther as for Aquinas and Calvin, it confuses everything if we think of God as an agent operating at the same level as other agents.

Human Freedom and the Problem of Sin

God's relation to human choices and actions, particularly sinful ones, focuses problems about the relation of God and world in particularly dramatic fashion. Here historians of doctrine would rightly point to greater differences among Aquinas, Luther, and Calvin. But in respect to the fundamental issues discussed in this chapter, here too they share a good deal of common ground—a common ground from which many of their modern successors moved away.

"God moves a person to act," Aquinas wrote,

> not only by presenting an object of desire to his senses or by effecting an organic change in his body, but also by setting in motion the will itself. Every activity, of both nature and will, comes from him as first mover. And as it is not incompatible for natural movement to spring from God in this manner, since nature is a tool in his hand, neither is it incompatible with voluntary activity for him to move the will. This is without detriment to that which both natural and voluntary movements share in common, namely the character of issuing from an intrinsic principle within the agent.[39]

A voluntary action, in other words, is one I choose to do—it "proceeds from a principle within the agent." But that choice can in turn proceed from an

36. Martin Luther, *Confession Concerning Christ's Supper*, trans. Robert H. Fischer, *Luther's Works*, vol. 37 (Philadelphia: Muhlenberg Press, 1961), 228.
37. Martin Luther, *The Bondage of the Will*, trans. Philip S. Watson, *Luther's Works*, vol. 33 (Philadelphia: Fortress Press, 1972), 41.
38. Ibid., 33:43.
39. Aquinas, *Summa Theologiae* 1a2ae.6.1 ad 3.

external cause. If you offer me a wonderful job, or a serving of my favorite desert, you are not destroying my freedom. I choose to take the job, or the piece of cake—that is what I want to do. But you made the offer so attractive that I was bound to do it—in that sense you determined my free action.

In this case as in others, however, analogies between God and other sorts of agents quickly break down. You did not make me the sort of person I am, with particular ambitions and tastes, and you do not sustain my being at every moment. God did make me and does sustain me. Indeed, God "acts in every agent immediately, without prejudice to the action of the will and of nature."[40] Thus divine shaping of my will is not an interference in the natural order; it *is* the natural order: "to give natural inclinations is the sole prerogative of Him Who has established the nature. . . . the only agent that can cause a movement of the will, without violence, is that which causes an intrinsic principle of this movement, and such a principle is the very power of the will. Now, this agent is God. . . . Therefore, God alone can move the will in the fashion of an agent, without violence."[41] God makes me—in a way that involves a whole chain of secondary causes but is also, in a different way, fully the action of God—someone with certain desires and inclinations. Through another set of secondary causes, but again also fully through divine action, God creates the pattern of external stimuli to which my desires and inclinations respond. All along, God is sustaining me as the being I am. Still, as I consider my options and choose according to my desires, I am acting voluntarily, and in relation to my acts of will as in other cases the way God "makes" or "creates" is so unlike other cases of such activities that I cannot understand it.[42]

Sometimes, however, I make the wrong choice—I choose evil rather than good. Aquinas struggled to explain how this should be possible. In his earlier writings, he regularly said that the reason determines the action of the will, so that the only way we can choose evil is out of ignorance—because reason told us it was the good. But this makes it seem as if we do not really commit moral faults. After all, we *thought* we were doing the good.[43] So, by the time he wrote the second part of his *Summa Theologiae,* he had to come up with a better explanation. He started with the conviction, already noted earlier in this chapter, that a gracious God will not rest content with divine perfection but will, in overflowing generosity, bring imperfect things into existence. Imperfect things that have wills can have "deficiencies" in their wills. If they saw the good, they would do it, but they can get distracted and fail to think about good.[44] Such a

40. Aquinas, *On the Power of God* 3.7, trans. English Dominican Fathers (Westminster, Md.: Newman Press, 1952).

41. Aquinas, *Summa contra Gentiles* 3.88.4 and 6.

42. See Aquinas, *Summa Theologiae* 1a2ae.9.4 ad 1, 1a.83.1, 1a.83.1 ad 3.

43. See James F. Keenan, *Goodness and Rightness in Thomas Aquinas's Summa Theologiae* (Washington, D.C.: Georgetown University Press, 1992), 23.

44. Aquinas, *Summa Theologiae* 1a2ae.10.2.

deficiency—the *capacity* for such failure to attend—is not itself a fault. In making creatures with such a capacity, God has, with unimaginably overflowing love, added to the richness of the universe and not done something wrong.

Since our wills control whether we really attend to something or not, however, a failure to attend to the good, and resulting evil act, really *is* a fault.[45] It "directly opposes the universal good itself, it conflicts with the fulfillment of the divine will."[46] God can and does bring good out of this evil, but it remains evil. Persecution by tyrants permits martyrs to witness to their faith, but the tyrants did not have that good end in mind. They had failed to attend to the good, and therefore willed evil.[47] In a crucial passage, Aquinas ducked the question of whether in so doing they were operating outside God's will: "Everything that takes place in the world proceeds from the plan of the divine intellect: except, perhaps [*forte*], in voluntary agents only, who have it in their power to withdraw themselves from the plan of the divine intellect; that is what the evil of sin consists in."[48]

That "perhaps" leaves the reader frustrated, but Aquinas resisted saying either yes or no. Sin really "conflicts with the fulfillment of the divine will." Yet no part of creation lies outside God's control. Aquinas did not pretend to be able to explain how to reconcile these two claims.[49] Given how little we can understand of words like "will" and "control" as applied to God, he argued, it would be surprising if we *could* understand how all these pieces fit together.

Some who choose evil continue to follow the path of evil until they arrive at eternal condemnation. "What is from freewill and what is from predestination," Aquinas explained, "are not distinct, no more than what is from a secondary cause and what is from the first cause. God's Providence procures its effects through the operation of secondary causes."[50] It is therefore not wrong to pray for the salvation of souls, on the grounds that their fate is predestined. Here too God chooses to work through secondary causes, and those secondary causes really do produce their effects, "so a person's salvation is predestined by God in such a manner that whatever promotes his salvation falls into the pattern of

---

45. Ibid., 1a.49.2 ad 3.
46. Ibid., 1a.48.6.
47. Ibid., 1a.19.9 ad 1.
48. Ibid., 1a.17.1, translation altered.
49. See, for instance, ibid., 1a.19.9 ad 3.
50. Aquinas, *Summa Theologiae* 1a.23.5. I have substituted "predestination" for "grace," the puzzling translation the Blackfriars edition offers of *praedestione* at the beginning of this passage.
The sense that Calvin invented any thought of predestination *ex nihilo* has grown common enough that it may be helpful to quote some basic texts of Aquinas: "For God the number of the predestined is determinate . . . not only by reason of his knowledge . . . but also by reason of his own defining decision and choice" (*Summa Theologiae*, 1a.23.7.) "Some people God rejects . . . Since by divine Providence human beings are ordained to eternal life, it also belongs to divine Providence to allow some to fall short of this goal. This is called reprobation." (Ibid., 1a.23.3.)

predestination."[51] Here too, the contingent events of the world really are, in their own order, contingent, while "the plan of predestination is certain, though the freedom of choice, from which predestination as an effect contingently issues, is not abolished."[52] Human beings should hope and pray and move toward their salvation, but never seeking some order of causation outside of God's predestinating grace. It is more important that we take our responsibility for our sins to heart, and that we give God alone the glory for the good that befalls us, than that we explain *why* doing both should be appropriate.

Calvin would have agreed. His critics often implore for some softening of the rigors of his doctrine of predestintation, but the request misunderstands the logic of his position. Calvin, like Aquinas, did not think that we do some things and God does other things. "We are robbing the Lord if we claim anything for ourselves either in will or in accomplishment. If God were to help our weak will, then something would be left to us."[53] Rather, he believed that God, on one order of efficacy, is the sustaining cause of every event, while at the same time each event has its own cause. Therefore, it just does not make sense to urge him to tilt the balance a bit so that God might do a bit less and human free will a bit more. God is in control of all things, and God "does not throw down men at random on the earth, to go wherever they please, but guides all by his secret purpose."[54]

And yet, we human beings really do perform actions. We obey God's laws and are zealous in good works, or we turn away and do evil.

> Satan and evildoers are not so effectively the instruments of God that they do not also act in their own behalf. For we must not suppose that God works in an iniquitous man as if he were a stone or a piece of wood, but He uses him as a thinking creature, according to the quality of his nature which He has given him. Thus when we say that God works in evildoers, that does not prevent them from working also in their own behalf.[55]

Calvin illustrated the point with a particular example. In the book of Job, God allows Satan to test Job, and, as part of the test, Satan arranges that the Chaldeans steal Job's property.

> How may we attribute this same work to God, to Satan, and to man as an author, without either excusing Satan as associated with God, or making God the author of evil? Easily, if we consider first the end, and then the manner of acting. The Lord's purpose is to exercise the

51. Ibid., 1a.23.8. See also Aquinas, *Summa contra Gentiles* 3.96.8.
52. Ibid., 1a.23.6.
53. Calvin, *Institutes* 2.3.9.
54. John Calvin, *Commentary on the Book of the Prophet Isaiah* (on Isa. 13:3), vol. 1, trans. William Pringle, *Calvin's Commentaries,* 7:411. See also J.K.S. Reid, "Introduction," John Calvin, *Concerning the Eternal Predestination of God,* trans. J.K.S. Reid (London: James Clarke, 1961), 26.
55. Calvin, "Against the Fantastic and Furious Sect of the Libertines," 245.

patience of His servant by calamity; Satan endeavors to drive him to desperation; the Chaldeans strive to acquire gain from another's property contrary to law and right.[56]

The Chaldeans, who really did act, who acted voluntarily in the sense that they were drawn by their wills to the goods they sought, and who acted from evil motives—the desire to steal somebody's property "contrary to law and right"— therefore deserve punishment.[57] Nevertheless, "Whatever implements God employs, they detract nothing from his primary operation."[58] God's will gets accomplished, even sometimes through evil agents.

Everything comes to us from God, Calvin wrote early in his career, "sin only being excepted, which is to be imputed to our own wickedness."[59] Does that mean that God occasionally lets go, so that there are parts of the world, those involving human wickedness, which are out of God's control? Not at all, Calvin would reply. Even Adam's fall has its "proximate cause" in Adam but its "hidden" or "remote" cause in God's providence.[60] "No one can deny that God foreknew what end man was to have before he created him, and consequently foreknew because he so ordained by his decree."[61] And yet, "Adam could have stood if he wished, seeing that he fell solely by his own will."[62] What God ordains is also what we do freely, and contrary to God's will. "If anyone object that this is beyond comprehension," Calvin admitted, "I confess it. But what wonder if the immense and incomprehensible majesty of God exceed the limits of our intellect?"[63]

As always with Calvin, in this we must acknowledge our inability to understand God, and then say what scripture calls us to say and what conduces to right piety, even as we admit that we cannot know how all the implications of everything we say would fit together. We could not trust in God and find

---

56. Calvin, *Institutes* 2.4.2. Similarly, in a famous passage at the end of the *Institutes,* Calvin reflected on how Assyrians and Babylonians were sometimes the instruments by which God punished the "ungratefulness of the kings of Judah and Israel." These invading armies "planned in their minds to do nothing but an evil act," and yet "however these deeds of men are judged in themselves, still the Lord accomplished his work through them." Ibid., 4.20.30–31.

57. Ibid., 2.5.2.

58. Ibid., 4.14.17.

59. Calvin, *Institutes* (1536), 66.

60. Even "the devil and the whole cohort of the wicked are completely restrained by God's hand as by a bridle, so that they are unable either to hatch any plot against us or, having hatched it, to make preparations or, if they have fully planned it, to stir a finger toward carrying it out, except so far as he has permitted, indeed commanded." Calvin, *Institutes* 1.17.11.

61. Calvin, *Institutes* 3.23.7. "He not only knew what was about to happen, but decreed it." John Calvin, "Brief Reply in refutation of the calumnies of a certain worthless person," *Calvin: Theological Treatises,* trans. J.K.S. Reid (Philadelphia: Westminster, 1954), 339.

62. Calvin, *Institutes,* 1.15.8.

63. He continued: "Those who seek to know more than God has revealed are crazy. . . . Let all the powers of the human mind contain themselves within this kind of reverence: in the sin of man God willed nothing but what was worthy of His justice." Calvin, *Concerning the Eternal Predestination of God,* 123.

peace in the midst of the world's chaos if there were any part of the world out of God's control. Yet we cannot deny the horror of sin, or our responsibility for it. Thus Calvin said of sinners, "As regards themselves, they did what God did not will; as regards God's omnipotence, they were by no means able to prevail against it."[64] "I am aware," he acknowledged, "how much absurdity and contradiction these things carry with them for profane men."[65] But Christian trust in God will live with its confidence in God's sovereignty and its confession of human responsibility, content not to understand more than it ought. Our confidence in God's sovereignty makes us grateful for God's benefits and confident as we live in a chaotic world; our acknowledgment of human responsibility fosters a proper attitude of humility and confession. Both claims have biblical warrants; both work rhetorically to contribute to an appropriate Christian piety. Calvin could trust that they fit together as God sees things in a way that we cannot see.

Luther agreed. He insisted that, "Whatever we do, God works it in us."[66] Indeed, in the full vigor of his polemic against Erasmus in *The Bondage of the Will*, Luther sometimes seemed to lose sight of the logic I have been describing. Rather than saying that God directs all things on one level, even as there is a combination of voluntary action, coercion, and chance on another, Luther made it sound as if God's ultimate control of events implies the denial of human freedom on any level: "If God foreknows things, that thing necessarily happens. That is to say, there is no such thing as free choice."[67] But such remarks, interpreted generously, just emphasize, by way of rhetorical flourish, God's ultimate control. Luther generally understood that people can voluntarily choose to do what God also determines. "If God foreknew that Judas would be a traitor," for instance, "Judas necessarily became a traitor, and it was not in the power of Judas or any creature to do differently or to change his will, though he did what he did willingly and not under compulsion, but that act of will was a work of God, which he set in motion by his omnipotence, like everything else."[68]

Thus, "free choice . . . wills good through grace alone," so that "the good will, the merit and the reward all come from grace alone."[69] Conversely, though Pharaoh, when the Lord hardens his heart, "is driven and carried along in his willing," there is no violence "done to his will, since it is not unwillingly com-

---

64. Calvin, "Brief Reply," 339.
65. Calvin, *Concerning the Eternal Predestination of God*, 98–99.
66. Luther, *The Bondage of the Will, Luther's Works*, 3:149.
67. Ibid., 3:195. "Free choice is in reality a fiction, or a name without reality. For no one has it in his own power to think a good or bad thought, but everything . . . happens by absolute necessity." Martin Luther, "Assertio omnium articulorum M. Lutheri per bullam Leonis X novissimam damnatorium" (1520), *D. Martin Luthers Werke*, vol. 7 (Weimar: Hermann Böhlaus Nachfolger, 1897), 146.
68. Ibid., 185.
69. Ibid., 152.

pelled but is carried along by the natural operation of God to will naturally, in accordance with its character."[70] "Those whom God hardens are those to whom He gives voluntarily to will to be and remain and sin and to love iniquity. Such people are necessarily in sin by the necessity of immutability, but not by force."[71] What God wills people to do voluntarily, they indeed do voluntarily, but they do not do it in a way that challenges God's control of all things.

Perhaps an analogy, with its limitations carefully noted, can summarize the conclusions of this chapter. In a play, the various actors act in the usual human mixture of determinism and free will. A character may move across the stage dragged against her will, or eagerly headed toward some goal, or more or less at random. And yet, at another level (assuming nonimprovisational theater and a firm directorial hand), playwright and director have determined everything. We can debate how many choices Willy Loman had in *Death of a Salesman* and what mix of forces and decisions shaped his tragedy. If someone interrupts our discussion of the relative importance of his family, the company that fired him, and his own character in his tragic fate, to say, "No, you all have it wrong—Arthur Miller was really the force that determined Willy Loman's actions," we do not feel so much that a new point of view has been introduced as that the interruption has changed the subject. *Of course,* the author determined all the characters' actions—but that is irrelevant to our discussion of the characters' motivations.[72]

Similarly, then, given the views of Aquinas, Luther, and Calvin, arguments about the relative weight to be assigned to chance and providence, free will and divine election, make no sense. The author is not one of the characters in the play, and those characters have their own motivations and freedom, independent of the divine author's determination of every outcome.[73] As chapter 9 will show, in the seventeenth century a whole series of "liberal" parties in debates about predestination urged giving God a bit less power and human beings a bit more in deciding our ultimate fates, thereby misunderstanding the logic of earlier discussions of divine causality. Unfortunately, many of their opponents accepted their premises and argued that a God who was one agent

70. Ibid., 184.

71. Martin Luther, *Lectures on Romans* (on Rom. 8:28), trans. Hilton C. Oswald, *Luther's Works,* vol. 25 (St. Louis: Concordia Publishing House, 1972), 376.

72. I will acknowledge that with regard to bad plays (as to bad theology?) our discussion *may* take this course. We can make no sense of the internal logic of the play at all, and so we start to wonder about the author's arbitrariness.

73. Tanner offers two rules for thinking about divine transcendence: "First, a rule for speaking of God as transcendent vis-à-vis the world: avoid both a simple univocal attribution of predicates to God and world and a simple contrast of divine and non-divine predicates. In the case of univocity, God is not really transcendent at all. In the case of simple contrast, God's transcendence is not radical enough. . . . The second rule is as follows: avoid in talk about God's creative agency all suggestions of limitation in scope or manner." Tanner, *God and Creation in Christian Theology,* 47.

among others in the world *should* have all the power, turning metaphysical distinction into simple tyranny.

Theologians must speak about such issues with particular caution when it comes to matters of evil and sin. It will not do to say that some metaphysical distinction or theological device adequately answers those who are angry or grieving over the tragedies of history or their own lives. Today's critics of "classical Christian theism" often accuse it of trying to do just that—as if Aquinas or Calvin or Luther thought they had "solved the problem" by insisting that evil was not real or double predestination manifested divine justice, or whatever. I have been arguing, in line with my accounts of their work in chapters 2, 3, and 4, that their theologies, on the contrary, were characterized by a willingness to leave problems unsolved. Their sense of God's transcendence left them content to say a number of things—admittedly sometimes puzzling when all said at once—that they thought needed to be said in the interests of Christian piety, and then admit how little they understood. Theologians are often justifiably criticized for appealing to mystery whenever the intellectual going gets tough. But in this case (I will return to this point in chapter 12), given the irrationality of evil and sin, one can explain why we should *not* be able to understand them. A neat account of how they make sense as part of God's world would make them less evil, less deeply irrational and at odds with the order of things, and for that reason would be wrong on the face of it.

The analogy of God to playwright, moreover, like all analogical talk about God, breaks down if we press it too far. We know something about both dramatic characters and playwrights; we can imagine or even observe the kind of causation at work as Willy Loman argues with his sons, and the different kind at work when Arthur Miller sits in his study writing a scene. In the theological case, however, we can observe or imagine only one order—that of the interaction of causes in the world. Christians believe, Aquinas and Luther and Calvin all argued, that all of this interaction finally has purpose and meaning within God's providential plan, and that whatever good we manage to do, and whatever ways in which we move toward salvation, the credit lies ultimately in God's hands. But *how* God does these things, what the relation actually is between these two orders of causation, remains unknown to us and indeed unimaginable.[74] Spinoza, who in some ways understood the earlier tradition better than nearly anyone else in the seventeenth century, once remarked that "intellect" and "will," when applied to God and human beings, have as little in common as "the celestial constellation of the Dog and the animal which

---

74. "When the word *causa* is applied to God on the one side and the creature on the other, the concept does not describe the activity but the active subjects, and it does not signify subjects that are not merely not alike, or not similar, but subjects that in their absolute antithesis cannot even be compared." Karl Barth, *Church Dogmatics,* vol. 3, part 3, trans. G. W. Bromiley and R. J. Ehrlich (Edinburgh: T. & T. Clark, 1960), 102. See also ibid., 189.

barks."[75] "Aquinas, Luther, and Calvin would not have agreed. If we saw matters from God's point of view, they would have responded, we would see *that* that is not true—but, they would have admitted, from our point of view we cannot comprehend *why* it is not true. Efforts to understand God's agency on too close an analogy to other forms of agency inevitably get it wrong. In that, as in much else, much Christian thought in the seventeenth century abandoned views held by many earlier theologians so radically that many writers could no longer even recognize the older position and its difference from their own.

75. Benedict de Spinoza, *Ethics,* trans. William Alan White, rev. trans. James Gutmann (New York: Hafner, 1949), 58.

8 Where God Is and What God Does
Some Modern Problems

For Aquinas, Luther, Calvin, and many other premodern Christian theologians, God's transcendence was not "contrastive." Emphasizing God's transcendence did not make God less immanent. On the contrary, the wholly other God, precisely because of a radical transcendence, could also be most present to all of creation. Since God was not one of the things in the world, it made no sense to locate God in one place, with creatures in another, such that one could ask about the distance between them. Since God was not one agent among others, but operated at a different level of agency, it made no sense to ask which things God had done and which things had been done by someone or something else. At the beginning of the modern era, however, theologians and philosophers began to worry about just where to put God in the universe. Debates about miracles and about grace and free will dominated the theology of the seventeenth and eighteenth centuries, and both those debates involved asking which things God, as opposed to someone or something else, did. Chapter 9 will consider questions about grace and free will; this chapter will look at worries about God's location and about miracles.

Finding a Place for God

In his vastly learned *Theology and the Scientific Imagination,* Amos Funkenstein has identified two factors that led modern thinkers to worry in new ways about God's location. First, many forces in their culture were moving language toward greater univocity. Second, people were thinking of space as more homogeneous—not as a hierarchy of places, with locations of greater and lesser honor, but as a geometric space in which every location had the same status as every other.[1] The two factors reinforced each other.

To medieval people, the natural world was full of multiple meanings. "The universe," in Michel Foucault's words, "was folded in upon itself: the earth echoing the sky, faces seeing themselves reflected in the stars, and plants holding within their stems the secrets that were of use to men."[2] If a plant contained the cure for the illnesses of some bodily part, the shape of the plant

---

1. Amos Funkenstein, *Theology and the Scientific Imagination from the Middle Ages to the Seventeenth Century* (Princeton, N.J.: Princeton University Press, 1986), 72.
2. Michel Foucault, *The Order of Things: An Archeology of the Human Sciences,* trans. Alan Sheridan (New York: Random House, 1973), 17.

would disclose it—aconite seeds, which look like eyes, must be good for vision problems, furrowed walnut seeds for diseases of the brain.[3]

The cross made by the celestial equator and the ecliptic, according to Dante, showed the glory of Christ built into the fabric of the heavens.[4] During the Renaissance too, Ian Hacking has noted, "there were signs, real signs, written by God on nature. People spoke with signs, but so did the world around us."[5] Such things strike modern readers as metaphorical flourishes, but medieval writers considered them part of the description of the world. Foucault illustrated the change in patterns of thought by contrasting two books of zoology: Aldrovandi's *History of Serpents and Dragons,* published in the sixteenth century, described for each species its anatomy, what it eats, how to capture it, how to cook it, and its allegorical significance. Jonston's *Natural History of Quadrupeds,* published in 1657, gave only name, anatomy, and habitat.[6] Both were studies in the science of zoology, but by the middle of the seventeenth century, allegorical meanings and the human uses of things were no longer considered part of the nature about which the scientist reported.

The seventeenth century had thus already arrived at the attitudes Peter Gay found in the eighteenth-century philosophes:

> It is not so much that the philosophes despised fancy, but that in their scientific way of thinking, they sharply separated fancy from reality. In their literary writings, allegory had become a useful, transparent convention, and in their scientific writings metaphor was being replaced by the severe unpictorial language of mathematics. . . . It was different in the Christian millennium. Allegory, metaphor, figurative interpretations, retained their place precisely because they were never reduced to mere linguistic devices or literary frills. This was only reasonable: since God had scattered traces of His intent throughout creation, the man schooled in the ways of the divine language might read sacred meanings everywhere.[7]

In the Middle Ages, in a universe rich in symbolic meanings, hell appropriately lay at earth's center, where all the weight of the world's sins could flow to it.

---

3. Ibid., 27.
4. Dante, *Paradiso* 14.100–08.
5. Ian Hacking, *The Emergence of Probability* (Cambridge: Cambridge University Press, 1975), 81.
6. Foucault, *The Order of Things,* 129.
7. Peter Gay, *The Enlightenment: The Rise of Modern Paganism* (New York: W. W. Norton & Co. 1966), 239–40.
"Don Quixote is the first modern work of literature, because in it we see the cruel reason of identities and differences make endless sport of signs and similitudes, because in it language breaks off its own kinship with things and enters into that lonely sovereignty from which it would reappear, in this separated state, only as literature.
"The written word and things no longer resemble one another. And between them, Don Quixote wanders off on his own." Foucault, *The Order of Things,* 48–49.

Modern readers want to ask, How far would you have to dig to reach hell, then—or are you just talking metaphorically? But to force that choice is to impose our ways of thinking on a very different culture. Similarly, before the seventeenth century, God could be, in Athanasius's phrase, "enclosing all things, and enclosed by none, within all according to His own goodness and power, yet without all in His proper nature."[8] As the preceding chapter indicated, God could be present everywhere in the universe in a way that implied no limitation, in part because God was also present, in a way that was symbolically appropriate but not just symbolic, "outside" the universe, beyond the limits of the finite cosmos. Modern thinkers tended to understand "in" and "out" only univocally and therefore, if they heard references to God's location, they wanted spatial coordinates.

The Copernican revolution reinforced tendencies to reject the earlier, richly symbolic pictures. A geocentric cosmos had a center and a periphery, with resulting rich symbolic possibilities. Heliocentrism, to be sure, initially offered alternative possibilities just as rich. Copernicus himself imagined the sun, "as though seated on a royal throne," governing "the family of planets revolving around it" like a "visible god."[9] Johannes Kepler argued as a reason for adopting the Copernican model that it put at the center of things the Sun, "King of the planets . . . in which the Most Good God, if he took pleasure in a corporeal home and had location, would dwell with the blessed angels."[10] Copernicus and Kepler believed in a finite universe, so it could still have an ordered center and periphery. But even Copernicans like the Englishman Thomas Digges, who argued for an infinite universe, could still think of the "Orbe" of the "lightes Celestiall," the realm of the stars, now boundless in expanse, as "the gloriouse court of a great god."[11] Particular places could still have symbolic significance.

Although new scientific theories thus did not require rejecting richly symbolic ways of thinking about the cosmos, those who held onto the older patterns of thought seem to have been swimming against a fairly strong historical current. Astronomers increasingly inferred that the earth was one planet among others, the sun one star among others, and moved toward something like Newton's model of space extending homogeneously and infinitely along geometrical coordinates in all directions.[12] Such a universe had no symboli-

---

8. Athanasius, *Defence of the Nicene Definition* 3.11, trans. Archibald Robertson, *Nicene and Post-Nicene Fathers*, 2nd ser., vol. 4 (Grand Rapids: Wm. B. Eerdmans Publishing Co. 1987), 157.

9. Nicholas Copernicus, *On the Revolutions of the Heavenly Spheres* 1.10, trans. Edward Rosen, *Complete Works*, vol. 2 (London: Macmillan & Co., 1978), 22.

10. Johannis Kepler, "Fragmentum Orationis de Motu Terrae," *Astronomi Opera Omnia*, vol. 8, part 1 (Frankfurt: Heyder & Zimmer, 1870), 267. See E. A. Burtt, *The Metaphysical Foundations of Modern Science* (Garden City, N.Y.: Doubleday & Co., 1954), 59.

11. Thomas Digges, *A Perfit Description of the Caelestiall Orbes*, published as addition to Leonard Digges, *A Prognostication Everlastinge* (Norwood, N.J.: Walter J. Johnson, 1975), no pagination.

12. Isaac Newton, *Mathematical Principles of Natural Philosophy*, trans. Andrew Motte, rev. trans. Florian Cajori (Berkeley: University of California Press, 1934), 6. "If it be granted that the

cally appropriate place for God, and it was emerging as the dominant model just as many were, as already noted, moving away from looking for such symbolism in the natural world anyway.[13]

So what to do with God? To oversimplify, as spatial language became increasingly univocal and models of space more homogeneous, there was no particular natural place for God, and the natural options were to say that God was either nowhere or everywhere. Descartes and Henry More, both writing in the early seventeenth century, represent these two possibilities.

Descartes's God causes the world, and not, as with the later Deists, simply by giving an initial push. Sustaining the world from each moment to the next requires just as much a divine act as the initial creation.[14] But, since God is not an extended substance, God does not have spatial location. Writing to Henry More, Descartes denied "that true extension as commonly conceived is to be found in God or in angels or in our mind or in any substance which is not a body. Commonly when people talk of an extended being, they mean something imaginable . . . distinguished into parts . . . which have determinate sizes and shapes." But "nothing of this kind can be said about God."[15] It is hard to imagine a clearer instance of the trends I have been discussing. Descartes wanted univocal language ("*true* extension") and appealed to ordinary usage with the confidence that it would support his position ("as commonly conceived," "commonly when people talk"). When it comes to location, the univocal language he sought must be devoid of mystery ("imaginable") and geometrically expressible ("determinate sizes and shapes"). He thus left no place

---

earth moves, it would seem more natural to suppose that there is no system at all, but scattered globes, than to constitute a system of which the sun is the centre." Francis Bacon, "Descriptio globi intellectualis," in *Philosophical Works* (London: G. Routledge & Sons, 1905), 685. The English scientist John Wilkins reported as one argument against Copernicus (he was himself a Copernican), that because of the earth's "vileness" it ought to be located at the center of the universe, "which is the worst place, and at the greatest distance from those purer incorruptible bodies, the heavens." John Wilkins, "Discovery of a New Planet" (1640), *Philosophical and Mathematical Works* (London: Vernor & Hood, 1802), 1:190. The argument recognized the loss of symbolic possibility inherent in Copernicanism. See Arthur O. Lovejoy, *The Great Chain of Being: A Study in the History of an Idea* (Cambridge: Harvard University Press, 1936), 102–10.

13. The seventeenth-century revolution in science led to "the destruction of the Cosmos, that is, the disappearance . . . of the conception of the world as a finite, closed, and hierarchically ordered whole (a whole in which the hierarchy of value determined the hierarchy and structure of being, rising from the dark, heavy and imperfect earth to the higher and higher perfection of the stars and heavenly spheres), and its replacement by an indefinite and even infinite universe which is bound together by the identity of its fundamental components and laws, and in which all these components are placed on the same level of being." Alexandre Koyré, *From the Closed World to the Infinite Universe* (New York: Harper & Brothers, 1958), 4.

14. René Descartes, "Meditations on First Philosophy," *Philosophical Writings*, vol. 2, trans. John Cottingham, Robert Stoothoff, and Dugald Murdoch (Cambridge: Cambridge University Press, 1984), 33, 254. See also Daniel Garber, "How God Causes Motion: Descartes, Divine Sustenance, and Occasionalism," *Journal of Philosophy* 84 (1987): 567–80.

15. Descartes to Henry More, 5 February 1649, *Philosophical Writings*, vol. 3, trans. John Cottingham et al. (Cambridge: Cambridge University Press, 1991), 361.

for most medieval ways of talking about God's presence in the world. Still, as chapter 5 explained, Descartes needed God to make his philosophy work, just as he needed human "thinking substances" which also could not have extension or physical location. He therefore pictured a geometrical world of extended substances, with which God and human souls somehow interacted in a way he notoriously could never quite explain.

The recipient of that letter from Descartes, the English poet and philosopher Henry More, reached conclusions very different from Descartes's but was inspired by many of the same motivations: "And so, through the very same gate by which Cartesian philosophy wishes to see God driven from the world, I in contrast . . . strive and contend to introduce him back."[16] More is a difficult figure for historians of philosophy, combining remarkable insights with a tendency to get scientific details wrong and a certain fuzziness in thinking, so that one is not quite sure what to make of him. Most contemporary philosophers think his mistrust of Descartes's dualism was one of the points More got right. Where Descartes said that my body is an extended substance and my mind a different, thinking substance (and then had to wrestle with the problem of how to get them connected), More thought it obvious that a human being is one substance with both bodily extension and the capacity for thought and will. Moreover, Descartes's claim that animals are purely robots with nothing like consciousness struck More as ridiculous; he believed they had mental as well as bodily properties. More's solution was to assign a fourth dimension to every substance with mind or spirit—he called it *spissitude*. Thus I can, in various dimensions, grow taller, put on weight, or—if I think more or grow in wisdom—add spissitude.[17] More insisted he was not just speculating, that there were particular experiments that would show the inadequacy of purely mechanical explanations and the need to posit the dimension of spirit in things.[18]

Once More had made the case for a dimension of spirit in an extended substance, he could then propose God as the spiritual dimension of the whole universe. "I believe," he wrote to Descartes,

> it to be clear that God is extended in His manner just because He is omnipresent and occupies intimately the whole machine of the world as well as its singular particles. How indeed could He communicate motion to matter . . . if He did not touch the matter of the universe in practically the closest manner, or at least had not touched it at a certain time? Which certainly he would never be able to do if He were not present

16. Henry More, *Enchiridium metaphysicum* 1.8.7 (London: E. Flesher, 1671), 69. See Koyré, *From the Closed World to the Infinite Universe*, 147.

17. See Funkenstein, *Theology and the Scientific Imagination*, 78; Koyré, *From the Closed World to the Infinite Universe*, 129.

18. See his letter to Joseph Glanville, cited in A. Rupert Hall, "Henry More and the Scientific Revolution," in Sarah Hutton, ed., *Henry More: Tercentenary Studies* (Dordrecht: Kluwer, 1990), 43, and his letter to Descartes, 23 July 1649, cited in Alan Gabbey, "Henry More and the Limits of Mechanism," ibid., 22.

everywhere and did not occupy all the spaces. God, therefore, extends and expands in this manner; and is, therefore, an extended thing.[19]

It was not a new idea that God is present "everywhere"; omnipresence was indeed one of the standard divine attributes in medieval theology. Luther's doctrine of the Lord's Supper had appealed to it with particular force. The body of Christ can be present in the bread of the sacrament because Christ's humanity shares the properties of his divinity, and one of those properties is "ubiquity," being everywhere. On the authority of God's word, we encounter in the sacrament the presence of a God who is present in all things.[20] But Luther also stated, with characteristic force, the kind of reservation most earlier theologians would have had about More's conclusions:

> We say that God is no such extended, long, broad, thick, high, deep being. He is a supernatural, inscrutable being who exists at the same time in every little seed, whole and entire, and yet also in all and above all and outside all created things.[21]

Drawing on the mystery regarding all language about God characteristic of so much pre-seventeenth-century thought, Luther could reject anything like a geometrical sense of God's location in the world while still affirming God's ubiquity. God's presence had a different sort of meaning. The particular conclusions he then drew with respect to the Eucharist were controversial, but the basic way of thinking about God's presence was a commonplace. In contrast, More moved from analogy to univocity, from metaphor to mathematics. He thought he *could* define the sense in which God was present, and in the terms of science and geometry: scientific experiments show that substances with spirit have a fourth dimension of spissitude; empirical evidence supports the claim that God is the Spirit of the whole world.[22] Indeed, it is "so *manifest,* that there is a *Principle* in the World that does tug . . . stoutly and resolutely against the *Mechanick* laws of Matter," that to doubt it would be "as ridiculous, as to doubt of the truth of any one plain and easy Demonstration in the first Book of Euclide."[23]

19. Henry More, Letter to Descartes, 11 December 1648, in *Oeuvres de Descartes*, vol. 5 (Paris: Librairie Philosophique J. Vrin, 1956), 238–239, quoted in Koyré, *From the Closed World to the Infinite Universe*, 111.

20. Martin Luther, "That These Words of Christ, 'This Is My Body,' etc., Still Stand Firm against the Fanatics," trans. Robert H. Fischer, *Luther's Works*, vol. 37 (Philadelphia: Muhlenberg Press, 1961), 58, 64.

21. Martin Luther, "Confession Concerning Christ's Supper," trans. Robert H. Fischer, ibid., 228.

22. For instance, the tilt of the earth's axis at just the proper angle to produce seasons fitted to agriculture and human life must have been "establish'd by a *Principle* that hath in it *Knowledge* and *Counsel,* not from a blind fortuitous jumbling of the parts of the *Matter* one against another." Henry More, *An Antidote against Atheisme*, in *A Collection of Several Philosophical Writings* (London: James Flesher, 1662), 42.

23. Ibid., 46, and Henry More, "The Immortality of the Soul," in *A Collection of Several Philosophical Writings*, 12. See John Henry, "Henry More versus Robert Boyle," in Hutton, *Henry More*, 58.

A contrast with the sixteenth-century scientist and philosopher Giordano Bruno makes the innovation in More's thought even clearer. Bruno had no interest in protecting theological orthodoxy; indeed, he was burned at the stake as a pantheist. More was theologically much more conservative. Yet, in terms of his conceptual world, Bruno had more in common with Aquinas, Luther, and Calvin than More did. He spoke of a God, present in all things, "which unfolds what is enfolded . . . a thing divine and an optimal parent, bearer, and mother of natural things, indeed nature itself in substance."[24] Such language assumes a world of symbols and similitudes.[25] More, in contrast, had come to live in a world of proofs and quantification, and therefore, when he talked about divine omnipresence, sought the precision and univocation of the new science and ended up with quite different meanings.[26]

Funkenstein sums up the story in a passage worth quoting at length:

> The medieval sense of God's symbolic presence in his creation, and the sense of a universe replete with transcendent meaning and limits, had to recede if not to give way totally to the postulates of univocation and homogeneity in the seventeenth century. God's relation to the world had to be given a concrete physical meaning. Descartes did so by maintaining . . . [that] the only relation of God to the world . . . was that of causality, a relation Descartes exploits to the extreme. More, on the other hand, rather translated the panpsychism, or even pantheism, of philosophers of nature in the Renaissance, into a "clear and distinct" language. God thus acquired a body of sorts. . . . It is clear why a God describable in unequivocal terms, or even given physical features and functions, eventually became all the easier to discard. . . . Once God regained transparency or even a body, he was all the easier to identify and kill.[27]

A God with a definable location would likely to be a God who did *some* things rather than the principle behind *all* things. The more things in the world that

---

More thought he had shown that the brain, considered in physical terms, cannot be the origin of human thoughts and motions, "And thus we have found a spirit . . . that . . . can both understand and move corporeal matter." But the cosmos is also in motion, and that motion similarly requires a nonmechanical cause, namely God. See Henry More, *An Antidote against Atheisme*, in *The Cambridge Platonists*, ed. Gerald R. Cragg (London: Oxford University Press, 1968), 193.

24. Giordano Bruno, "De la causa, principio ed uno," in *Dialoghi italiani*, ed. Giovanni Gentile (Firenze: Sansoni, 1958), 234; quoted in Louis Dupré, *Passage to Modernity: An Essay on the Hermeneutics of Nature and Culture* (New Haven: Yale University Press, 1993), 62–63.

25. "Bruno's use of the organic metaphor of the immanent origin of movement is indeed, viewed formally, a step back into a mode of assertion that verges on the mythological." Hans Blumenberg, *The Legitimacy of the Modern Age*, trans. Robert M. Wallace (Cambridge, Mass.: MIT Press, 1983), 584.

26. Nor was More unique. For parallels, see Nicholas Malebranche, *Méditations chrétiennes et métaphysiques* 9.9, *Oeuvres Complètes*, vol. 10 (Paris: Librairie Philosophique J. Vrin, 1959), 99; Joseph Raphson, "On the real space or the Infinite Being," appendix to idem, *Analysis aequationum universalis* (London: A. & L. Churchill, 1702), 193, 196.

27. Funkenstein, *Theology and the Scientific Imagination*, 116.

science could explain in other terms, therefore, the less potential need there would be for such a God.

The Debate about Miracles

Such concerns took clear shape in the "debate on miracles," one of the central episodes of seventeenth- and eighteenth-century theology. Earlier Christian theologians had generally made no sharp distinction between the "natural" and the "miraculous."[28] Augustine saw all creation as *both* nature *and* miracle.[29] He could not understand the category "contrary to nature": "For how can an event be contrary to nature when it happens by the will of God, since the will of the great Creator assuredly is the nature of every created thing? A portent, therefore, does not occur contrary to nature, but contrary to what is known of nature."[30] God may produce some events in different ways than others, but God makes everything happen, and anything might provide the occasion for reflecting on God's power and goodness—though events whose causes we cannot discern may particularly evoke such reflection.[31] Similarly, Aquinas noted that "the word miracle is taken from *admiratio*. Now we experience wonder when an effect is obvious but its cause is hidden." Thus a peasant will find an eclipse miraculous, where an astronomer, understanding its cause, will not. We best call miracles those events whose cause is "hidden absolutely and from everyone," so that we can think of them only as actions of God and regard them with wonder.[32] Still, in a world where God sustains everything at every moment, what distinguishes miracles is our inability to understand their causes and the wonder that results, not the fact that God acts in them but not elsewhere.

Calvin likewise refused to set aside one class of events as uniquely miraculous. "For there are as many miracles of divine power," he wrote, "as there are kinds of things in the universe, indeed, as there are things either great or small."[33] Each human being contains "enough miracles to occupy our minds,

---

28. "Our normal definition of 'miracle' as the direct intervention of God in the normal running of events is a narrow and modern concept, which had little meaning before the sixteenth century at the earliest." Benedicta Ward, *Miracles and the Medieval Mind* (Philadelphia: University of Pennsylvania Press, 1982), 214.

29. Augustine, Letter 102.5, trans. J. G. Cunningham, in *Nicene and Post-Nicene Fathers*, 1st ser., vol. 1 (Grand Rapids: Wm. B. Eerdmans Publishing Co., 1988), 415.

30. Augustine, *The City of God* 21.8, trans. Henry Bettenson (Harmondsworth, Middlesex: Penguin Books, 1972), 980.

31. See Anselm, "The Virgin Conception" 11, in *Why God Became Man and The Virgin Conception*, trans. Joseph M. Colleren (Albany, N.Y.: Magi Books, 1969), 186–87; see also R. M. Grant, *Miracles and Natural Law in Greco-Roman and Early Christian Thought* (Amsterdam: North Holland Publishing Co., 1952).

32. Aquinas, *Summa Theologiae* 1.105.7, trans. English Dominican Fathers (London: Blackfriars, 1963–).

33. John Calvin, *Institutes of the Christian Religion* 1.14.21, trans. Ford Lewis Battles (Philadelphia: Westminster Press, 1960).

if only we are not irked at paying attention to them."[34] The occasional event in radical violation of the normal order of things serves only to "renew our remembrance" that God was directing every event in the normal order as well.[35]

Interactions between "nature" and "miracle" grew particularly complex during the Renaissance. Neo-Platonic traditions then prominent saw "occult forces" at work in all sorts of places—alchemy, magic, and astrology all aroused great interest. More mechanistically oriented scientists saw this interest in the occult as the enemy of empirical, predictive science. Christian theologians often joined in that opposition, since magic and the like involved appeal to powerful forces not under the control of the church—and possibly access to the demonic. Many scientists and many theologians therefore made common cause in trying to draw a sharper line between the ordinary, scientifically explicable course of the world and the occasional, but rare, divine intervention.[36] Miracles, they argued, are very different from other events, and there are not many miracles.

Thus the Englishman Joseph Glanville, in the middle of the seventeenth century, wrote that a miracle is not just a strange act (for that would include all things we do not understand) or something we consider beyond natural powers (for we do not know the limits of nature) or something done by supernatural agents (for there are many such agents), but something done in violation of the natural order by divine power.[37] God is, his contemporary Walter Charleton wrote, a "supernatural Nature" who can "infringe, transcend, or pervert" the ordinary course of nature in whatever way "his own prudence shall think expedient."[38]

In the previous chapter, I offered a rough analogy to the way Aquinas, Luther, and Calvin thought about the relation of God and world: the actors in a play interact in a mixture of determined and free behavior, but the author—or in the case of creation, God—is directing *all* the action. Writing in the seventeenth century, the English philosopher-theologian Ralph Cudworth also thought of God as a "skillful dramatist," but he changed the image. Human beings, he said, can "insert something of our own" into the dramatic action, so that God has to

34. Ibid., 1.5.3.

35. Ibid., 1.16.2. Nor is there anything uniquely divine in the violation of the normal order of things. In that sense God "permits false prophets [like Pharaoh's magicians] to work miracles." John Calvin, *Commentaries on the Four Last Books of Moses* (on Ex. 7:12), vol. 1, trans. Charles William Bingham, *Calvin's Commentaries*, 2:149.

36. See William B. Ashworth, Jr., "Catholicism and Early Modern Science," in David C. Lindberg and Ronald L. Numbers, eds., *God and Nature* (Berkeley: University of California Press, 1986), 138. Sylvester of Ferrara, for instance, a sixteenth-century commentator on Aquinas, distinguished "supernatural" and "natural" orders in a way that Aquinas never did. See Dupré, *Passage to Modernity*, 171–72.

37. Joseph Glanville, *Sadducismus Triumphantes* (Gainesville, Fla.: Scholar's Facsimiles and Reprints, 1966), 124–25.

38. Walter Charleton, *The Darknes of Atheism Dispelled by the Light of Nature: A Physico-Theological Treatise* (London: William Lee, 1652), 130.

exercise divine skill by always finding a way to connect "that of ours which went before with what of his follows after." God sometimes does that by appearing, "as it were, miraculously upon the stage," no longer operating at a different level of agency, but as one actor among the others in the drama.[39]

Thus Robert Boyle, gifted scientist and devout Christian, acknowledged that "some of the arbitrary laws" God has established "in that little portion of his workmanship that we inhabit should now and then (though very rarely) be controlled or receded from."[40] But we cannot expect that such miracles will occur very often: "It became the divine Author of the universe . . . to establish among its parts such general and constant laws, as best suited with his purposes in creating the world" and "it seems very congruous to his wisdom to prefer . . . catholic laws, and higher ends, before subordinate ones, and uniformity in his conduct before making changes in it according to every sort of particular emergencies."[41] It would be beneath the dignity of God to intervene in the order of nature for trivial reasons.

Notice the picture that Boyle presupposed: God as First Cause set the universe running according to fixed laws, and thereafter intervenes only rarely to perform the occasional miracle. Given such a picture, miracles now had evidentiary value. As long as our mystified wonder defined a miracle, it had no more status as "evidence" for the truth of faith than any other event, properly understood. But if the defining characteristic of a miracle was that it violated the laws of nature, then a properly established miracle constituted good evidence that something existed beyond the (newly defined) natural order. As Samuel Clarke proclaimed, Christian faith is

> positively and directly proved, to be actually and immediately sent us from God; by the many infallible Signs and Miracles, which the Author of it worked publicly as the evidence of his divine Commission.[42]

---

39. Ralph Cudworth, "The True Intellectual System of the Universe," *The Cambridge Platonists,* 207–08.

40. Boyle Manuscripts, Royal Society London, vol. 7, folios 113–14, quoted in Robert M. Burns, *The Great Debate on Miracles* (Lewisburg, Pa.: Bucknell University Press, 1981), 54.

41. Robert Boyle, "A Free Inquiry into the Received Notion of Nature," *Works,* vol. 5 (London: W. Johnston, 1772), 251–52. Boyle was already approaching the position of a Deist like Toland: "God is not so prodigal of *Miracles,* as to work any at random. The Order of Nature is not alter'd, stopp'd, or forwarded, unless for some weighty Design becoming the Divine Wisdom and Majesty." John Toland, *Christianity not Mysterious* (London: n.p., 1696), 152–53.

42. Samuel Clarke, *A Discourse concerning the Being and Attributes of God, the Obligations of Natural Religion, and the Truth and Certainty of the Christian Revelation,* 6th ed. (London: James Knapton, 1725), 216. "The Course of Nature," Clarke added, "truly and properly speaking is nothing else but the *Will of God,* producing certain Effects in a continued, regular, constant and uniform Manner: Which Course or Manner of Acting being in every Moment perfectly *Arbitrary,* is as easie to be *altered* at any time, as to be *preserved*" (ibid., 222). Therefore, contrary to the assumptions of the Deists, it is as easy for God to alter the natural order as to sustain it. And, in fact, there are "rare and extraordinary" events that could not be caused by God's "constant and uniform acting on matter"—in other words, miracles (ibid., 224). Clarke thus sought to preserve the old sense of God's sustaining work in all things while allowing for the evidentiary value of the miraculous.

Thus, while the seventeenth- and eighteenth-century debate about miracles in some ways paralleled the late medieval discussion of the absolute power of God, a new context made the implications very different. Reflections on God's absolute power had led in the fourteenth century to doubts about the reliability of divine promises, which Luther addressed by his appeal to trust in Christ. In the seventeenth century, on the other hand, the pressing issue was not whether one could trust God not to act too arbitrarily, but whether occasional interventions in the normal order of things provided evidence for God's existence and continued activity.

Once one began to take miracles as evidence for religious claims, they were being discussed in discourse about evidence, and it became natural to ask more aggressively about the evidence for the miracles themselves. Thus by the early eighteenth century a Deist like Thomas Woolston, while still believing in a divine Creator, dismissed the evidence even for biblical miracles: if such tales "had not been reported of *Jesus* but of *Mahomet,* in the same disorder of Time, by three different Historians, you would presently have scented the Forgery and Imposture."[43] Woolston's tracts against miracles sold 30,000 copies and generated over sixty published replies from irate Christians.[44] For his time, he was too outrageous to gain many supporters, but his opponents generally accepted the terms of the argument as he had defined them. Granted that God as first cause made the world, does God intervene once things have started off? Woolston and other Deists doubted it; his opponents, with considerable passion, laid out the contrary evidence as they saw it. Neither side grasped that, until a century before their time, most Christian theologians would have rejected that way of framing the question.

Newton versus Leibniz

The debate in the early eighteenth century between Gottfried Wilhelm Leibniz and Isaac Newton's friend Samuel Clarke (with Newton at least giving Clarke regular advice and possibly drafting parts of his responses[45]) provides a fitting conclusion for this chapter. It engaged, in Leibniz and Newton, perhaps the two greatest minds of the time. It centered on the two issues discussed in this chapter's two previous sections—God's location and miracles. And everyone involved accepted the new framework the seventeenth century had established for thinking about such problems.

---

43. Thomas Woolston, *Fifth Discourse on the Miracles of Our Saviour* (London: printed for the author, 1728), 11.

44. See Burns, *The Great Debate on Miracles,* 10.

45. Newton "collaborated fully with Clarke in his replies." Alexandre Koyré and I. Bernard Cohen, "Newton and the Leibniz-Clarke Correspondence," *Archives Internationales d'Histoire des Sciences* 15 (1962): 67.

Newton hated Leibniz, whom he suspected of having stolen from him the idea of calculus, and they had already had a long feud when, in 1715, Leibniz wrote a letter to Caroline, Princess of Wales, that was soon being widely circulated. Leibniz lamented the decay of natural religion in England, and, among other causes or symptoms of this decay, noted,

> Sir Isaac Newton says, that space is an organ, which God makes use of to perceive things by. But if God stands in need of any organ to perceive things by, it will follow, that they do not depend altogether upon him, nor were produced by him.

Furthermore,

> Sir Isaac Newton, and his followers, have also a very odd opinion concerning the work of God. According to their doctrine, God Almighty wants to wind up his watch from time to time. . . . Nay, the machine of God's making, is so imperfect, according to these gentlemen; that he is obliged to clean it now and then by an extraordinary concourse, and even to mend it.[46]

The tone managed to be not only condescending but nasty, and Newton's fury was redoubled. He did not deign to enter into direct communication with Leibniz himself but commissioned his young friend Samuel Clarke to write on his behalf, and so began a remarkable correspondence in which, as these quotations indicate, God's relation to space and God's intervention in nature proved central topics.

The issue of God's "sensorium," the sense "organ" that God supposedly "makes use of to perceive things by," was particularly awkward for Newton. In the original Latin edition of his *Opticks,* published in 1706, he had referred to "infinite space" as the "Sensorium of a being incorporeal, living, and intelligent, who sees the things themselves intimately, and thoroughly perceives them, and comprehends them wholly by their immediate presence to himself." Even as the book was being published, he evidently got nervous about the phrase, and some copies, presumably later in the publishing run, referred to a Being who, "*as it were* in his Sensorium [*tanquam Sensorio suo*] sees the things themselves intimately."[47] The addition of that *tanquam*—"as it were"— reflected caution, but Leibniz had gotten hold of an early copy, and Clarke found himself defending "the Sensorium of God."

"Sensorium," Leibniz initially complained, meant a sense organ or a medium or some sort of device by way of which God would interact with the world,

46. Gottfried Wilhelm Leibniz, "Mr. Leibniz's First Paper," H. G. Alexander, ed., *The Leibniz-Clarke Correspondence* (New York: Philosophical Library, 1956), 11.

47. See Alexandre Koyré and I. Bernard Cohen, "The Case of the Missing *Tanquam*," *Isis* 52 (1961): 555–56.

and that in turn implied an imperfection in a God who could not know or act on the world directly and immediately.[48] It was as if God needed eyeglasses because of failing sight or a prosthetic device because of limited strength. No, Clarke protested, God has no "need of any medium at all, whereby to perceive things: but on the contrary . . . he, being omnipresent, perceives all things by his immediate presence to them." Newton had only been using a "similitude" in order "to make this more intelligible." Just as the human mind sees pictures and images in a sort of sensory field, so God sees all things "by his immediate presence to them." Space is to God as our sensory field is to a human mind.[49] But that, Leibniz repeatedly complained, "seems to make God the soul of the world" and thereby led to pantheism.[50] "Space," he wrote acidly in a letter to Bernoulli, "is the idol of the English."[51]

Newton thought he needed absolute space and time, extending infinitely and unchangeably in all directions, in order to be able to distinguish between absolute and relative motion—this was a crucial point for Einstein's challenge centuries later.[52] He therefore felt he had to reject Leibniz's relational account of space. But what was this infinite space? It could not be a material object; it had, for instance, no mass. Yet it had to be something. So Newton proposed that it was, "as it were," the sensory field of God, by virtue of which, Clarke explained, God, "being omnipresent, is really present to everything, essentially and substantially."[53] Newton insisted that he was not a pantheist: "We are not to consider the World as the Body of God, or the several Parts thereof, as the Parts of God."[54] But given a geometrical understanding of space and univocal meanings for terms like "present" and "existence," he was hard put to explain why his thought would not lead in that direction.

Leibniz had problems too. He identified God as a monad, and monads, the basic components of his system, he elsewhere explained, are defined by their place in relation to other monads. Except that God has no location, and is in fact "absolutely infinite."[55] Since Leibniz generally defined the relations among monads spatially and did not know how to give God a spatial location, it is

48. Leibniz, "Leibniz's First Reply," *The Leibniz-Clarke Correspondence*, 17.
49. Ibid., "Clarke's First Reply," 13.
50. Ibid., "Leibniz's Fourth Paper," 40. See also ibid., "Leibniz's Fifth Paper," 82.
51. Leibniz to Bernoulli, 27 May 1716, *The Correspondence of Isaac Newton*, vol. 6 (Cambridge: Cambridge University Press, 1976), 536.
52. Newton, *Mathematical Principles of Natural Philosophy*, 6.
53. "Clarke's Third Reply," *Leibniz-Clarke Correspondence*, 33–34.
Newton's friend David Gregory recorded an account of a conversation they had: "The plain truth is, that he believes God to be omnipresent in the literal sense . . . for he supposes that as God is present in space where there is no body, he is present in space where body is also present." "Memorandum of Conversation with Newton, 21 December 1705," quoted in Richard S. Westfall, *Never at Rest: A Biography of Isaac Newton* (Cambridge: Cambridge University Press, 1980), 647.
54. Isaac Newton, *Opticks* (New York: Dover Publications, 1952), 403.
55. Nicholas Rescher, *G. W. Leibniz's Monadology: An Edition for Students* (Pittsburgh: Pittsburgh University Press, 1991), 143.

not surprising that he could not come to a clear resolution on the relation between God and creatures. In April 1676 he wrote to his friend Arnold Eckhard, "God . . . is everything. Creatures are some things." But a a year later he wrote, "It seems to be impossible for there to be a Being that is everything,"[56] and from 1678 on, he consistently insisted that creatures were independent substances, not modes of the one divine substance. Still, Robert Merrihew Adams has documented what he calls "the tenuousness of the creatures' independence from God in the Leibnizian scheme of things."[57] To preserve creatures' independence in their relations with God, God needed a location—but there was no place in Leibniz's universe to put God.

The debate over Leibniz's first comment to Princess Caroline thus repeated issues Descartes and More had argued a generation or two earlier. Like More, Newton saw God as somehow suffusing all things—and then had to protect himself from pantheism.[58] Like Descartes, Leibniz came to think of God as a separate substance, but then could not figure out where to put God or the mechanism for how God would interact with other substances. In all four cases, increasingly mathematical understandings of space and the demand for clear and distinct ideas forced questions earlier thinkers had been able to avoid, without providing viable answers.

In his initial letter to Princess Caroline, Leibniz had also referred to the "odd opinion" of Newton and his followers that "God Almighty wants to wind up his watch from time to time." Newton indeed held that the interaction of all the planets and comets in the solar system produces gradually increasing irregularities, which God must adjust from time to time.[59] Leibniz found this simply silly; it made God seem like an incompetent mechanic who could not build a device correctly and had to keep adjusting it. Clarke offered an alternative analogy: If God is like a king over all the universe, then a king is *more* powerful, *more* regal, if regularly involved in the affairs of his kingdom. "If a king had a kingdom, wherein all things would continually go on without his government or interposition . . . it would be to him, merely a nominal kingdom;

56. Quoted in Robert Merrihew Adams, *Leibniz: Determinist, Theist, Idealist* (New York: Oxford University Press, 1994), 130.

57. Ibid., 132.

58. For two quite different views of More's influence on Newton, see Stephen Toulmin, "Criticism in the History of Science: Newton on Absolute Space, Time, and Motion," *Philosophical Review* 68 (1959): 214, and W. von Leyden, *Seventeenth-Century Metaphysics* (New York: Barnes & Noble, 1968), 259–60.

59. Newton, *Opticks,* 402. Perhaps the most famous story about later Newtonianism speaks to this point. Napoleon, the story goes, asked Pierre Laplace where God fit into his model of the solar system, and Laplace replied, "I have no need of that hypothesis." Whether or not this event really took place, it would not have represented just a clever turn of phrase on Laplace's part; he had actually figured out a more precise model of planetary interactions, in which things would not, it turned out, gradually run down. See Roger Hahn, "Laplace and the Vanishing Role of God in the Physical Universe," in *The Analytic Spirit,* ed. Harry Woolf (Ithaca, N.Y.: Cornell University Press, 1981), 85–86.

nor would he in reality deserve at all the title of king or governor."[60] Indeed, if "God does not concern himself in the Government of the World . . . it will follow that he is not an Omnipresent, All-powerful, Intelligent and Wise Being; and consequently, that he is not at all."[61] Leibniz was leading his readers, Clarke claimed, down a road that led not merely to Deism but to atheism.

Moreover, Clarke insisted he and Newton were not claiming that God came up with an initial plan, discovered its flaws, and unexpectedly had to fix it. God had a plan from the start that involved interventions from time to time in the order of nature, so that every stage of the divine activity is part of that single divine plan. Human beings build weights and springs, which then can operate independently of us, but in that sense there are "no powers of nature independent upon God." At the same time, he spoke of God's "amendment" of the original order of nature and, as earlier noted, argued that God must intervene in creation from time to time in order not to be merely a nominal ruler.[62] So was God always directly involved, or merely from time to time? Newton faced the same question in relation to the topic most associated with his name—gravity.

Newton thought that matter is "passive," acting only when acted on by an outside force, so that of themselves material objects should not be doing anything. Like most of his scientific contemporaries, he also believed that force could be exerted only through a medium. No matter how hard I swing a bat, I cannot make a ball move unless I either hit the ball or else hit something that in turn hits the ball. And yet, material objects just by themselves seem to exert gravitational force, and they seem to do it on objects at a distance.

At least at some points in his career, Newton tried to solve the problem by saying that material objects do not exercise gravitational force at all, but that God directly causes gravitational attraction:

> For two planets separated from each other by a long distance that is empty do not attract each other by any force of gravity . . . except by the mediation of some active principle interceding between them. . . . And therefore those Ancients who rightly understood the mystical philosophy taught that a certain infinite spirit pervades all space & con-

60. Leibniz, "Clarke's First Reply," *Leibniz-Clarke Correspondence,* 14. But, Leibniz responded, a king "who should originally have taken to have his subjects so well educated, and . . . preserve them so well in their fitness for their several stations . . . as that he should have no occasion ever to be amending any thing amongst them" would not be "only a nominal king." Ibid.,"Leibniz's Second Paper," 19–20.

Leibniz was employed by the ruling house of Hanover, whose imminent assumption of the British throne was of some concern to many in Newton's circle, so the debates about how to understand the role of a king had a political context. See Stephen Shapin, "Of Gods and Kings: Natural Philosophy and Politics in the Leibniz-Clarke Disputes," *Isis* 72 (1981): 187–215.

61. Samuel Clarke, "A Discourse Concerning the Unchangeable Obligations of Natural Religion," in *Works* (London: James Knapton, 1738), 2:602.

62. Leibniz, "Clarke's Second Reply," *Leibniz-Clarke Correspondence,* 22–23.

tains and vivifies the universal world . . . according to the Poet cited
by the Apostle: In him we live and move and have our being.[63]

But if God causes *every* instance of gravitational attraction, then what does it
mean to talk about God intervening from time to time to make adjustments?
Even more, why would those adjustments count as the necessary evidence that
God is not a merely "nominal" monarch, if God is fully engaged in making
things happen at every moment and place?[64]

Leibniz's position, however, seems at least as tangled. His central argument
against Clarke, stated again and again, was, in effect, "If God made things right
in the first place, why would God ever have to intervene? But surely God made
things right in the first place." To make his argument work, he therefore
wanted to hold his opponents to a straightforward sense of "divine intervention." At least three times in the correspondence he insisted that, " 'tis not usual-
ness or unusualness that makes a miracle properly so called," for then any oddity would count as a miracle.

But if "miracle" means something stronger, then did Leibniz believe in miracles? At one of those points he went on to say that, although he conceded
that "there are miracles of an inferior sort, which an angel can work. He can,
for instance, make a man walk upon the water without sinking," yet "there are
miracles, which none but God can work; they exceed all natural powers."[65]
Yet the other two passages seem to reject the introduction of miracles altogether, as "the very thing which all men endeavour to avoid in philosophy."
A miracle can explain *anything,* and therefore abandons the effort to explain
the world of our experience according to orderly principles which is central
to science and philosophy.[66] Moreover, it was central to Leibniz's philosophy

63. Newton, Add MS 3965.6 f269, quoted in Westfall, *Never at Rest,* 511. See Newton to Richard
Bentley, 25 February 1692/3, in *The Correspondence of Isaac Newton,* vol. 3 (Cambridge: Cam-
bridge University Press, 1961), 254. See also J. E. McGuire, "Force, Active Principles, and Newton's
Invisible Realm," *Ambix* 15 (1968): 161–65; James E. Force, "Newton's God of Dominion," in James
E. Force and Richard H. Popkin, eds., *Essays on the Content, Nature, and Influence of Isaac New-
ton's Theology* (Dordrecht: Kluwer Academic Publishers, 1990), 85; and, for the more general back-
ground, Ernan McMullin, *Newton on Matter and Gravity* (Notre Dame, Ind.: University of Notre
Dame Press, 1978).

64. "With regard to God," Clarke suggested at one point, "no one possible thing is more miraculous than another; and . . . therefore a miracle does not consist in any difficulty in the nature of
the thing to be done, but merely in the unusualness of God's doing it." ("Clarke's Fifth Reply,"
Leibniz-Clarke Correspondence, 114.) "Miracles are so called not because they are the actions
of God but because they happen seldom and by happening seldom create wonder." (Isaac Newton, Portsmouth College, Cambridge University Library Add 3968 fol. 587, quoted by Koyré and
Cohen, "Newton and the Leibniz-Clarke Correspondence," 74.)

65. Leibniz, "Leibniz's Fourth Paper," *Leibniz-Clarke Correspondence,* 43. He elsewhere wrote,
"God can exempt creatures from the laws that he has prescribed for them, and produce in them
that which their nature does not bear by performing a *Miracle.*" G. W. Leibniz, *Theodicy,* trans.
E. M. Huggart (La Salle, Ill.: Open Court, 1985), 74.

66. Leibniz, "Leibniz's Second Paper," *Leibniz-Clarke Correspondence,* 20; ibid.,"Leibniz's Fifth
Paper," 90–91.

that God would make the best of all possible worlds, and he thought such a world is one in which natural laws perfectly and without interference realize the moral goods of what he called "the kingdom of grace."[67] The reality of a miracle would appear to be a failure in this ideal.

At some point thinking about these matters leads to the long debated question of whether Leibniz was really being honest. Two generations ago Bertrand Russell forcefully developed the case that Leibniz had two philosophies, a public one compatible with orthodox Christianity and a private one very close to Spinoza's pantheism.[68] I suspect Leibniz was more ambivalent and confused, but less dishonest, then Russell claimed, but it is undeniably very difficult to construct a consistent picture of his views. Within a single page of a letter to Bernoulli, Leibniz first criticized Newton for believing that "the world-machine . . . repeatedly requires some extraordinary correction, which is hardly worthy of God its architect," and then criticized Clarke for holding that miracles are distinct from other events "only according to our apprehension," whereas "according to theology and truth miracles (at least those which are of a higher order, such as to create or destroy) transcend all natural created forces."[69] The meaning of that parenthetical phrase is unclear—does it suggest that there has been only one miracle, at the beginning of all creation, or not? But the most natural reading of the criticism of Clarke is that God does interfere in an otherwise independent natural order—just the sort of thing the criticism of Newton seemed to deny. Even in private correspondence, Leibniz seems to be trying to have it both ways.

Whatever Leibniz's relation to him, Spinoza does turn out to hover in the background of much of this story. With respect to God and space, he was the one major thinker in the seventeenth century cheerfully ready to say that, if God is omnipresent and language is univocal, then God occupies all space and is identical with the totality of the world.[70] With respect to miracles, he insisted that the natural order, identical with God, necessarily worked out its own nature, and had no room for miraculous interventions.[71] Spinoza transferred some of the implications of the premodern vision of God into the new world of univocal predication and mechanical causation. His horrified critics rightly recognized that in the process he had lost central elements of Christian (and

---

67. See Rescher, *G. W. Leibniz's Monadology,* 289; Adams, *Leibniz,* 84.

68. See Bertrand Russell, *A Critical Exposition of the Philosophy of Leibniz* (London: Allen & Unwin, 1964), and, more briefly, Bertrand Russell, *A History of Western Philosophy* (New York: Simon & Schuster, 1945), 587, 590–91. Even Leibniz's contemporaries were raising similar questions; see the early reviews cited in Catherine Wilson, *Leibniz's Metaphysics* (Princeton: Princeton University Press, 1989), 297. Given the quite nasty things Leibniz said about Spinoza on occasion, the charge that he was a crypto-Spinozist is a morally serious one. See David Bell, *Spinoza in Germany from 1670 to the Age of Goethe* (London: Institute of Germanic Studies, 1984), 7.

69. Leibniz to Bernoulli, 27 May 1716, *The Correspondence of Isaac Newton,* 6:356.

70. Benedict de Spinoza, *Ethics,* book 1, prop. 8, trans. William Alan White, rev. trans. James Gutmann (New York: Hafner Publishing Co., 1949), 45.

71. Ibid., book 1, appendix, 75.

Jewish) faith. Rejecting Spinoza, the Deists posited a God who created every-thing and then stepped out of the picture, while their opponents invented a God who jumped in and out of creation in a way earlier theologians would not have recognized. No one knew quite what to say about where God was. Newton, Clarke, and Leibniz all seem at different times to have taken several positions on these issues, as they struggled to talk about God in a new intel-lectual language. Few of the intellectuals involved in these conversations rad-ically challenged the new modes of thinking, and the challenge of affirming central elements of the old faith in the new terms remained unmet.

9 Grace and Works in Modern Thought

The previous chapter described how many Christian theologians in the seventeenth century came to a different understanding of God's relation to the world. Aquinas, Luther, and Calvin, retaining a more radical sense of God's transcendence, had thought of God as everywhere sustaining and directing the world at a different dimension of things. Many in the seventeenth century, as they pushed toward univocity of language and clarity of argument, thought of God as one agent among others in the world, so that they started to ask where God was and which things God did. This chapter focuses on the particular question of God's relation to the actions of human beings. The same pattern emerges. Where earlier theologians had thought of many acts as *both* wholly the result of divine grace *and* the result of free human decisions, many in the seventeenth century wanted to divide up the responsibility. Which things did God do? Which things did human beings do? If both were involved, how much did each contribute? As a result, I believe, they often lost sight of earlier insights about the power of God's grace.

This chapter is also related to chapter 6. There I talked about how new understandings of God led many seventeenth-century theologians to try to define the nature of divine grace more precisely, and in doing so lost the transcendence that made it truly God's grace. Obviously, the way we understand grace and the way we understand the relation between grace and human freedom are two sides of the same coin, so there is a kind of arbitrariness to the division of material between chapter 6 and this one. That earlier chapter focussed on those who in theory most emphasized the power of grace (Jansenists, Lutheran Pietists, and Puritans), arguing that even they in practice distorted earlier ways of thinking about grace's freedom. This chapter will turn to those in the seventeenth century who modified earlier accounts of grace not just in practice but in theory. It also happens that, among Reformed theologians, chapter 6 considered examples from England and Massachusetts, while this chapter will look at figures from the European continent and Scotland. Here too that Reformed story has Catholic and Lutheran parallels. Since the idea of grace was so central to Luther's reformation, it seems appropriate to begin by looking briefly at what happened with Lutheranism.

Melanchthon and His Critics

In 1559, the same year as the final edition of Calvin's *Institutes,* Philipp Melanchthon published the *Loci praecipui theologici,* his final effort at a sys-

146

tematic statement of Reformation theology. Luther had praised a much earlier version, the *Loci communes* of 1521, as the greatest book since the Bible, and the young Melanchthon, professor of Greek at Wittenberg when only twenty-one, had been Luther's right-hand man in the beginnings of the Reformation. But Luther had been dead since 1546, and Melanchthon was by 1559 himself a year away from death, worn down by bitter debates in which he had been accused of betraying Luther's principles.

Early in his book, Melanchthon turned to the question of human freedom, divine grace, and their roles in salvation. He attacked

> those who excuse their cessation from activity on the ground that the will, as they believe, does nothing. On the contrary, it is the eternal and changeless command of God that you should obey the Gospel. . . . "I cannot," you say? Yes, you can, in a certain sense: sustaining yourself with the Word of the Gospel, you can ask to be helped by the Holy Spirit; then you shall know that . . . when we strive with ourselves, when, aroused by the promise, we call upon God and resist our distrust and other vicious desires, that is the very way God desires to convert us. . . . This, rightly understood, is true, and . . . will make clear this combination of causes: The Holy Spirit, the Word of God, and the will.[1]

That last sentence invites us to think of God's Word and Spirit and human free will as causes on the same level, interacting so that each makes a partial contribution to the result. Earlier parts of the passage suggest that God will help us with grace when we on our part do the best that is in us—precisely the conclusion of later medieval theology that Luther attacked with greatest vehemence.

Thus a good many of Melanchthon's contemporaries, like a good many Lutheran theologians since, denounced him for "synergism," the doctrine that human will and divine grace each play a partial role in justification. He certainly used language that implied such shared efforts, whether about justification or human moral efforts generally.[2] For example, he said that the Holy Spirit helped Joseph resist seduction by Potiphar's wife, but that it played only a partial role, which would have been inadequate without Joseph's own efforts: "the will of Joseph might have shaken off the Holy Spirit."[3] Part of his problem was that Melanchthon wanted to locate theology as part of a universal

---

1. Philipp Melanchthon, *Loci praecipui theologici* (1559), *Melanchthons Werke* 2/1 (Gütersloh: C. Bertelsmann Verlag, 1952), 245–46; the whole section is translated into English in C. B. Gohdes, "The Second Article of the Form of Concord," *Lutheran Church Review* 28 (1909): 331–32.

2. See the selection of passages quoted in Clyde L. Manschreck, *Melanchthon: The Quiet Reformer* (New York: Abingdon Press, 1958), 297, 300. Manschreck's book informs much of my discussion of Melanchthon, though he is much more sympathetic than I am.

3. Philipp Melanchthon, *Liber de anima*, in *Corpus Reformatorum*, vol. 13 (Halle: C. A. Schwetschke et filium, 1846), col. 162. Similarly, God's hardening of Pharaoh's heart was "permissive, not causative." Melanchthon, *Explicatio Symboli Niceni*, in *Corpus Reformatorum*, vol. 23 (Brunsvigae: C. A. Schwetschke et filium, 1855), col. 392.

system of knowledge, within which both human psychology and the workings of divine grace would be explained, with theological concepts subsumed under more general philosophical categories.[4] For all his admiration of his young friend, Luther had always resisted this—there is, he once wrote Melanchthon, a topic called "faith" that never finds a place in your philosophy—and only faith can apprehend the significance of grace.[5] For Luther, God's grace was not one cause among others to be fit into a world-system philosophically understood.

Many of Melanchthon's opponents, however, also misinterpreted Luther. The loudest of them, Matthias Flacius Illyricus, proclaiming his fidelity to Luther, insisted that in conversion the human will was "purely passive." "Through Adam's fall," he wrote, "the nature and substance of man is totally destroyed." No longer the image of God, we are now the image of Satan, and God does not, and could not, work on us as agents with our own freedom and responsibility, but has to treat us as *things* to be moved to salvation with no participation on our own part.[6] Like Melanchthon, Flacius assumed that God operates as an agent in competition among others. Therefore, wanting to preserve the sovereignty of God's grace, he concluded that he had to deny that, when it came to salvation, human beings did anything at all. Neither side in the debate could understand that God might operate, at a different order, so that human beings were *also* engaged as responsible agents in a process that yet owed everything to God.

Molina and His Context

Similar debates occurred among Roman Catholics. For Aquinas, as noted in chapter 7, God and human beings are not competing centers of agency but operate on different levels; God sustains the activity of *all* being. Thus, "What is from freewill and what is from grace are not distinct, no more than what is from a secondary cause and what is from the first cause; as we have seen, God's Providence procures its effects through the operation of secondary causes. Hence what is through freewill is also from predestination."[7] Therefore, Aquinas felt no need to limit God's role in order to preserve a place for human freedom.

The Council of Trent, worried that Protestant theologians were denying any

4. "His theological-philosophical double project gave evangelical theology a positive relation to systematic knowledge [*Wissenschaft*], first to humanistic philology, which becomes its indispensable tool, fundamental to every true systematic knowledge of truth." Heinrich Bornkamm, *Philipp Melanchthon* (Lüneburg: Heliand Verlag, 1947), 14.

5. Luther To Melanchthon, 29 June 1530, trans. Gottfried G. Krodel, *Luther's Works*, vol. 49 (Philadelphia: Fortress Press, 1972), 331.

6. See Jaroslav Pelikan, *Reformation of Church and Dogma* (Chicago: University of Chicago Press, 1984), 143.

7. Aquinas, *Summa Theologiae* 1a.23.5, trans. English Dominican Fathers (London: Blackfriars, 1963–).

place for human moral responsibility, introduced a warning: "If anyone says that man's free will . . . in no way cooperates toward disposing and preparing itself for obtaining the grace of justification; that it cannot refuse its consent if it would, but that, as something inanimate, it does nothing whatever and is merely passive, let him be anathema."[8] In spite of that firm anathema, however, it is not quite clear what this canon actually condemned. Obviously, it ruled out Flacius, who really had said that the human will does nothing but is acted on as something inanimate. But Calvin and—most of the time—Luther agreed with Aquinas that human free will cooperates in preparing for its justification—while remembering that, as Aquinas put it, "whatever is in man disposing him towards salvation is all included under the effect of predestination, even the preparation for grace," so that all the credit ought ultimately to go to God.[9] Was Trent attacking such a view? It is worrisome that the council claimed that people can refuse consent to grace, and elsewhere defined "freedom" as "indifference"—that is, if I freely choose A over B, then, all causal factors in place, nothing yet determined my choice.[10] Such assumptions might well imply a forced option—*either* human freedom *or* divine direction as the cause of salvation—the mistake I have been arguing was characteristic of seventeenth-century theology. But is is just not clear how far the council had thought through these issues.

Later Catholic theologians, however, began to think them through with some precision. The Spanish Jesuit Luis de Molina (1535–1600) played a central role in these debates. Like the Council of Trent, Molina defined freedom as indifference: We are free when we can, in the face of all external causes, either act or not act.[11] Therefore, if human beings are to have any freedom in matters of salvation, then, God having done all that God is going to do, the human choice to accept or reject must remain genuinely open: "It is possible that of two who are given equal internal help from God, one is by his free will converted, and the other remains in unfaithfulness."[12] Indeed, sometimes it is the person given *less* grace who responds better and is saved.[13] Otherwise, "contingency would be taken away from all the effects of secondary causes and everything would have to happen by a kind of fatalistic necessity."[14]

8. Council of Trent, session 6, canon 4 on justification, *Canons and Decrees of the Council of Trent*, ed. H. J. Schroeder (St. Louis: B. Herder Book Co., 1941), 42–43.

9. Aquinas, *Summa Theologiae* 1a.23.5.

10. See Trent, session 6, decree concerning justification, chapter 6, Schroeder, *Canons and Decrees of the Council of Trent*, 31–32.

11. Luis de Molina, *Concordia liberi arbitrii cum gratiae donis* 14.13.40 (Paris: P. Lethielleux, 1876), 230–31. For the following discussion, see also Mark John Farrelly, *Predestination, Grace, and Free Will* (Westminster, Md.: Newman Press, 1964), and Reginald Garrigou-Lagrange, *Predestination*, trans. Bede Rose (St. Louis: B. Herder, 1953).

12. Luis de Molina, *Concordia liberi arbitrii* 14.13.12.

13. Ibid. And this is "because they of their own will refused to use their innate freedom that they might be saved." Ibid., 23.4 & 5.1.11.

14. Luis de Molina, *On Divine Foreknowledge* (part 4 of the *Concordia*) 47.9, trans. Alfred J. Freddoso (Ithaca, N.Y.: Cornell University Press, 1988), 93.

If what decides the issue is the human response, however, then why would God bother to give some more grace than others? To answer, Molina introduced his great innovation, the *scientia media,* "in-between knowledge" or "conditional knowledge" by which God knows what someone *would* do in a particular hypothetical circumstance.[15] Thus, before Peter was saved, God knew just how much grace it would take to save him. Since the amount of help required differs from person to person, what saved Peter might not have sufficed to save Paul, but God knows what is needed and gives just the required amount to those chosen for salvation.[16] Why does God choose some and not others? Because, by the *scientia media,* God foresees that some will make better use of grace than others: "In this sense there is a reason for their predestination . . . in that God foresees their merits and the use of their free will."[17] Peter gets the help he needs because God knows what good use he would make of it.

Molina recognized that at this point he had abandoned Aquinas's position.[18] Aquinas had maintained that, since God's "love is the cause of things," one creature is better than another because God gives it more grace.[19] Molina had turned things around: God gives one person more grace than another because God knows that that person will make better use of it. He was not, however, consistent on the point; as already noted, he also said that sometimes person A needed less grace than B to be saved, but B got what he needed and A did not. But if A really needed less help, would not God, seeing that by the *scientia media,* have given the help needed? Molina seems caught in a contradiction. The general drift of his thought, however, is clear: he thought that, in order to preserve a measure of human freedom, he needed to assign a role to human efforts independent of divine guidance. God acts in a particular way only because God knows how God will, independently, respond.

These views got Molina into a good bit of trouble, and as he lay dying rumors swirled that he was about to be condemned by the Pope. But the condemnation never came. Molina had published the *Concordia* in 1588. In 1597 Pope Clement VIII established a commission on grace (*Congregatio de auxiliis*) to consider the issues, and its debates continued for many years, with

15. James Brodrick, *Robert Bellarmine, Saint and Scholar* (Westminster, Md.: Newman Press, 1961), 200. For further discussions, see Robert M. Adams, "Middle Knowledge and the Problem of Evil," *American Philosophical Quarterly* 14 (1977): 109–17; William Hasker, "A Refutation of Middle Knowledge," *Nous* 20 (1986): 545–57. Molina cited Matthew 11: Christ knew that, *if* the wonders worked in Chorazin and Bethsaida had been done there, the inhabitants of Tyre and Sidon *would* have repented and been saved. Molina, *On Divine Foreknowledge* 49.9.

16. "By that mediate foreknowledge . . . God knew before a free act of his will, what in any particular case the created free will would do. . . . And we see by this principle how the freedom of the created will coheres with divine foreknowledge." Molina, *Concordia* 23.4 & 5.1.

17. Ibid.

18. Ibid., 22.1, 2.2.

19. Aquinas, *Summa Theologiae* 1a.20.3. "The reason why some are better is that he wills them more good." Ibid., 1a.20.4.

Molina's fellow Jesuits supporting his position and Dominicans, who sought to be more faithful to Aquinas, attacking it. But in the end, in 1607, Pope Paul V decided not to decide. "The Dominicans," he declared, "say that grace does not destroy but perfects free will, and its power is such that man acts in his own way, which is freely." Since they insisted on human freedom, they did not fall into the error of Calvin, whom the Pope took to be a complete determinist. The Jesuits, on the other hand, did not fall into Pelagianism, because they held that the beginning of our salvation does not originate with us but with divine grace. Since neither side fell into heresy, the Pope concluded, there was no need to make a judgment between them.[20]

Robert Bellarmine, the most politically skilled theologian of the time, whose influence probably lay behind the final decision, actually distinguished three positions on efficacious grace. (1) Molina, he said, taught that grace owes its efficacy to the consent of the human will; God provides enough grace to enable us to accomplish salvation, but it is human cooperation that turns "sufficient grace" into "efficacious grace." Therefore, two people can receive the same grace, and only one of them be converted. Bellarmine did not find this actually heretical, but he thought it was wrong—while Molina acknowledged that grace begins the process of salvation, and therefore was not actually a Pelagian, he made the question of who gets saved entirely dependent in practice on human response. (2) In contrast, Bellarmine said, the Dominicans said that consent is physically and intrinsically determined by grace. When God decides to give saving grace, the human recipient is utterly powerless to resist. Bellarmine thought that such a view, while again not actually heresy, was not acceptable, since it both contradicted the Council of Trent and destroyed the freedom of the human will.[21] (3) Bellarmine, like his fellow Jesuit Suárez, therefore opted for a position often called "congruism." God does not, they said, really leave our salvation up to us. But neither does God force us down one path. Rather, God knows how much help each of us will need to move (freely) toward salvation, and, if we are among the elect, provides us with exactly that much help, thus preserving our freedom, while yet assuring that the elect will in fact be saved.[22]

It is a neat solution to a hard problem, but it creates an odd picture, whose oddity parallels some problems noted in the preceding chapter. When Newton said that God intervened from time to time to adjust a planetary system running down, Leibniz protested that such a God would seem to have botched

---

20. Garrigou-Lagrange, *Predestination*, 151–52.

21. "They who by sin had been cut off from God, may be disposed through His guiding and helping grace to convert themselves to their own justification by freely assenting to and cooperating with that grace." Trent, session 6, Decree concerning justification, chapter 5, Schroeder, *Canons and Decrees of the Council of Trent*, 31–32.

22. See Brodrick, *Robert Bellarmine*, 197–99; Thomas U. Mullaney, *Suárez on Human Freedom* (Westminster, Md.: Newman Press, 1950), 86, 59.

the job of creation in the first place. More generally, I argued, Newton's God seems to be one of the competing agents among the other agents in the world in a way that denies divine transcendence. The same awkwardness arises with a God who carefully intervenes with the calculatedly right amount of help in each situation. God lets pass the things that would not tempt me anyway, gives me a boost over difficult moral obstacles, and—so congruists like Alphonsus Ligouri held—intervenes with infallible efficaciousness in a really tough case.[23] I retain my freedom, but under the panoptic gaze of a busybody God who will never let me fatally misuse it. The idea of God, at a different dimension, sustaining and directing *all* things has simply disappeared.

Arminius

Reformed theologians in the same period also faced many of the same issues. Lacking a pope to declare a compromise, they found these matters even more divisive. The Dutch theologian Jacob Arminius became the symbol of many of their divisions. Arminius was born in 1559, the same year that Calvin published the final edition of his *Institutes* and Melanchthon published his *Loci praecipui theologici*. When he was only a teenager, off at school, his family was slaughtered by the Spanish army in the siege of Oudewater, one of the nastier episodes in the wars of religion in the Netherlands. Young Arminius turned to theology and studied with Theodore Beza, Calvin's successor at Geneva, before returning to be first a pastor in Amsterdam and then a professor at the University of Leiden.

Beza's relation to Calvin interestingly parallels Melanchthon's to Luther. In both cases, the younger theologian tried to make his mentor's work more systematic and to fit it into an overall philosophical context, using Aristotelian categories.[24] When scriptural evidence was ambiguous and nothing central to Christian piety seemed at stake, Calvin, as noted in chapter 4, was willing to leave questions unanswered. Beza, often, was not. For example, Calvin left it unclear whether God had predestined some to damnation from the beginning or only after the fact of original sin. Beza unambiguously favored the "supralapsarian" position—even before the Fall (*super lapsum*) God had determined to abandon some to perdition. Calvin gave no clear answer on whether Christ died for all or only for the elect.[25] Beza insisted on limited atonement—Christ

---

23. Farrelly, *Predestination, Grace, and Free Will,* 28–29.
24. For instance, he said that the free mercy of God was the efficient cause of salvation; Christ, the material cause; faith, preaching, or the imputation of Christ's righteousness, the instrumental cause; and the glory of God the Father, the final cause. John S. Bray, *Theodore Beza's Doctrine of Predestination* (Nieuwkoop: De Graaf, 1975), 52.

For the similar story of a Reformed theologian roughly contemporary to Beza, Girolamo Zanchi, see Otto Gründler, *Die Gotteslehre Girolamo Zanchis und ihre Bedeutung für seine Lehre von der Pradestination* (Neukirchen: Neukirchener Verlag des Erziehungsvereins, 1965).

25. On this much-disputed point, see R. T. Kendall, *Calvin and English Calvinism to 1649* (Oxford: Oxford University Press, 1979), 13–28; James B. Torrance, "The Incarnation and 'Limited

died only for the elect. It is a very tough understanding of predestination, and it focuses *all* attention onto the question of whether you are among the elect. To answer that question, Beza taught people to look within themselves. Calvin had urged Christians to trust in Christ as the mirror in whom they could see their election. Like many of the seventeenth-century theologians discussed in chapter 6, Beza wanted evidence of a particular individual's salvation, and found it in the evidence of one's transformed life. "That I am elect," he wrote, "is first perceived from sanctification begun in me."[26] As Charles Cohen has written, "The path of assurance which for Calvin ascends from the believer to the Redeemer at God's right hand, for Beza descends back into the self."[27]

One story goes that, back in Holland, Arminius, as Beza's former student, was invited to present an account of his thought, and in the process of preparation discovered how deeply he disagreed with it. He simply could not accept that some are abandoned to perdition without being less worthy than the saved. "Grace," Arminius concluded, "is present with all men, by which their free will may be actually bent to good; but . . . there is in all men such a will as is flexible to either side upon accession of grace."[28] No one can be saved without grace, but sufficient grace is available to all, and therefore what distinguishes the saved from the damned is how they make use of that grace. "It always remains within the power of the free will to reject the grace bestowed . . . because grace is not an omnipotent action of God which cannot be resisted by man's free will."[29]

If we sin, then, our actions are purely and simply our fault. Since sin is "a voluntary transgression of the law," we "could avoid it." After all, "An act which is inevitable on account of the determination of any decrees does not deserve the name of sin."[30] True, scripture speaks of God's "hardening of the heart" of

---

Atonement," *Evangelical Quarterly* 55 (1983): 83–94; Mark R. Shaw, "Drama in the Meeting House: The Concept of Conversion in the Theology of William Perkins," *Westminster Theological Journal* 45 (1983): 45–57; Charles L. Cohen, *God's Caress: The Psychology of Puritan Religious Experience* (New York: Oxford University Press, 1986), 10.

26. Theodore Beza, *A Little Book of Christian Questions and Responses,* trans. Kirk M. Summers (Allison Park, Pa.: Pickwick Publications, 1986), 96. Robert Letham defends Beza on this last point. See Robert Letham, "Theodore Beza: A Reassessment," *Scottish Journal of Theology* 40 (1987): 25–40. But even Letham admits, "Calvin uses the fact of election being made in Jesus Christ as the basis of our assurance of salvation. . . . Insofar as Beza adopted a more rigorously logical and speculative predestinarianism, a thorough-going supralapsarinism, this Christocentric and soteric focus of election was precariously poised and in later years as scholastic interests became more dominant it was ultimately threatened." Ibid., 39.

27. Cohen, *God's Caress,* 11.

28. James Arminius, *Examination of Perkins's Pamphlet,* trans. James Nichols and William Nichols, *Works* (Grand Rapids: Baker Book House, 1986), 470–71.

29. Ibid., 470.

30. James Arminius, "Analysis of the Ninth Chapter of Romans," trans. W. R. Bagnall, *Writings* (Grand Rapids: Baker Book House, 1956), 3:548.

some who turn to sin, but in so doing God is only inflicting an additional punishment on people who had already chosen the path of sin for themselves.[31]
To be sure, if we live righteously and achieve salvation, this is not entirely our
own doing, for human beings cannot achieve this without the help of God's
grace. In sin, free will has been "destroyed and lost . . . it has no powers whatever except such as are excited by divine grace."[32] We ought to be grateful for
the help. Still, grace was there, available to everyone, and what distinguishes
the saved is simply that they made better use of it.[33] Any doctrine that some
are predestined to salvation and others to damnation

> prevents . . . godly sorrow for sins . . . removes all pious solicitude
> about being converted . . . restrains all good and studious regard for
> good works . . . extinguishes the zeal for prayer . . . takes away all that
> most salutary fear and trembling with which we are commanded to
> work out our own salvation . . . [and] produces within men a despair
> both of performing that which their duty requires and of obtaining that
> toward which their desires are directed.[34]

On the particular issues, Arminius came out on the opposite side from Beza,
but with respect to methodological questions, they turned away from Calvin
in the same way. As Peter White has written, "Arminius' confidence in the capacity of human reason exceeded even that of Beza. . . . He refused to take
refuge in the inscrutability of God; if a doctrine was incomprehensible, it ought
to be repudiated."[35] Neither Beza nor Arminius was as willing as Calvin had
been to remain unsystematic and trust what they could not understand.

In 1619 the Synod of Dort rejected Arminius's views. The "grace whereby
we are converted to God," Dort declared, is not "only a gentle advising"; grace
and free will are not "partial causes which together work the beginning of conversion."[36] We are saved by an irresistible grace. Dort developed the classic
five points of Reformed orthodoxy: unconditional election, limited atonement,
total depravity, irresistible grace, and the perseverance of the saints. Christ died
only for the elect, whose election is guaranteed, who cannot resist God's grace,
and who will not fall to damnation. Those predestined to retribution can do
nothing to help themselves. Those gathered at Dort thought they were de-

---

31. "Nothing is more plain in Scripture than that sinners persevering in their sins against the
long-suffering of God, who invites them to repentance, are those whom God wills to harden."
Arminius, "Analysis," 550.
32. Arminius, "Disputation on the Free Will of Man and Its Powers," trans. James Nichols, *Writings*, 1:526–29.
33. Grace is "the commencement, the continuance, and the consummation of all good," but is
not an "irresistible force." Arminius, "Declaration of Sentiments," *Writings*, 1:253.
34. Ibid., 1:230–31.
35. Peter O. G. White, *Predestination, Policy, and Polemic* (Cambridge: Cambridge University
Press, 1991), 25.
36. Canons of the Synod of Dort, third and fourth heads of doctrine, rejection of errors, para-
graphs 7 and 9, in *Crisis in the Reformed Churches*, ed. Peter Y. De Jong (Grand Rapids: Reformed
Fellowship, 1968), 252–53.

fending Calvin against Arminius; my argument is that, in theological method—in their insistence on clear answers, their refusal to admit how many questions Christians cannot understand—they had more in common with Arminius than with Calvin. In particular, like Beza, like so many of the seventeenth-century figures discussed in chapter 6, *and* like Arminius but unlike Calvin, Dort acknowledged the importance of finding clear assurance that I am among the elect, and said that people could find this out by looking within themselves: "not by inquisitively prying into the secret and deep things of God but by observing in themselves . . . infallible fruits of election."[37]

Federal Theology

That quest for assurance also haunted the most systematic effort among Reformed theologians to find a middle ground between a radical doctrine of predestination and Arminianism: the covenant or federal (from *foedus,* the Latin word for "covenant") theologies. The idea of covenant of course goes back to the Bible and played an important role in Reformed theology from the beginning. Zwingli, for instance, appealed to their membership in a covenant people as a justification for baptizing infants. In the first two generations of the Reformed tradition, however, two innovations emerged in talking about covenants. First, the earliest Reformers thought about divine-human covenants in unilateral terms as the gifts of God's grace. Israel, for instance, was in covenant with God simply because God had chosen them, irrespective of any actions or qualities on their side. Heinrich Bullinger (1504–1575), Zwingli's successor at Zurich, however, thought about covenants more as bilateral agreements, contracts between God and human beings in which each made a commitment.[38] As an English covenant theologian wrote in the seventeenth century, a covenant "implies two things, something on God's part which is the promise, and something on man's part, which is the duty, and unto both these consent of parties is required; God's consent unto the promise, and man's consent unto the service."[39]

37. Ibid., first head of doctrine, article 12, 233.
38. See Kenneth Hagen, "From Testament to Covenant in the Early Sixteenth Century," *Sixteenth Century Journal* 3 (1972): 1–24. See also J. Wayne Baker, *Heinrich Bullinger and the Covenant: The Other Reformed Tradition* (Athens, Ohio: Ohio University Press, 1980). The distinction even appears linguistically. The Septuagint generally translated *berith,* the Hebrew word for "covenant," as *diatheke,* meaning an unconditional, unilateral agreement, in contrast to the Greek word *syntheke,* which suggests equal parties bargaining and negotiating an agreement. Beginning with Bullinger, Reformed theologians were shifting to the connotations of *syntheke.* See James B. Torrance, "Covenant or Contract?" *Scottish Journal of Theology* 23 (1970): 51–76.
39. William Strong, *A Discourse of the Two Covenants* (London: Francis Tyton, 1678), 241. Some theologians distinguished between a covenant and a testament—a covenant is a contract with mutual demands, but a testament is a will from which you receive inheritance without any action on your part: "a covenant requireth something to be done. In a testament, there is nothing but receiving the legacies given." Richard Sibbes, "The Faithful Covenanter," *Complete Works* (Edinburgh: James Nichol, 1862), 6:4.

Second, the first Reformers generally talked about a single covenant. Zacharias Ursinus (1534–1583), one of the coauthors of the Heidelberg Catechism, however, distinguished between two covenants—a covenant of works and a covenant of grace. Calvin had never mentioned these two covenants, and in all the church fathers only one brief passage in Augustine refers to the idea.[40] Indeed, even Ursinus's Heidelberg Catechism coauthor, Caspar Olevianus, talked about only one covenant. But it was Ursinus's view that came to be dominant among Reformed theologians in the seventeenth century.[41] Indeed, as Karl Barth put it, by the second half of the seventeenth century, bilateral, two-covenant theology had become "the ruling orthodoxy of the Reformed Church."[42]

These two changes made for a real difference in how people thought about covenants. If a covenant is a bilateral agreement, then the divine-human covenant holds only if human beings keep to their part of the bargain. If there is both a covenant of works and a covenant of grace, then it was natural to think of them in the same conceptual framework, and thus to think about the covenant of grace as rather like the covenant of works, only with easier demands. Both changes thus limited the dominance of sheer grace in thinking about covenants. The resulting patterns of thought fit a businessperson's experience of contracts with mutual terms. One could even imagine a practical God, with everyone failing to meet the terms of the covenant of works, renegotiating for the best he could get and settling for the covenant of grace.

For Ursinus, for instance, a covenant was "a mutual contract, or an agreement between two parties" in this case between human beings and God.[43] God initially made a covenant with Adam, a "covenant of works," whereby God promised eternal life in return for full obedience to God's commands. Adam, of course, failed to live up to the terms of the agreement, and so has everyone since, but God has subsequently offered a better deal, a "covenant of grace," a

> mutual promise and agreement, between God and men, in which God gives assurance to men that he will be merciful to them, remit their sins, grant unto them a new righteousness, the Holy Spirit, and eternal life by and for the sake of his Son our Mediator. And, on the other side, men bind themselves to God in this covenant that they will exercise

40. Augustine, *City of God* 16.27, trans. Henry Bettenson (Harmondsworth, Middlesex: Penguin Books, 1972), 688–89. See David Weir, *The Origins of Federal Theology in the Sixteenth-Century Reformation* (New York: Oxford University Press, 1990), 10–12.

41. See Robert Letham, "The Foedus Operum: Some Factors Accounting for Its Development," *Sixteenth Century Journal* 14 (1983): 463–64. Charles Cohen cites Dudley Fenner, in 1585, as the first English theologian to use the idea of two covenants. Cohen, *God's Caress,* 56.

42. Karl Barth, *Church Dogmatics,* vol. 4, part 1, trans. G. W. Bromiley (Edinburgh: T&T Clark, 1956), 55.

43. Zacharius Ursinus, *Commentary on the Heidelberg Catechism,* trans. G. W. Willard (Phillipsburg, N.J.: Presbyterian and Reformed, 1990), 97.

repentance and faith, or that they will receive with a true faith this great benefit which God offers, and render such obedience as will be acceptable to him.[44]

Though the terms are easier, the covenant still imposes conditions—of faith and obedience—on the human parties.[45] Ursinus acknowledged that God predestines some to salvation, but he appealed to Aristotle's classification of the different types of causation to explain how human efforts too play their role. He managed the neat trick of writing a lengthy Reformed treatise on predestination without making a single reference to Calvin.[46]

One could trace the development of covenant theology on the European continent or in England, but, for purposes of simplicity, let us look at Scotland, where the story has fewer key characters and a clearer narrative line. John Knox already spoke of a covenant whereby the "Obedience gevin to Godis preceptis in this case, is the cause why God schawis his mercie upon us."[47] The covenant served at least two pragmatic functions in his thought. First, it provided the organizing principle for the Scottish commonwealth. Not everyone was among the saved, but those who were not still stood under the covenant of works, so that Christian magistrates had religious grounds for keeping moral order, without regard for the inner state of their subjects.[48] Second, individual Christians could be reassured as to their election, for works are an "outward testimony to faith," and a faith that produces such works is the mark of election.[49] If you want to know if you are among the elect, you can look to your works for evidence.

A generation after Knox, Robert Rollock (1555–1599), the first principal of Edinburgh University, was the first in Scotland to develop a full two-covenant theology, with a covenant of works and of grace.[50] "All the word of God," he wrote, "appertains to some covenant; for God speaks nothing to man without the covenant."[51] For Rollock, the two covenants were stages not merely in history but in the life of each believer. We have to be prepared for grace, and a key element in that preparation is a meditation on the covenant of works

44. Ibid.
45. "Every mediator is the mediator of some covenant and the reconciler of two opposing parties." Ibid., 96.
46. Richard A. Muller, *Christ and the Decree: Christology and Predestination in Reformation Theology from Calvin to Perkins* (Durham, N.C.: Labyrinth Press, 1986), 106, reference to *Epistola D. Zachariae Ursini ad amicum de praedestinatione* (Heidelberg: Johannis Lancelloti, 1612).
47. John Knox, "A Godly Letter to the Faithful in London," *Works* (New York: AMS Press, 1966), 3:193.
48. Knox, "The Appellation," *Works*, 4:491.
49. Knox, "A Briefe Summarie of the work by Balnaires on Justification," *Works*, 3:20; "On Predestination," *Works*, 5:210.
50. See M. Charles Bell, *Calvin and Scottish Theology* (Edinburgh: Handsel Press, 1985), 52. I am drawing on Bell's work in much of this section.
51. Robert Rollock, "A Treatise of God's Effectual Calling," *Select Works*, vol. 1 (Edinburgh: Wodrow Society, 1849), 33.

through which we realize that, by its standards, we are inevitably con-demned.[52] In the covenant of grace, Rollock was clear, our good works are God's doing and not ours, and our faith itself is a gift from God.[53] Yet even in the covenant of grace, we must exercise "care, thought, and labor to keep grace," and our "firm and certain assent" is necessary to receive assurance of our salvation.[54] Even "being freed from the covenant of works," the Christian "is not to become a libertine, or not subject to any covenant, or as it were law-less, but forthwith he is admitted to the covenant of grace"—which has its own conditions.[55] Covenants involve obligations on both sides, and the difference in the covenant of grace lies in the reduction of our obligations to manageable proportions.

Samuel Rutherford (1600–1661), who was born the year after Rollock died, developed many of these ideas a stage further. We have to be "ploughed," he said, before Christ can be sown in us, and the ploughing must take the form of recognizing the inevitable condemnation we face under a covenant of works. It is "mere presumption, not Faith," to claim to believe in Christ before having been broken by the realization of our inability to fulfill the covenant of works. In short, we have to understand the full extent of our sin *before* we can encounter grace.[56]

The covenant of grace, in turn, is "a joint and mutual bargain between two, according to which, they promise freely such and such things to each other: hence God and man made up a solemn bargain in Christ. They both consent, Christ forced not his spouse to marry against her will, nor was God forced to make a covenant."[57] God promises us forgiveness and eternal life, "upon con-dition of beleeving in Christ."[58] While faith is "the only condition of Justifica-

---

52. Ibid., 43.

"Both Luther and Calvin insist that the conscience—whether of the infidel or of the believer—cannot testify to itself as to God's will toward us. Rather, the conscience must always look to the Word of God, in matters of faith as well as matters of obedience. The testimony of a good con-science has a legitimate place in both Luther's and Calvin's theology; yet such testimony does not tell us about the grace or favor of God toward us, but only about the sincerity of our response to that grace in faith and love." Randall C. Zachman, *The Assurance of Faith* (Minneapolis: Fortress, 1993), 6.

53. Ibid., 36.

54. Ibid., 217, 234.

Randall Zachman seems to me to get these issues exactly right: for Calvin, as for Luther, it is God's self-revelation in Jesus Christ, known through the illumination of the Holy Spirit, that is the foundation (*fundamentum*) of Christians' confidence in our salvation. Inward assurance and sanc-tification can provide at most a posteriori confirmation (*confirmatio*). But, once one has conceded an importance to such a confirmation, "such a distinction remains inherently unstable. The possi-bility of the testimony of a good conscience founding the assurance of faith cannot in principle be avoided, even if neither theologian intended it." And, with Beza and others, just such a rever-sal occurs. (Zachman, *The Assurance of Faith,* 221; see also 211–13, 246.)

55. Ibid., 52.

56. Samuel Rutherford, *The Trial and Triumph of Faith* (Keyser, W.Va.: Odom Publishing, 1990), 148–50. See also the passages cited in Bell, *Calvin and Scottish Theology,* 77.

57. Ibid., 75; see also 89.

58. Samuel Rutherford, *The Covenant of Life Opened* (Edinburgh: Andro Anderson, 1655), 310.

tion," "holy walking," a morally good life, "as a witnesse of faith, is the way to the possession of the kingdome."[59] The moral quality of one's life witnesses to one's faith, which is the condition of one's justification. Having adopted the model of divine and human agency operating on the same level as competing forces, Rutherford insisted that, while we are "(as it were) patients in obeying Gospel-Commands," we are not "meer patients," since "in Gospel-obedience we offer more of the Lord's own, and lesse of our own."[60] The relation between human and divine contributions has become a zero-sum game, and thus the power of grace is finally the enemy of human freedom.

Covenant theology came particularly to grief on the same issue that created problems for the Puritans discussed in chapter 6: the assurance of one's election. (Indeed, I should emphasize, many of those Puritans were themselves covenant theologians. These stories are more intertwined than my telling of them acknowledges.) Where Calvin urged Christians to look to Christ for assurance of their salvation, Rutherford concluded that this would not work. If I happen not to be among the elect, recognizing the mercy of Christ would be beside the point, since it will not benefit me. Rutherford was clear on this point: "I have no assurance, hope, nor comfort to rest on a generall good will that God beareth to all," since not all are among the elect.[61] Therefore, our search for assurance needs to turn inward: "We may know our selves to bee in the state of grace, by holy walking and acts of beleeving, and we may know our holy walking to be true, by other acts of holy walking and beleeving."[62] Like smoke evidencing the presence of fire, or the morning star signaling that the sun will soon rise, Rutherford wrote elsewhere, "so doth Sanctification give evidence of Justification . . . as markes, signes, and gracious effects giveth evidence of the cause."[63] Covenants set out clear rules, some of those rules concern the ethical quality of my life, and I can measure myself against the standard those rules define, and see where I stand.[64]

Covenant theology like Rutherford's increasingly came to dominate theology in Scotland—though not only there—through the seventeenth century. An episode early in the eighteenth century illustrates its impact. When a book called *Marrow of Modern Divinity*, originally published by Edward Fisher in

59. Samuel Rutherford, *Christ Dying and Drawing Sinners to Himselfe* (London: Andrew Crooke, 1647), 263.

60. Samuel Rutherford, *The Covenant of Life Opened* (Edinburgh: Robert Brown, 1655), 198–99, quoted in John von Rohr, *The Covenant of Grace in Puritan Thought* (Atlanta: Scholars Press, 1986), 152. This particular edition of Rutherford's book was not available to me, and I was unable to verify the citation.

61. Rutherford, *Christ Dying and Drawing Sinners to Himselfe*, 432.

62. Samuel Rutherford, *A Survey of the Spirituall Antichrist* (London: Andrew Crooke, 1648), 2:84.

63. Rutherford, *Christ Dying and Drawing Sinners to Himselfe*, 109.

64. "To gather up assurance from the conditions of the covenant," wrote the English federal theologian Thomas Blake, "is . . . the highest pitch of Christianity." Thomas Blake, *Vindiciae Foederis*, 2nd ed. (London: A. Roper, 1658), 197.

1645, was reprinted in Scotland in 1717, it aroused great controversy, and the General Assembly of 1720 both condemned the book and urged ministers to warn against it. Among the propositions condemned were a believer's conviction that, "There is no more for him to do, but only to know and believe that Christ hath done all for him," and, "I confess . . . that I am neither godly nor righteous; but this yet I am sure of, that he [Christ] is godly for me."[65] These are, perhaps, statements open to misinterpretation, but outright condemnation of them is a signal of how far covenant theology had moved from the piety of the Reformation. M. Charles Bell summarizes the changes:

> Calvin taught that faith is fundamentally passive in nature, is centered in the mind or understanding, is primarily to be viewed in terms of certain knowledge, such that the assurance of salvation is of the essence of faith, and is grounded *extra nos,* that is, outside ourselves in the person and work of Jesus Christ. Scottish theology, on the other hand, gradually came to teach that faith is primarily active, centered in the will or heart, and that assurance is *not* of the essence of faith, but is a fruit of faith, and is to be gathered through self-examination and syllogistic deduction, thereby placing the grounds of assurance *intra nos,* within ourselves.[66]

As already noted, these changes were occurring not only in Scotland. Samuel Rutherford was one of the six Scottish commissioners to the Westminster Assembly, and Westminster, which has long served as the benchmark of Reformed theological orthodoxy, manifested many of the characteristics of federal theology. Its chapter on "Christ the Mediator" was immediately preceded by one on "God's Covenant with Man," so that Christ's work was placed in the context of thought about covenant. Its discussion of covenant laid out the two covenants of works and of grace, specifying that, people being unable to meet the terms of the former, the latter specifies easier requirements.[67] The Westminster Confession, moreover, declared good works to be "the fruits and evidence of a true and lively faith."[68] Even "true believers may have the assurance of their salvation divers ways shaken, diminished, and intermitted," but, when that happens, they must note their "life of faith, that love of Christ and the brethren, that sincerity of heart and conscience of duty, out of which, by the operation of the Spirit, this assurance may in due time be revived."[69] When in doubt about our salvation, in short, Westminster invited us to look at the moral and spiritual quality of our own lives.

---

65. Bell, *Calvin and Scottish Theology,* 152.

66. Ibid., 8. "The covenant theology . . . was a means of overcoming the absolute decrees, a smuggling 'works' into Calvinism. . . . It reestablished moral obligation on a clearer, more rational basis." Christopher Hill, *Puritanism and Revolution* (New York: Schocken Books, 1958), 245.

67. Westminster Confession of Faith 7.3; Philip Schaff, *The Creeds of Christendom,* vol. 3 (Grand Rapids: Baker Books House, 1993), 617.

68. Ibid., 16.2.

69. Ibid., 18.4.

Moralism and Reasonableness

The federal theology of the early seventeenth century, like Melanchthon, Molina, and Arminius, at least had *theological* reasons for its modification of the theology of grace. By the end of the century, Anglican preaching increasingly downplayed the role of grace for quite pragmatic reasons. The language of covenants still appeared, but in service of a practical and often unreflective Arminianism. Jeremy Taylor (1613–1667), the most famous writer on spiritual topics of his age, and one of its great preachers, offers a good example of these trends.[70] Taylor appealed to the language of two-covenant theology:

> The whole Gospel is nothing else but that glad tidings which Christ brought to all mankind, that the covenant of works, or exact measures, should not now be exacted; but men should be saved by second thoughts, that is, by repentance and amendment of life, through faith in the Lord Jesus Christ. That is, if we become disciples (for that is the condition of the covenant), we shall find mercy, our sins shall be blotted out, and we shall be saved if we obey heartily and diligently, though not exactly.[71]

Because of Christ's work, the terms we have to meet for salvation are considerably reduced, but the model of a contract with mutual obligations remains firmly in place. This is gentle legalism, but legalism nonetheless.[72] Taylor could even sound like a Protestant caricature of bad late-medieval theology, as when he declared in a sermon, "Every deadly sin destroys the rewards of a seven years' piety."[73] It seems significant that the subtitle of his book on the life of Christ should be, "The Great Exemplar"—Christ functions by giving us a moral example to follow.

Like many of his contemporaries, Taylor was terrified of "antinomianism," the belief that, thanks to grace, moral laws simply did not apply to Christians.[74] Calvin's idea that they do indeed apply—as guides to how we might display our gratitude, and rules that just make sense for life—but have nothing to do

---

70. "Few divines of the seventeenth century (and probably no Anglicans) had so vast an influence." Of his two best-known works, *Holy Living* had gone through fourteen editions by 1686, and *Holy Dying*, twenty-one editions by 1710. C. FitzSimons Allison, *The Rise of Moralism: The Proclamation of the Gospel from Hooker to Baxter* (New York: Seabury Press, 1966), 193. I am indebted to Allison for much of my discussion of Taylor.

71. Jeremy Taylor, "The Doctrine and Practice of Repentence," *The Whole Works of the Right Rev. Jeremy Taylor* (London: Ogle, Duncan, & Co., 1822), 8:315.

72. "A hearty endeavour and an effectual general change shall get the pardon; the unavoidable infirmities, and past evils, and present imperfections, and short interruptions, against which we watch, and pray, and strive, being put upon the accounts of the cross, and paid for by the holy Jesus." Jeremy Taylor, "The Rule and Exercises of Holy Living," *Works*, 4:256–57.

73. Taylor, Sermon 17, part 2, "Of Growth in Sin," *Works*, 6:50.

74. See for instance Jeremy Taylor, "An Answer to a Letter . . . concerning the Chapter of Original Sin in the Unum Necessarium," *Works*, 9:379. See also John Tillotson, Sermon 103, "Christianity doth not destroy, but perfect the Law of Moses," *Works* (London: Richard Priestly, 1820), 5:33.

with how we get saved was no longer heard in public. In Taylor's private prayers, he consistently threw himself on the mercy of Christ's righteousness alone. The insistence on the importance of our own efforts, the picture of salvation as a joint project, quite disappeared in a theology of radical grace. But apparently he thought this unsafe for public consumption. In FitzSimons Allison's words, "Apparently Taylor fundamentally believed what he said in his prayers, but his profound concern lest antinomianism be encouraged by preaching and teaching gratuitous forgiveness led him publically to exhort holy living as the only hope for justification."[75] Even under the covenant of grace, he said in public, only minor sins can be forgiven. His private and deeply moving prayers before the Eucharist referred to the sacrament as providing a nurture that will lead us away from sin, but he warned others against the dangers of receiving the Eucharist unless one is already fully repentant.[76] For the social good, one simply had to be careful in talking about grace.[77]

When John Locke, at the very end of the seventeenth century, came to define "the reasonableness of Christianity," he too drew on the language of covenant theology. Locke was arguing with Deists for whom Christ served *only* as a moral example; he wanted to preserve *some* salvific role for Christ—but a reasonable one. The rules are, he explained, that for those who "believe Jesus to be the Messiah, the promised King and Saviour, and perform what other conditions were required of them by the covenant of grace, God would justify them because of this belief."[78] But it is still a matter of clear rules and mutual obligations: "The difference between the law of works, and the law of faith, is only this: that the law of works makes no allowance for failing on any occasion. . . . But by the law of faith, faith is allowed to supply the defect of full obedience."[79] A modest function in helping human moral efforts seemed the only role for grace compatible not only with good social order but also with reasonableness.

In the understanding of the mystery of grace that the Reformers shared with Aquinas, we owe God everything. Our salvation is not a matter of owing and paying, but comes from God as gift. Ethics is not a matter of earning or winning, but of spontaneous gratitude for what we have already received. In chapter 6, I indicated that even those in the seventeenth century who claimed to retain this ideal betrayed it in practice. This chapter has considered those who gave it up even in theory. Lutheran synergists, Catholic Molinists, Arminians, and covenant theologians—the differences are important, but the similarities

---

75. Allison, *The Rise of Moralism*, 185.

76. Ibid., 86–87.

77. "Whatsoever is said of the efficacy of faith for justification is not to be taken in such a sense as will weaken the necessity and our carefulness of good life." Jeremy Taylor, Sermon 3, "Fides Formata," *Works*, 6:268, 279.

78. John Locke, *The Reasonableness of Christianity* (Washington, D.C.: Regnery Gateway, 1965), 124.

79. Ibid., 13.

are quite striking. All thought of God and human beings as operating in some sense on the same level, so that, if human beings were to do something toward their salvation, then one had to reduce the divine contribution. All wanted to decrease mystery, and find clear rules, so that people could look at themselves and measure their chance of salvation. All worried that telling people that their own moral efforts were irrelevant to their salvation would lead to moral chaos. If they considered at all that earlier ideal of a morality based purely on gratitude, which would honor God and serve the neighbor without relevance to reward, they decided not to risk it.

10 The Marginalization of the Trinity

On October 27, 1553, in Geneva, Michael Servetus was publicly burned to death for having denied the doctrine of the Trinity. It was a horrible event, though Calvin has gotten something of a bum rap when it is regularly cited as the proof of his intolerance. The sentence was actually ordered by the Genevan council; Calvin pleaded for a less barbarous means of execution. More significantly, Servetus would likely have received the same fate nearly anywhere in Europe. He was arrested while passing through Geneva on the run from Catholic France, and from the Lutheran camp, Melanchthon soon passed his congratulations on to Calvin for proper punishment of the heretic.[1] But the pervasiveness of persecution should not disguise the evil fact that, in sixteenth-century Europe, denying the Trinity put you at risk of your life.

Sometime in the early eighteenth century (so Voltaire told the story) Queen Anne of England wanted to make Newton's friend Samuel Clarke her Archbishop of Canterbury. But Clarke did not believe in the Trinity, and so, Voltaire explained, Bishop Gibson of London had to demur: " 'Madam,' he said to the Queen, 'Mr. Clarke is the wisest and most honorable man in the kingdom; he lacks only one thing.' 'What?' asked the Queen. 'He is not a Christian.' "[2] Writing as a citizen of a Catholic country of events in a Protestant one, Voltaire wittily assumed that intelligent people in either tradition would get his joke— how antiquated it was that belief in the Trinity should still make any serious difference.

Something dramatic had happened in the intervening years. It would be pleasant to report that educated Europeans had grown more tolerant of people whose fundamental views differed from their own, or at least less inclined to react to disagreement with violence. It would be pleasant—but it probably would not be true, for eighteenth-century Europe still saw bloody warfare and religious persecution. It seems more correct to say that the Trinity had, for a great many Christians, simply ceased to be a matter of fundamental importance. The story of how and why that happened, involving, as Nicholas Lash

---

1. "I have read the writings in which you have refuted the fine, horrible blasphemies of Servetus. I give thanks to the Son of God who was the arbiter of your conflict. To you the church now and in the future owes and will owe gratitude. I agree completely with your judgment. I also affirm that your magistrates acted justly in putting to death this blasphemous man by judicial procedure." Melanchthon to Calvin, 14 October 1554, John Calvin, *Opera,* vol. 15 (Brunsvigae: C. A. Schwetschke et filium, 1876), col. 268.

2. Voltaire, *Lettres Philosophiques* (Oxford: Basil Blackwell, 1951), letter 7, variant, 129. The standard English translations omit the variant.

has written, "puzzles whose roots lie deep in the history of modern Western culture,"[3] can here be given only the briefest of sketches.

Changes discussed in earlier chapters provided an important context for this diminution of the Trinity's importance. Prior to the seventeenth century, Christians whose fundamental belief was in a *Triune* God thought of God as engaging in self-revelation, as reaching out toward humankind in grace. Self-revelation and grace were central to God's identity as they knew it. As the doctrine of the Trinity was moved to the margins of Christian faith, "God" increasingly referred to the creator of the universe and the basis of moral law. We could know about that God by inference from the order of creation, figuring out God's existence and attributes by our reason. We could shape our own lives by living up to the precepts of that God's law, if perhaps with a bit of help or a lowering of standards thanks to grace. Revelation and grace were less important, and the shift away from the God who fits neither human metaphysical schemes nor human ethical systems came all the more naturally. To ask which came first—a change in thinking about the Trinity or a change in thinking about revelation and grace—is like asking about the chicken and the egg. Enough to say that they were happening at roughly the same time, and in complex interrelation.

To be sure, historians of Christian theology have identified many historical periods as crucial to the decline of a lively interest in the Trinity. The Reformation, for instance, made the issues of works and grace, the sacraments, and ecclesiology more central to theological discussions than the Trinity, which both Calvin and Luther tended to affirm without discussing it much.[4] Aquinas comes in for his share of blame for having, in contrast to the classic medieval pattern of Peter Lombard, separated the discussion of *de Deo uno* from that of *de Deo trino,* developing a discussion of the existence and attributes of God before turning to the Trinity.[5] In an important recent book Catherine LaCugna has argued that the age of a healthy doctrine of the Trinity was over virtually before it began, since as early as the fourth century theologians increasingly discussed the Trinity in relative isolation from the economy of salvation, so that it became an abstract nexus of technical issues unrelated to the life and liturgy of Christian people.[6] I do not want to enter this field with a counter-argument for the seventeenth century as *the* crucial period in the decline of Trinitarian

---

3. Nicholas Lash, "Considering the Trinity," *Modern Theology* 2 (1986): 183.

4. Luther's "trinitarian doctrine remained largely a simple, devout expression of his belief in the traditional dogma." Edmund J. Fortman, *The Triune God: A Historical Study of the Doctrine of the Trinity* (Philadelphia: Westminster Press, 1972), 239. While Calvin gave "indeed a thoroughly correct and respectful exposition of the doctrine of the Trinity . . . it is noteworthy that the author's interest in this matter is not exactly burning." Karl Barth, *Church Dogmatics,* vol. 1, part 1, trans. G. T. Thomson (Edinburgh: T&T Clark, 1936), 477.

5. See Karl Rahner, *The Trinity,* trans. J. Donceel (New York: Herder & Herder, 1970), 16–17.

6. Catherine Mowry LaCugna, *God for Us: The Trinity and Christian Life* (San Francisco: Harper, 1991).

faith, but I do want to argue that something changed. Looking at Aquinas, Luther, and Calvin can again provide examples of some patterns of thought common in the Christian tradition before that change occurred.

Aquinas, Luther, and Calvin

Aquinas began the *Summa Theologiae* with a discussion of the existence and attributes of God before turning to the Trinity, but the section on the Trinity is nearly as long as what precedes it. Before Aquinas moved on to discuss any topic other than God, in other words, he explored the Trinity in considerable detail. Nor, once he did move on, did he leave the Trinity behind. The story he told of human salvation consistently presented it in Trinitarian terms. The five "ways" of arguing for the existence of God at the beginning of part 1 of the *Summa,* as I argued in chapter 2, do not represent some sort of summary of Aquinas's own theology but a review of open questions raised in a variety of philosophical contexts. It was at the beginning of part 3 that Aquinas made his own "way" clear. Christ, he wrote, is "the way of truth which, in rising again, we can follow to the blessedness of eternal life."[7] And, he said elsewhere, it is the Holy Spirit who was the active principle in Christ's conception[8] as well as being the means of our appropriation of Christ's salvific work.[9] "Therefore the Son teaches us doctrine," Aquinas explained in his commentary on John, "for he is the Word, but the Holy Spirit makes us able to receive his doctrine."[10] For Aquinas, the relations that matter in knowing and loving God are not to an abstract "God," but to and through the Trinitarian Persons.

Though Luther rarely engaged in much technical Trinitarian theology, reference to the Trinity regularly served him as a way of pointing to the God of grace known in faith, in contrast to the God imagined by human reason. Reason, he said, turns into foolishness when it seeks to know God apart from Christ.[11] Furthermore, "Knowledge of Christ and of faith is not a human work but utterly a divine gift. . . . This sort of doctrine which reveals the Son of God . . . is revealed by God first by the external Word and then inwardly through the Spirit."[12] "For the Spirit kills the 'wisdom of the flesh' and makes the inner

---

7. Thomas Aquinas, *Summa Theologiae* 3a, prologue, trans. English Dominican Fathers (London: Blackfriars, 1963–). As noted in chapter 2, though the Blackfriars translation has "path of truth," the Latin is *via,* the same word used of the "five ways."

8. Ibid., 3a.32.1.

9. "As grace is given the Holy Spirit himself is possessed and dwells in a person and so it is he himself who is given and sent." Ibid., 1a.43.3.

10. Thomas Aquinas, *In Joannem Evangelistam Expositio,* chap. 14, lect. 6, *Opera Omnia* (New York: Musurgia Publishers, 1949), 10:559. See Bruce D. Marshall, "Thomas, Thomisms and Truth," *The Thomist* 56 (1992): 523.

11. Martin Luther, "Heidelberg Disputation," trans. Harold J. Grimm, in *Luther's Works,* vol. 31 (Philadelphia: Muhlenberg Press, 1957).

12. Martin Luther, *Lectures on Galatians* (1535) (on Gal. 1:11–12 and 1:15–17), trans. Jaroslav Pelikan, *Luther's Works,* vol. 26 (St. Louis: Concordia Publishing House, 1963), 64, 72.

man alive and causes men to despise death and to give up life and to love only God above all things."[13] Those who employ human reason will move to an abstract God who cannot save us and who is not really God, instead of the Triune God revealed by the Word and through the Spirit. Luther summarized his position in a sermon for Trinity Sunday:

> The Scriptures gradually and beautifully lead us to Christ: first revealing him to us as a man, then as the lord of all creatures, and finally as God. But the philosophers and the wise men of this world would begin at the top and so they have become fools. . . . Therefore, we cling to the Scriptures, those passages which testify of the Trinity of God, and we say: I know very well that in God there are the Father, the Son, and the Holy Spirit; but how they can be one I do not know, neither should I know it.[14]

He knew the self-revealing God of grace, in other words, as Triune, and it was in the face of the *unity* of God that his understanding broke down completely—quite the reverse of the later view that reason can get us to a single God, while the Trinity remains a mysterious "matter of faith."

The Trinity functions less often by way of explicit contrast to reason's ways of knowing God in Calvin, and Calvin's nervousness about "speculation" led him, to my mind, to an excessive reticence in reflecting about the Trinity,[15] but he was just as clear that, unless we think of God as Triune, "only the bare and empty name of God flits about in our brains, to the exclusion of the true God."[16] It is only in Christ, Calvin wrote, that we know God: "For God lowers himself to us. He shows us only in his Son—as though he says, 'Here I am. Contemplate me. And realize how I have adopted you to be my children.' "[17] But apart from the Holy Spirit, no one would appropriate that christological work, for it is the Spirit who is "the inner teacher by whose effort the promise of salvation penetrates into our minds, a promise that would otherwise only strike the air or beat upon our ears."[18] It is only in Christ and through the Spirit

---

13. Martin Luther, *Lectures on Romans* (on Rom. 8:3), trans. Jacob A. O. Preus, *Luther's Works*, vol. 25 (St. Louis: Concordia Publishing House, 1972), 349.

14. Martin Luther, Sermon for Trinity Sunday (on John 3:1–15), *Sermons of Martin Luther*, trans. John Nicholas Lenker (Grand Rapids: Baker Book House, 1988), 410–11.

15. Though he makes the case for that reticence beautifully: "Here, indeed, if anywhere in the secret mysteries of Scripture, we ought to play the philosopher soberly and with great moderation; let us use great caution that neither our thoughts nor our speech go beyond the limits to which the Word of God itself extends. . . . Let us then willingly leave to God the knowledge of himself. For, as Hilary says, he is the one fit witness to himself and is not known except through himself. But we shall be 'leaving it to him' if we conceive him to be as he reveals himself to us, without inquiring about him elsewhere than from his Word." John Calvin, *Institutes of the Christian Religion* 1.13.21, trans. Ford Lewis Battles (Philadelphia: Westminster Press, 1960).

16. Ibid., 1.13.2.

17. John Calvin, *Congregation on Eternal Election*, trans. Philip C. Holtrup, in Philip C. Holtrup, *The Bolsec Controversy on Predestination from 1551 to 1555*, vol. 1, book 2 (Lewiston, N.Y.: Edwin Mellen Press, 1993), 717.

18. Calvin, *Institutes* 3.1.4.

that we appropriate knowledge of God or God's salvific work, so anything important we say about God has to be Trinitarian.

Here, even more than in earlier sections, Aquinas, Luther, and Calvin exemplify a fairly consistent pattern in the Christian tradition before the seventeenth century. Like Christian creeds and Christian liturgy, Christian theology was Trinitarian, not just in the sense that it affirmed the doctrine of the Trinity, but in that—even conceding LaCugna's point that Trinitarian doctrine was not as closely linked with the economy of salvation as it should have been—theologians still thought about the way we come to know about God and the way God saves us in Trinitarian terms. By the end of the seventeenth century, however (and I have indicated as much in earlier chapters), arguments to God as the creator and sustainer of the universe and debates about the role of God in the accomplishment of our salvation tended simply to talk about "God"—the Trinitarian Persons did not play much role in the analysis. Christ increasingly functioned in a subordinate role, with the Holy Spirit, in Patricia Wilson-Kastner's phrase, "reduced to a ghostly whisper."[19] When Arians like Newton and Clarke and then out-and-out Deists explicitly challenged the Trinity, most of their critics could only denounce them for heresy. It was not *orthodox* to deny the Trinity, but almost no one could explain why belief in the Trinity was *important*. As Michael Buckley puts it, "In the absence of a rich and comprehensive Christology and Pneumatology of religious experience, Christianity entered into the defense of the Christian God without appeal to anything Christian."[20] Indeed, what is striking is how little difference there was in practice between the theology of most in the seventeenth century who affirmed Trinitarian orthodoxy and that of their more radical opponents.

Seventeenth-Century Changes

As already suggested, how and why so much had changed are complex questions. I can only suggest some tentative answers. Among Protestants, the very structure of confessions and theological systems points to one sort of explanation. Calvin's *Institutes,* like the Lutheran Augsburg Confession, began with a discussion of God, and in both cases that discussion talked about the Trinity. Calvin then subsequently presented scripture as a gift of the Triune God he had already identified. The Westminster Confession, written in the 1640s, however, *begins* with a chapter on scripture. "Of God, and of the Holy Trinity" comes only in chapter 2. In chapter 1, "the Word of God" consistently refers to the Bible, not to Christ. Much seventeenth-century theology, in both

19. Patricia Wilson-Kastner, *Faith, Feminism and the Christ* (Philadelphia: Fortress Press, 1983), 123.

20. Michael J. Buckley, *At the Origins of Modern Atheism* (New Haven: Yale University Press, 1987), 67.

Lutheran and Reformed traditions, likewise discussed scripture first and then the Triune God.[21]

One consequence was a change in the basis of scriptural authority. For Calvin, "those who wish to prove to unbelievers that Scripture is the Word of God are acting foolishly," since "Scripture will ultimately suffice for a saving knowledge of God only when its certainty is founded upon the inward persuasion of the Holy Spirit."[22] A seventeenth-century Reformed theologian like Francis Turretin, on the other hand, could review the antiquity of the biblical texts, their accurate preservation, the candor of their writers in admitting their own faults, the majesty of their style, the harmony of their doctrine, and so on, and conclude, "The Bible . . . proves itself divine ratiocinatively by an argument artfully made from the marks which God has impressed upon the Scriptures and which furnish indubitable proofs of divinity."[23] No need then for the Spirit's inward illumination to establish scripture's authority.

Luther's view had been more like Calvin's. The Bible, he said, remained the letter, a purely human word, unless illuminated by the Holy Spirit.[24] But the seventeenth-century Lutheran theologian Abraham Calov, like a number of his contemporaries, insisted that the Word of God (by which he here meant the Bible) was not an "inanimate instrument" but could itself accomplish conversions, without the need of the illumination of the Spirit.[25] Both reformed and Lutheran theologians, then, began a pattern that continues down to contemporary evangelical theology in which "orthodoxy" has more to do with beliefs about biblical authority than about Trinitarian doctrine. More than that, while such theologians thought of themselves as defending biblical authority in the face of a rising tide of rationalism, they were in their own way rationalists. Human reason, Turretin insisted, could figure out the Bible's authority. That authority, then, served as a foundation for a theology that did not need to appeal in the ways earlier theologians had to the mysteries of grace and revelation.

At the same time, among Reformed theologians, the decrees and covenants of theology were moving more to the center of things. Both the Westminster Confession and Turretin's *Institutes,* for instance, having moved from a section on scripture to one on God then went on to a discussion of God's decrees.

21. See for instance, Francis Turretin, *Institutes of Elenctic Theology,* trans. George Musgrave Giger (Phillipsburg, N.J.: Presbyterian & Reformed, 1992), and Johann Gerhard, *Loci Theologici* (Frankfurt: Z. Hertel, 1657).

22. Calvin, *Institutes* 1.9.13.

23. Turrentin, *Institutes,* 63–64.

24. "He instructs us how the Word of God must be heard or read, namely, so that we do not approach it with our own powers, nor are content with the letter and the openly heard word, but that we seek to hear the Spirit Himself: For however many words there may be in the open, they are nothing but an utterance." Martin Luther, *First Lectures on the Psalms* (on Ps. 45:1), trans. Herbert J. A. Bouman, *Luther's Works,* vol. 10 (St. Louis: Concordia Publishing House, 1974), 212.

25. Abraham Calovius, *System locorum theologicorum,* vol. 1 (Witebergae: A. Hartmann, 1655), 705, 717. For a still more helpful discussion, see J. A. Dorner, *History of Protestant Theology,* trans. George Robson and Sophia Taylor (Edinburgh: T&T Clark, 1871), 132.

Eternal predestination (the first and most important of the decrees) thus came to serve as the basic framework of the story of salvation, within which the works of Christ and the Spirit took their place. In the words of Westminster, "As God hath appointed the elect unto glory, so hath he, by the eternal and most free purpose of his will, fore-ordained all the means thereunto. Wherefore they who are elected being fallen in Adam are redeemed by Christ, are effectually called unto faith in Christ by his Spirit working in due season; are justified, adopted, sanctified, and kept by his power through faith unto salvation."[26] The pattern of divine decrees, rather than the activity of the Triune God, thus became the shaping principle for theology, and it was a principle that emphasized the rules at work at each stage rather than an always unexpected and excessive divine grace. Chapter 9 traced how federal theology qualified earlier accounts of grace; it was also making the Trinity less important in theology.

Among Catholics a quite different set of events led to many of the same results; I will survey this story even more quickly since it has already been told so well by Michael Buckley in *At the Origins of Modern Atheism*. He begins with Lessius and Mersenne, two quite orthodox seventeenth-century theologians engaged in refuting atheism who shifted the theological ground by arguing for the existence of God with virtually no reference to Christ or the Holy Spirit.

Leonard Lessius (1554–1623) became a Jesuit in 1572 and studied with Suárez from 1581 to 1584 before going on to his own teaching career at Louvain. He adopted Suárez's interpretation of Aquinas, and taught Aquinas's *Summa Theologiae* by careful commentary on each passage, starting at the beginning. As a result, the question of the existence of God got discussed in relation to the "five ways" in question 2 of part 1, not the whole sweep of the *Summa* leading to Christ as the "way of truth" at the beginning of part 3. One can talk about God without reference to Christ, the Spirit, or the Trinity. In Buckley's works, Lessius "did not excuse himself from referring to Christology or properly religious experience; it seems never to have occurred to him."[27] In his most important book, *De Providentia Numinis et Anime immortalitate,* published in 1613, Lessius took on atheism, which was emerging into public debate for the first time since antiquity. His refutation took the form of rehearsing the arguments for the existence of God developed by pre-Christian philosophers. He did not take atheism as a reaction against Christianity; nor did he offer distinctively Christian arguments against it. The argument proceeded as if the first century B.C. led directly into the seventeenth century A.D. and Christianity had never happened.[28]

---

26. Westminster Confession of Faith, chapter 3, *Book of Confessions,* Presbyterian Church (U.S.A.), 6.019.
27. Buckley, *At the Origins of Modern Atheism,* 341.
28. Ibid., 42–43, 47.

Lessius set a pattern for Catholic theologians. Marin Mersenne (1588–1648) followed it a generation later. Mersenne knew everybody: he was in lively correspondence with Descartes and with the Jansenist Antoine Arnauld. He was a priest and a friar of the Minim order and no one seems to have doubted his orthodoxy. Yet his *L'Impiété des Déistes, Athées, et Libertins de ce temps,* published in 1624, again sought to refute atheism in terms of the debates of classical antiquity. His key argument was that "everyone recognizes the great mover of the universe as the creator of all things,"[29] and he made no effort to connect that "great mover" with the Trinity or Christology,[30] a pattern followed by many Catholics discussing the existence of God or arguing with atheism down into the twentieth century.[31] To quote Michael Buckley again:

> The person and teaching of Jesus or the experience and history of the Christian church, did not enter the discussion. The absence of any consideration of Christology is so pervasive through serious discussion that it becomes taken for granted, yet it is so stunningly curious that it raises a fundamental issue of the modes of thought: How did the issue of Christianity vs. atheism become purely philosophical?[32]

Lessius's connection with Suárez suggests one answer. Catholics reading Aquinas through the lenses of Suárez had, as I discussed in chapter 5, grown far more confident than Aquinas was in the capacity of human thought and language to comprehend God. If one thought (as Aquinas, like Luther and Calvin, did) of God as a mystery we can come to know at all only as the result of initiatives on God's part, then talk of God naturally included talk of those initiatives in the work of Christ and the Holy Spirit. If, on the other hand, one thought that reason could grasp the existence and attributes of God, but that the Trinity remained a mystery of faith, then it made sense, when arguing with atheists, to focus on God, the great mover of the universe, and ignore the Trinity. Lessius and Mersenne led the way.

Another factor played a role in the French context of these debates. Back in the sixteenth century, the essayist Michel de Montaigne had linked the appeal to Christian faith with philosophical skepticism. His friend the theologian Pierre Charron (in *Les Trois veritez,* published in 1594) developed the connection between philosophical skepticism and Catholic apologetics even more explicitly. Reason, they said, cannot give us certainty about *anything.* To escape the most radical kind of skepticism, we need to turn to faith in Christian

29. Marin Mersenne, *L'Impiété des Déistes, Athées, et Libertins de ce temps* (Paris: Pierre Bilaine, 1624; reprinted in photostat, Stuttgart: Friedrich Fromann Verlag, 1974), 72.

30. Buckley, *At the Origins of Modern Atheism,* 61.

31. On the existence of God, "a theologian cannot do much more than apply to the philosophers for philosophical information. The existence of God is a philosophical problem." Etienne Gilson, *Elements of Christian Philosophy* (Garden City, N.Y.: Doubleday & Co., 1960), 43.

32. Buckley, *At the Origins of Modern Atheism,* 33.

revelation.[33] By the time of Mersenne, the philosophical climate had changed. His friend Descartes was arguing powerfully for a much more optimistic picture of the capacities of human reason. Jansenists around Arnauld were making the case for probabilistic reasoning that did not leave us in radical skepticism.[34] Discussion of the existence of God located in the context of Christian faith and the Trinity seemed to place itself in the now out-of-date philosophical tradition of Montaigne and Charron, so that most Catholic theologians followed Lessius and Mersenne in making philosophical arguments for God's existence and leaving the Trinity out of the picture.[35]

For quite different reasons, then, much of Protestant and Catholic theology was moving in the seventeenth century toward similar conclusions. For Protestants the authority of scripture, and decrees and covenants, were replacing the Trinity at the center of theological debate, and reason and the scriptural authority it could warrant were replacing grace and the inner testimony of the Holy Spirit as what energized and undergirded belief. Catholic theologians were arguing for the existence of God against atheism in a way that made little appeal to the particularities of Christian faith. In both cases a marginalization of the Trinity went hand in hand with greater optimism about the use of human reason to move toward God, and greater optimism about the capacity of human moral efforts to cooperate in accomplishing our salvation.

As chapter 1 mentioned, the intellectual developments of the early seventeenth century were taking place against a background of horrific religious warfare. To be sure, in the Thirty Years War, some Protestants were fighting on the Catholic side, some Catholics for the Protestants, and along the way the French king made an alliance with the Turks, so it does not take too cynical a mind to wonder if political and economic factors may have been at work behind the religious slogans. Still, on the Continent the appeal to arms often called for a defense of the true faith—and in England too, conflicts over religion became as prominent as constitutional disputes between king and parliament. As a result of a generation of carnage, many thoughtful people began to wonder if doctrinal disputes were really worth killing and dying for. A generation or so after the end of the English Civil War, Archbishop Tillotson, probably the most admired English preacher of his day, noted in a sermon that, while it was true that the Socinians, who denied Christ's divinity, did not be-

---

33. See Richard H. Popkin, *The History of Skepticism from Erasmus to Descartes* (Assen: Van Gorcum, 1960), 57–59.

34. See Ian Hacking, *The Emergence of Probability* (Cambridge: Cambridge University Press, 1975).

35. Buckley, *At the Origins of Modern Atheism*, 66. Pascal, in this as in many things, was willing to be out of fashion: "All of those who seek God apart from Christ, and who go no further than nature, either find no light to satisfy them or come to devise a means of knowing and serving God without a mediator, thus falling into either atheism or deism, two things almost equally abhorrent to Christianity." Blaise Pascal, *Penseés,* no. 449, trans. A. J. Krailsheimer (London: Cox & Wyman, 1977), 169–70.

lieve in the Trinity, "I must own, that generally they are a pattern of the fair way of disputing and of debating matters of religion without heat and unseemly reflections upon their adversaries . . . virtues to be praised wherever they are found."[36] They were decent folk, in other words, so should we really worry too much concerning what they believed about the Trinity?

Tillotson himself believed that "the great business of religion is to make men truly good, and to teach them to live well."[37] To that end, he suspected that too much worry about doctrine was a mistake: "We have but a finite heat, and zeal, and activity; and if we let out much of it upon small things, there will be too little left for those parts of religion which are of the greatest moment and concernment."[38] Most of what makes Christianity distinctive apparently seemed to Tillotson small things. "Natural religion," he wrote, "requires piety, and justice, and charity, the due government of our appetites and passions, as well as Christianity does." The difference is that it "does not discover to us the rewards of another world, by many degrees, so clearly, as our Lord and Saviour, who . . . by his resurrection from the dead, and ascension into heaven, hath given us full assurance of another life after this."[39] In other words, "whatever was doubtful and obscure before is now certain and plain; the duties are still the same, only it [Christianity] offers us more powerful arguments, and a greater assistance to the performance of those duties."[40] Thanks to Christianity, we can reason our way to God more easily, and our moral struggles too will be less difficult, but the God Tillotson urged Christians to worship was not in any central sense either the God self-revealed in Christ or the source of a grace so amazing as to astonish every human ethical understanding, but essentially reason's God, the orderer of things both physical and moral. Tillotson did not deny that God is Triune—that denial would have stirred up trouble in a different way—but he saw no reason to risk religious conflict by arguing about it very much.

Christians might have responded to the horrors of the age's warfare in a different way. The Trinity itself, after all, with its vision of mutual deference among equals and its identification of a crucified preacher of peace as the Word of God incarnate, offers a starting point for condemnation of the world's violence. Christians in various eras have made passionate christological and Trinitarian witness against violence's evil.[41] But in the seventeenth century, many Christian writers saw such doctrines as part of the problem rather than part of the solution. Particular beliefs about Christ or the Trinity divided

36. John Tillotson, Sermon 44, "Concerning the Divinity of Our Blessed Saviour," *Works* (London: Richard Priestly, 1820), 3:310–11.
37. Tillotson, Sermon 21, preached at Whitehall, 4 April 1679, *Works*, 2:280.
38. Tillotson, Sermon 153, "The Spirituality of the Divine Nature," *Works*, 7:185–86.
39. Tillotson, Sermon 117, "The Prejudice against Christianity," *Works*, 6:19–20.
40. Tillotson, Sermon 101, "Of the Great Duties of Natural Religion," *Works*, 5:292.
41. For one form such an appeal might take in the intellectual conversation of today, see John Milbank, *Theology and Social Theory: Beyond Secular Reason* (Oxford: Basil Blackwell, 1990), chaps. 10 and 12.

Christians, they concluded, and passion about those beliefs led to bloodshed. A century later, David Hume summarized the drift of a long argument. Philosophers too, he conceded, inevitably fall into error, but, "Generally speaking, the errors in religion are dangerous; those in philosophy only ridiculous."[42] If religious differences lead to conflict, let us learn not to care too much about them. Since Christian theologians were already refuting atheism, reflecting on ethics, and arguing for the Bible's authority without much reference to the Trinity, it seemed a good candidate for the sort of doctrine not worth a fight.

The Rebirth of Arianism

An implicit agreement not to worry too much about the Trinity left the doctrine in some measure still in place, but very vulnerable to challenge. One challenge emerged in the mind of the greatest thinker of the age. Sometime in the 1670s, a recent biographer writes of Isaac Newton, "The conviction began to possess him that a massive fraud, which began in the fourth and fifth centuries, had perverted the legacy of the early church."[43] He grew convinced, as he later wrote to John Locke, that the biblical passages cited often in support of Trinitarian doctrine were in fact later corruptions, deliberately inserted by nefarious Trinitarians.[44] The biblical authors and the whole early church were Arian—they believed that Christ was divine, but a created being lesser than God the Father. Not until 381, when the Council of Constantinople ratified the doctrine of the Trinity, was "the year . . . in which this strange religion of ye west which has reigned ever since first overspread the world, & so ye earth with them that dwell therein began to worship ye Beast & his Image."[45] Newton did not arrive at these conclusions casually; his notebooks indicate the remarkable range of his reading in scripture and patristic texts. While he shared his opinions only with a few close friends, he avoided renewing his fellowship at Cambridge, at some risk to his career, when he would have had to be ordained and affirm the Trinity in order to keep it. (At the last minute the Lucastian professor was granted a special exemption from having to be ordained, and Newton was given the job.)

"When ever it is said in the scriptures that there is but one God," he wrote in his notebooks, "it is meant of ye Father. . . . The son in several places confesseth his dependence on the will of the father. . . . The son confesseth ye father greater than him, calls him his God, &c."[46] It is noticeable that Newton

---

42. David Hume, *A Treatise of Human Nature* (Oxford: Clarendon, 1888), 272.

43. Richard S. Westfall, *Never at Rest: A Biography of Isaac Newton* (Cambridge: Cambridge University Press, 1980), 313.

44. Isaac Newton, letter to a friend [John Locke?], November 1690, *The Correspondence of Isaac Newton* (Cambridge: Cambridge University Press, 1961), 3:138.

45. Newton, Yahuda MS 1.4, f.50, quoted in Westfall, *Never at Rest,* 323.

46. Newton, Yahuda MS 14, f.25, quoted in Westfall, 315–16.

saw the argument as a purely historical one. The question was what the Bible and the earliest church taught, and he thought it clear, on empirical evidence from historical research, that they taught Arianism. What was *theologically* at stake in affirming or denying the Trinity never much entered his reflections—a sign, probably, of how little the Trinity functioned theologically among his contemporaries.

Around 1690, as the newly published *Principia* was making Newton famous, a number of debates about the Trinity did emerge in public in England. William Babcock has described them as the "culmination" of the "crucial developments" in the decline of the doctrine of the Trinity that took place in the seventeenth century.[47] Yet, on the pro-Trinity side, it is hard to find anyone who made a strong case that much was at stake.

In 1690 Arthur Bury, the rector of Exeter College, Oxford, published *The Naked Gospel*, arguing that Christianity had grown most quickly in its earliest days, before its simple biblical faith had been overlaid with theological technicalities. Bury nowhere explicitly identified the Trinity as one of these excessively complex doctrines that Christianity would be healthier without, but some of his enemies accused him of heresy. (Bury had made enemies shortly before, when he had expelled one of the fellows of the college for alleged immorality with one of the women who made the college beds every morning.) A flurry of conflict ensued, with the representative the bishop sent to investigate barricaded out of the college by Bury's supporters and Bury himself eventually expelled from his position.[48]

Also in 1690, William Sherlock published his *Vindication of the Holy and Blessed Trinity.* Heretics and atheists, he said, try to show contradictions in doctrines,[49] so his goal was to make the Trinity "a very plain and intelligible notion."[50] He sought to do so by using Descartes's notion of a thinking substance. What unites a thinking substance is that all its thoughts are thought by a single consciousness: "This makes a finite Spirit numerically One, and separates it from all other Spirits, that every Spirit feels only its own Thoughts and Passions, but is not conscious to the Thoughts and Passions of any other Spirit." Suppose, however, that more than one spirit had exactly the same content of thoughts and passions.

> I cannot see any reason why we might not say, that Three such Persons were numerically One, for they are as much One with each other,

---

47. William S. Babcock, "A Changing of the Christian God: The Doctrine of the Trinity in the Seventeenth Century," *Interpretation* 45 (1991): 135. I am grateful to Maurice Wiles for calling my attention to this helpful article.

48. John Redwood, *Reason, Ridicule, and Religion: The Age of Enlightenment in England 1660–1750* (London: Thames & Hudson, 1976), 157–58.

49. William Sherlock, *A Vindication of the Doctrine of the Holy and Ever Blessed Trinity and the Incarnation of the Son of God,* 3d ed. (London: W. Rogers, 1694), 5.

50. Ibid., 73.

as every Spirit is One with it self; unless we can find some other Unity for a Spirit than Self-consciousness; and, I think, this does help us to understand in some measure this great and venerable Mystery of a *Trinity in Unity*.[51]

Sherlock deserves credit for taking the Trinity seriously enough to try to think it through, but the storm of opposition his book generated had some justification. As one of his critics, John Wallis, noted, Sherlock seemed to assume that "person" meant the same thing as applied to human beings and to God.[52] Given that Sherlock's project was to take the mystery out of the Trinity and make everything clear and consistent, it is not surprising that the results diverged substantially from classic doctrines.

The principal effect of the controversy over Sherlock's book (and Bury's), however, was not to lead people to more careful reflection on the Trinity but to reinforce the sense that talking about the Trinity got one into trouble, and it was perhaps best to avoid the subject. Archbishop Tillotson, as already noted, was offering a good example of how to avoid it; John Locke provided another. In Locke's notebooks from the 1690s there is a volume entitled *adversaria theologica,* with biblical passages collected on a variety of topics. The entry under *Non Trinitas* includes many quotations; under *Trinitas* only two are listed.[53] Locke complained to Edward Stillingfleet, after reading that bishop's defense of the Trinity, "Whether the not being able to get clear and distinct apprehensions concerning nature and person, from what your lordship has said of them, be the want of capacity in my understanding, or want of clearness in that which I have endeavoured to understand, I shall not presume to say; of that the world must judge."[54] But that we need "clear and distinct apprehensions"—or that they would be hard to come by in connection with the Trinity—did not seem to him in doubt. In *The Reasonableness of Christianity,* published in 1699, Locke concluded that biblical faith turns out to be very simple:

> What we are now required to believe to obtain eternal life is plainly set down in the gospel. St. John tells us, John 3:36, "He that believeth

51. Ibid., 48–49. "That the essential unity of a Spirit consists in self-consciousness every Man may feel in himself, for it is nothing else which makes a Spirit One, and distinguishes it from all other Spirits; and therefore if Two Spirits were conscious to all that is in each other, as they are to what they feel in themselves, they would be united to each other by the same kind of unity which makes every individual Spirit One: And why then should not this be thought an essential unity between the Divine Persons of the Ever Blessed Trinity." Ibid., 74. In Germany, Christoph Wittich was trying a somewhat analogous move at roughly the same time. See Christoph Wittich, *Theologia pacifica* (Lugduni Batavorum: Cornelium Bontesteyn, 1683), nos. 228, 231. J. A. Dorner, *History of the Development of the Doctrine of the Person of Christ,* 2nd division, vol. 2, trans. D. W. Simon (Edinburgh; T. & T. Clark, n.d.), 356.

52. See Fortman, *The Triune God,* 245. See John Wallis, *Theological Discourses* (London: Thomas Parkhurst, 1695).

53. Redwood, *Reason, Ridicule, and Religion,* 162.

54. John Locke, "Reply to the Bishop of Worcester's Answer," *Works* (London: W. Otridge & Son, 1812), 4:180.

on the Son hath eternal life . . . " . . . it is plain that believing on the
Son is believing that Jesus was the Messiah, giving credit to the miracles he did and the profession he made of himself.[55]

Biblical references to "the Son of God" should not lead us into Trinitarian speculations, for in the New Testament this is simply another term for "Messiah."
When confessing Jesus' identity, after all, "Peter answers in these words, Mark
8:29, 'Thou art the Messiah.' Luke 9:20, 'The Messiah of God.' and, Matt. 16:16,
'Thou are the Messiah, the Son of the living God,' which expressions, we may
hence gather, amount to the same thing."[56] Locke did not make an issue of
challenging Trinitarian orthodoxy, but it is hard to find a place he had left for
it. As a good seventeenth-century theologian, he appealed to reason and a certain kind of historical reading of the Bible, and as a result, the Trinity fared
none to well.

At this point the story arrives at the figure with which this chapter began,
Samuel Clarke. Where his friend Newton had kept his views private, and Locke
and Tillotson simply avoided the topic, Clarke tackled it head-on and in public: "The word God, in its absolute and primary sense, signifies the First Cause,
even Him who alone has all perfections, and all dominion absolutely in and
of himself, original, underived, and independent on any."[57] And in the Bible,
therefore, it always means the Father. Scripture leaves it unclear whether the
Son was or was not made out of nothing, but it is clear that the Son derives
his being from the Father, and hence only the Father is really God. "It appears
beyond contradiction that the words God and the Father, not God and the
Three Persons, are always used in Scripture as synonymous terms."[58] Newton's
piety had centered on "the *pantocrator* Lord of all things which an irresistible
& boundless power & dominion that we may not hope to escape if we rebell
& set up other Gods or transgress the laws of his monarchy, & that we may
expect great rewards if we do his will."[59] Clarke shared that vision of God
as sovereign first cause and moral judge, not as gracious redeemer. When
process theologians or other contemporary critics protest against an exclusively "transcendent" God, this is often the picture they have in mind. It is a
way of thinking about God that came into clearest focus as these seventeenth-
century figures turned away from the Trinity.

Just before Clarke published *The Scripture Doctrine of the Trinity* in 1712,
he took the precaution of buying a house, in case he should lose his job and
be expelled from his rectory. The expected attacks did appear, but in 1714 the
upper house of convocation of the province of Canterbury voted to take no

55. John Locke, *The Reasonableness of Christianity* (Washington, D.C.: Regnery Gateway, 1965),
16–17.
56. Ibid., 65–66.
57. Samuel Clarke, *A Modest Plea* (London: J. Knapton, 1720), 5.
58. Samuel Clarke, *The Scripture Doctrine of the Trinity,* 3rd ed. (London: J. Knapton, 1732), 232.
59. Newton, Yahuda MS 15.3, f.46v, quoted in Westfall, *Never at Rest,* 827.

action on charges against him, and Clarke, relieved, sold the house.[60] He promised not to preach on the Trinity ever again, and it gives a significant picture of the state of Trinitarian thought at the time that the promise of silence satisfied his critics. The leaders of the church accepted keeping quiet about it as an adequate attitude to Trinitarian orthodoxy.[61]

In the eighteenth century the issue did not keep quiet, and anti-Trinitarianism and Deism became more prominent. I have been arguing, however, that the battle had already been lost. In the seventeenth century, as earlier chapters have noted, Christian theologians increasingly thought of God as comprehensible in human terms, as the First Cause of the universe (who might or might not subsequently intervene in its affairs), and as the support of human efforts at moral improvement. Their imagining of this God primarily as a cosmic ruler and supporter of ethical standards put the divine on the side of most of the dominant forms of social order. Neither revelation nor grace, with their disruptive potential, was as central to their understanding of the divine. It is hardly surprising that the Trinity came, to many of them, to seem less important. If most did not deny the doctrine, it was often mostly out of respect for tradition and the desire not to stir up trouble. The British Museum has Samuel Clarke's copy of the prayer book: every Trinitarian passage is slashed through with violent strokes of his pen.[62] It would have been hard to find any of his contemporaries who brought the same passion to affirming the Trinity.

60. J. P. Ferguson, *An Eighteenth-Century Heretic, Dr. Samuel Clarke* (Kineton, Warwickshire: Roundwood Press, 1976), 48, 89.

61. See ibid., 85.

62. Frank E. Manuel, *The Religion of Isaac Newton* (Oxford: Clarendon Press, 1974), 61.

Part 4

Some Critical Retrievals

11   The Image of the Invisible God

It is time to try to draw some lessons—some implications for contemporary Christian theology—from the historical inquiries that have occupied most of this book. These final two chapters can only begin to sketch such implications; to do more would require at least another book. Still, since I have been saying that theology took some wrong turns in the seventeenth century and that we cannot simply return to the world as it was before those turns were taken, I owe the reader at least some hints of how I think some of those mistakes could be fixed—of how one might critically retrieve and then rethink for our putatively postmodern time some elements from theology before its turn to modernity.

A basic lesson: theologians get in trouble when they think they can clearly and distinctly understand the language they use about God. In Cajetan's and Suárez's reinterpretations of Aquinas on analogy, in Protestant scholasticism's restatements of the Reformation in philosophical categories, and in the quest for precision and certainty that in Descartes and others shaped the beginnings of modern philosophy, early modern thinkers sought and claimed to achieve such clarity. At least three sorts of trouble emerged as a result:

1. Many theologians came to think of God as one of the entities or agents in the world among the others, and of God's properties as differing from those of created things in degree rather than in kind. If we insist on a clear understanding of our language about God, then we have to think of God's love or power as rather like the love of a human being or the power of a steam engine—only greater. Thinking of God in such terms leads to asking where God is, and which are the things that God does, and attempts to answer such questions in ways compatible with Christian faith have often made theology the *enemy of science,* fighting to preserve a place for the "God of the gaps" in the face of ever-more-comprehensive scientific explanations. (See chapters 5 and 8.[1])

2. The effort to make God, and God's agency, comprehensible also leads to thinking about the relation of God to human freedom and responsibility as a zero-sum game. The more we contribute to our actions, and to our salvation, the less God does, and vice versa. On the one hand, this leads to niggling accounts of grace, in which we debate the degree of our own contribution rather than simply acknowledging in gratitude that we owe all things to God. On the

---

1. And see Amos Funkenstein, *Theology and the Scientific Imagination from the Middle Ages to the Seventeenth Century* (Princeton, N.J.: Princeton University Press, 1986), 116.

other hand, it makes faith in God's sovereignty and grace the *enemy of human freedom,* since whatever we claim God does comes at the cost of our own free responsibility. (See chapters 6 and 9.[2])

3. Theologians who think of God as one thing in the world alongside others often then try to preserve some sense of divine transcendence by emphasizing that God is the most distant, most powerful thing in the world, at the peak of all the world's hierarchies of being and value. This often makes God the *enemy of transformative justice,* since God's place at the peak of hierarchies gives divine sanction to those hierarchies, and a God defined in terms of distance, power, and unaffectability gives such qualities the imprimatur of divinity. (See chapters 5, 6, 8, and 9.)

An alternative—which I have argued tended to get lost in the seventeenth century—would be to think of God as transcendent in a more radical sense, admitting that in important ways we do not know what we mean when we talk about God, and that God is not the most distant of the things in the world but a transcendent mystery to whom none of our categories of distance or closeness apply. Not all Christians, or even all Christian theologians, before the seventeenth century held this view, and those who did hold it expressed and understood it in very different ways. But Aquinas, Luther, Calvin, and many other premodern theologians, with all their differences, did share such a view of God and our language about God. (See chapters 2, 3, and 4.) Given such a view, one could accept that God is engaged in *all* the realities of the world around us. It need not be incompatible to say *both* that we act freely *and* that our action is part of God's providential plan. Far from reinforcing the world's hierarchical structures, such a radically other God would serve as continuing reminder of their limitations and critique of their pretensions. (See chapter 7.)

Human reason cannot figure its way to such a God, since a God we could figure out, a God fitted to the categories of our understanding, would therefore not be transcendent in an appropriately radical sense. We can know the transcendent God not as an object within our intellectual grasp but only as a self-revealing subject, and even our knowledge of divine self-revelation must itself be God's doing. Christian faith finds here confirmation of God's Triune character: We come to know this gracious God not merely in revelation but in self-revelation in Jesus Christ, and we come to trust that we do know God in Christ through the work of the Holy Spirit.

Obviously, such a way of thinking about God did not simply disappear for four hundred years. It has shaped the thinking of many important theologians

---

2. One end of this intellectual trajectory would be Sartre's assertion that, if we are God's creatures, then even if our acts flow from our own essence, "the single fact that our essence has not been chosen by us [but created by God] shows that all this freedom in particulars actually covers over a total slavery." Jean-Paul Sartre, *Being and Nothingness,* trans. Hazel E. Barnes (New York: Philosophical Library, 1956), 538.

in our own century as in every earlier one.[3] Still, if this alternative needs recovery, then much modern theology went astray, and several of the movements discussed in chapter 1, which claim to be inaugurating postmodern theology, are headed even further in wrong directions. Process theologians, in thinking of God as the chief exemplification of all metaphysical principles and tracing the interaction of God and other free agents in the world, are losing God's authentic transcendence. Deconstructionist theologians have a better sense of God's radical otherness, but, lacking any place for revelation, they either qualify their original insight so that it turns out we can figure out something about God after all, or else they are reduced to silence. Functionalists who would construct God in the service of human concerns, even if they do so in the name of transcending the symbols and doctrines of particular religious traditions, lose what makes God God by making God a means to some other end.

So how should we do theology? In tracing what I claim went wrong in the seventeenth century, I have already said a good bit about the dangers of using the categories of human reason to work our way to God. But what about pushing the deconstructionist project to its limits and simply accepting, in Wittgenstein's famous phrase, that that which cannot be said must be passed over in silence? This chapter will begin with a brief note about why I reject negative theology as the *only* theological approach. The alternative to figuring out God for ourselves or saying only what God is not involves some kind of revelation from God, so I need to explain what I mean by *revelation* and defend the viability of the concept. That account in turn raises three questions that will be the concern of the rest of the chapter: (1) What can it mean to think of God as a character who speaks and acts within human history? (2) Does a God who acts in the world and whose character traits we can identify thereby cease to be radically transcendent? (3) Why should we believe that any particular persons, events, or stories in fact reveal the transcendent God?

A Note on Negative Theology

"Negative theology" has functioned, in Christianity as in other religious traditions, as a way of safeguarding the divine mystery and as a way of praising God. To speak of God paradoxically by noting what we cannot say does function to remind us of divine transcendence and as a negative form of the activity Whitehead once called "paying metaphysical compliments to God." And

---

3. My own thinking lies primarily in the tradition of Karl Barth, but see also Paul Tillich, *Systematic Theology* (Chicago: University of Chicago Press, 1951), 1:235; Karl Rahner, *Foundations of Christian Faith*, trans. William V. Dych (New York: Seabury, 1978), 46; Wolfhart Pannenberg, *Systematic Theology*, vol. 1, trans. Geoffrey W. Bromiley (Grand Rapids: Wm. B. Eerdmans Publishing Co., 1991), 189; Robert P. Scharlemann, *Inscriptions and Reflections: Essays in Philosophical Theology* (Charlottesville: University Press of Virginia, 1989), 41–43.

these are worthy activities for Christians. Yet if theology confines itself exclusively to the negative, it seems to fall into one of four problematic positions.

First, negative propositions can contain hidden positive claims. If I have already argued that everything is either body or spirit, then to say, "God is not body," is equivalent to saying, "God is spirit." If I say, "God is unchanging," I may in fact be making, with a negative term, a positive claim about how God remains always the same. This is not in any distinctive sense negative theology at all.

Second, more subtly, the piling up of negations may be designed to evoke positive conclusions about God. Authors as different as pseudo-Dionysius and Karl Barth (in the second edition of his Romans commentary) have sometimes seemed engaged in such an enterprise. The lists of negations come to have a certain dramatic force, and their order implies a certain trajectory (not at all like X, not like Y, not exactly like Z, but getting closer); they lead us toward a not, then, unexpected glory. As Aquinas noted, much so-called negative theology takes this form, for it clearly implies that the right way to talk about God lies in one direction rather than another, even as it claims not to be stating anything "positive."[4] To repeat: nothing is wrong with such strategies as cautionary note or as praise. But, located at the center of theological method, negative theology understood in this way offers only a more sophisticated human way of trying to move toward God.

Third, negative language about God can claim to refer to a particular sort of experience of God. The language cannot, of course, capture the experience but somehow recalls for the speaker and hopes to recall or invoke for the reader some inexpressible moment prior to all language or conceptual thought.[5] George Lindbeck has made the point, drawn in part from the later works of Wittgenstein, that such "experiential-expressivism" gets the relation between language and experience wrong.[6] We do not have profound but prelinguistic religious experiences, which the languages of various religious traditions then, more or less adequately, attempt to express. When a deaf-mute, Mr. Ballard, quoted by William James, speaks of the fascinating thoughts he had about the first cause of the universe before he learned language, I for one simply do not believe him.[7] It is the images and languages of religious traditions that make such reflection and indeed religious experience possible.[8] The Buddhist contemplating nirvana and the Catholic meditating on the cross of

4. Aquinas, *Summa Theologiae* 1a.13.2, trans. English Dominican Fathers (London: Blackfriars, 1963–).
5. See Friedrich Schleiermacher, *On Religion: Speeches to its Cultured Despisers,* trans. John Oman (New York: Harper, 1958), 43, though I am not claiming that this was Schleiermacher's last word on the matter.
6. See George A. Lindbeck, *The Nature of Doctrine: Religion and Theology in a Postliberal Age* (Philadelphia: Westminster Press, 1984), 34.
7. William James, *Principles of Psychology* (New York: Henry Holt, 1908), 1:267.
8. "The presupposition of listening to Christian preaching is not that everything is language, it is rather that it is always within a language that religious experience is articulated. . . . More pre-

Christ are not using different means to try to arrive at a common inexpressible goal. They are engaged in different activities, differently experienced, each made possible only by a particular framework of shared language and practice.[9] Therefore, an understanding of negative theology as only pointing beyond itself to a prelinguistic experience would have it leading away from the particular languages and associated forms of life that matter centrally to religious traditions.

Fourth, negative theology in the strongest sense can intend to leave us simply with silence. We can say nothing at all about God, period. But here I think that Feuerbach was right: if we get rid of all the predicates, we get rid of the subject too.[10] If we can literally say nothing at all about God, then we are atheists, and, sooner or later, just have to get on with talking about something else.

Revelation

Theologians dissatisfied with human reason's efforts to grasp the divine and with a purely negative theology have often talked of revelation. Pointing to problems in other approaches, to be sure, does not magically open the door to revelation, for the very idea of revelation implies that one can only wait for a God who in divine freedom may choose to speak—or may not. Still, it is not as if, in contemporary theology, we have to invent the idea of revelation for our current purposes; the Christian tradition has laid claim to the reception of revelation for a long time. Revelation is—no question—a problematic concept, but perhaps the difficulties that arise in alternative theological strategies make it worth reexamination.

Revelation has certainly become a controversial word in contemporary theology.[11] Exegetes argue that it is not really a biblical category; philosophical theologians announce that they can make no sense of it. Many see "appeals to revelation" as the enemy of reflection and therefore the friend of intellectual oppression. "Thus saith the Lord . . .," which is the sort of phrase *revelation*

---

cisely . . . faith . . . is instructed—in the sense of being formed, clarified, and educated—within the networks of texts that in each instance preaching brings back to living speech. This presupposition of the textuality of faith distinguishes biblical faith ('bible' meaning book) from all others. In one sense, therefore, texts do precede life. I can name God in my faith because the texts preached to me have already named him." Paul Ricoeur, "Naming God," trans. David Pellauer, Union Seminary Quarterly Review 34 (1979): 216.

9. See J. A. DiNoia, *The Diversity of Religion* (Washington, D.C.: Catholic University of America Press, 1992), 35.

10. Ludwig Feuerbach, *The Essence of Christianity,* trans. George Eliot (New York: Harper & Brothers, 1957), 15. See also David Hume, *Dialogues concerning Natural Religion,* in *On Religion* (Cleveland: Meridian Books, 1963), 131; Karl Barth, *Church Dogmatics,* vol. 2, part 1, trans. T.H.L. Parker et al. (Edinburgh: T&T Clark, 1957), 193.

11. See for instance F. Gerald Downing, *Has Christianity a Revelation?* (London: SCM Press, 1964); James Barr, *The Bible in the Modern World* (New York: Harper & Row, 1973), 120–32; Gordon Kaufman, *The Theological Imagination* (Philadelphia: Westminster Press, 1981), 21–57.

often calls to mind, can indeed sound like, "Shut up and do as you're told."
By *revelation,* however, I mean rather that we have a way of talking about
God appropriate to who God is, a way that is not something we can figure out
by our reason and does not turn God into an object but that comes to us from
God as a free gift. As Eberhard Jüngel puts it:

> Revelation is by no means an authority which renders something in-
> fallible. It is as little that as it is an instance which immunizes against
> the labor of thought. . . . revelation means only that God is the un-
> conditional subject of himself and as such is accessible only because
> and to the extent that he makes himself accessible. Apart from the ac-
> cess to himself which he himself *affords,* no thinking will ever find its
> way to him.[12]

Our encounters with other human persons offer the closest analogy. When
I observe an object as a thing—the pencil on the table, the corpse in the
morgue, even the prisoner in handcuffs—then the initiative lies with me to
grasp what I can, to understand in my terms of reference. In an encounter with
a person, encountered *as* a person, on the other hand, much initiative lies on
the other side. You choose what you wish to show or tell me about yourself
through your words and actions. If I want to understand as fully as possible, I
will have to come to terms with your ways of presenting yourself. To be sure,
in any human encounter both parties remain objects as well as subjects. If we
meet on the street, your physical appearance tells me something about you,
whether you want it to or not, and your unconscious may betray you into revealing more. When Jüngel (or Karl Barth) says that in revelation God is the
unconditional subject, they mean that there is nothing about God that we can
know whether God wants us to or not.[13] If God is really transcendent, then
there is no epistemological path from us to God, and everything we know
about God comes at God's initiative.

This does not render our encounter with God contentless. At one point in
his career, Emil Brunner spoke of our encounters with God in language much
influenced by Martin Buber. *Any* statements "about" God, he seemed to say,
any objective content, would inappropriately turn God into an object. "When
I stand opposite to God," he wrote, "I am face to face with Him who uncon-
ditionally is no 'something', who in the unconditional sense is pure 'Thou.' "[14]

---

12. Eberhard Jüngel, *God as the Mystery of the World,* trans. Darrell L. Guder (Grand Rapids: Wm.
B. Eerdmans Publishing Co., 1983), 158. From such a definition it follows that all revelation is, at
least indirectly, self-revelation. (Let me do here what I have resisted doing until now in this book,
and apologize for all the masculine pronouns in this passage—but the insight here is an important one.)

13. See for instance Karl Barth, *Church Dogmatics,* vol. 1, part 1, trans. G. T. Thomson (Edinburgh: T&T Clark, 1936), 280–83.

14. Emil Brunner, *The Divine-Human Encounter,* trans. Amandus W. Loos (Philadelphia: Westminster Press, 1943), 86–87.

As critics like Ronald Hepburn have pointed out, however, this God who was so resolutely not an object was one about whom we could know nothing, and therefore our knowledge of God had no content and finally no meaning—so back to pure negative theology.[15]

Christians, however, have generally not thought of revelation as a content-less encounter but as an encounter with a God whose identity the biblical stories narrate. Narratives provide one way of limning personal identity that keeps resisting the reduction of persons to objects. I can tell you the sort of person Jane is by listing properties she possesses—generous, a bit foolhardy, etc.—or I can *show* the sort of person she is by telling you stories about her. In the latter case, you may come to a sense of her richer than would be preserved by any attempt to reduce what you learned to a list of attributes, and the telling of the stories can honor her own "subjecthood" better than any scheme of classification. As David Kelsey explains,

> Narrative can "render" a character. A skillful storyteller can make a character "come alive" in a way that no number of straightforward propositional descriptions of the same personality could accomplish. He can bring one to know the peculiar identity of this one unique person. Moreover, what one knows about the story's central agent is not known by "inference" from the story. On the contrary, he is known quite directly in and with the story, and recedes from cognitive grasp the more he is abstracted from the story. So too, biblical narrative can be taken as rendering an agent whose identity and actions theology is then to discuss.[16]

In reading the Bible or hearing it preached, Christians encounter a figure called "God" whose "character traits" they learn in these stories.[17] This God is faithful even when human covenant partners are faithless; this God hears the cries of slaves, and loves radically imperfect creatures. The actions of this character do not seem arbitrary; they form recognizable patterns. Like human beings, God has freedom such that we cannot always predict what God will do. Indeed, this is even more true of God, since the limitations of our particular bodies and situations always limit what human beings can do in a way that has no equivalent in God's case. Still, as with a human being, we can identify the sorts of things God might do, and other things that would be completely "out of character." The stories invite such reflections, for even within them God speaks and acts with reference to a pattern of past activity. The mysterious Lord who speaks to Moses from the burning bush is "the God of your ancestors, the God of

15. See Ronald W. Hepburn, *Christianity and Paradox* (New York: Pegasus, 1966), 31–35.

16. David H. Kelsey, *The Uses of Scripture in Recent Theology* (Philadelphia: Fortress Press, 1975), 39.

17. See Thomas F. Tracy, *God, Action, and Embodiment* (Grand Rapids: Wm. B. Eerdmans Publishing Co., 1984), 3–6; Ronald F. Thiemann, *Revelation and Theology: The Gospel as Narrated Promise* (Notre Dame, Ind.: University of Notre Dame Press, 1985), 107.

Abraham, the God of Isaac, and the God of Jacob" (Ex. 3:15). The one who tells Amos to condemn Israel is the very one who brought them out of the land of Egypt (Amos 3:1). In Acts, Stephen sets his preaching of Christ in the context of God's whole history with Israel (Acts 7). The God who delivers promises and warnings is a God who in the story has already proven trustworthy in fulfilling, in whatever unexpected ways, past promises and warnings.[18]

In emphasizing stories or narratives as the central form of biblical revelation, I do not want to claim too much. As Paul Ricoeur and others have pointed out, the Bible contains a range of different ways of speaking about God: "narration that recounts his acts, prophecy that speaks in the divine name, prescription that designates God as the source of the imperative, wisdom that seeks God as the meaning of meaning, and the hymn that invokes God in the second person. . . . The referent 'God' is thus intended by the convergence of all these partial discourses."[19] Yet Ricoeur himself acknowledges, "The whole of contemporary exegesis has made us attentive to the primacy of the *narrative* structure in the biblical writings."[20] One can take the biblical narratives as a framework within which prophecy, prayer, and the like find their place, while (I claim no more than this) none of the other elements seems to work so well as a starting point.[21]

The biblical narratives, however, function for Christian believers in an unusual way, such that "God" is not "just a character in a story," not even the dominant character in a very good story. Robert Scholes and Robert Kellogg, two literary critics who have written a recent study of narrative, explain how narratives "mean":

> Meaning, in a work of narrative art, is a function of the relation between two worlds: the fictional world created by the author and the "real" world, the apprehendible universe. When we say we "understand" a narrative, we mean that we have found a satisfactory relationship or set of relationships between these two worlds.[22]

If I read a history of the Civil War, I understand its meaning when I insert its narratives within the framework of my knowledge of American history. If I read a novel, I recognize that its "narrative world" does not fit into the world of historians and ordinary experience; no need to check New England archives for records of Hester Prynne, no chance of meeting Rabbit Angstrom on the street.

---

18. See Martin Luther, *Lectures on Galatians* (1535) (on Gal. 5:6), trans. Jaroslav Pelikan, *Luther's Works*, vol. 27 (St. Louis: Concordia Publishing House, 1964), 29.

19. Ricoeur, "Naming God," 222.

20. Ibid., 220.

21. It offers, Hans Frei said, a better organizing principle, that is, one with "a wider range of applicability within the New Testament canon, than many another." Hans W. Frei, *Theology and Narrative* (New York: Oxford University Press, 1993), 43.

22. Robert Scholes and Robert Kellogg, *The Nature of Narrative* (New York: Oxford University Press, 1966), 82.

The biblical narratives, however, neither offer to fit into a framework already constructed by experience and historical reflection, nor do they stand aside in a secondary world. Rather, they claim to *define* the framework within which we might understand our experience and the rest of history.[23] These stories, they say, are what the world is really about, and your own story and the other stories you know can be properly understood only if you fit them into these stories, so that, in George Lindbeck's phrase, "It is the text, so to speak, which absorbs the world, rather than the world the text."[24] Further, these narratives portray a world defined by the character of this God. The world is God's creation. Israel's history works out a covenant with God. In general, the world is the way it is, and what is important and of value in it are what they are, in these stories, because God is who God is.[25]

To say that the biblical narratives constitute *revelation*, then, is to say (1) that they claim to be defining of all reality, and (2) that their internal sense of things is in turn defined by the identity of the character they call "God," about whom they claim to provide trustworthy language to use, even as the divine nature remains utterly mysterious. If God's identity has this defining role in the stories, and the stories claim a defining role for all things, then to read these stories is to be addressed by a claim on one's life from this God. This is how things are, they say; this is the context in which your life, or anyone's life, has whatever meaning it possesses—in the context shaped by the character called "God" whose identity is herein narrated and who is the transcendent, sustaining beginning and end of all things. Scripture constitutes revelation from a subject both because it presents God as an agent acting in its stories and—an issue to which the last section of this chapter will return—because the personal agency of the Holy Spirit shapes our acceptance of them. To accept scripture as the revelation of God, however, is not to think that we have grasped the divine nature, but to trust that, in ways we cannot understand, we will be speaking rightly of God if we tell the stories these texts recount and cautiously note, in creed and theology, some of the character traits we perceive of this God, without ever letting the results of such reflection take the primary place of the stories themselves.[26]

Such an account of revelation, particularly in the context of themes traced elsewhere in this book, raises a host of questions. As already noted, the rest of this chapter will deal with three of them.

23. See Erich Auerbach, *Mimesis: The Representation of Reality in Western Literature,* trans. Willard R. Trask (Princeton, N.J.: Princeton University Press, 1968), 15, and Hans W. Frei, *The Eclipse of Biblical Narrative* (New Haven: Yale University Press, 1974), 3.

24. Lindbeck, *The Nature of Doctrine,* 118.

25. Pannenberg points out, in response to arguments that the Old Testament has no word for "history," that the equivalent term would be some variation on "the acts of God." See for instance Josh. 24:31 or Isa. 5:12. Pannenberg, *Systematic Theology,* 1:230–31. There is not some history independent of what God does.

26. Hans W. Frei, *Types of Christian Theology* (New Haven: Yale University Press, 1992), 126.

Divine Action

First, *what can it mean to think of God as a character who speaks and acts within human history?* Talk of revelation seems inevitably to involve such claims, but as Langdon Gilkey stated in a classic article, it is hard to know how people today can make sense of them:

> The causal nexus in space and time which Enlightenment science and philosophy introduced into the Western mind . . . is also assumed by modern theologians and scholars; since they participate in the modern world of science both intellectually and existentially, they can scarcely do anything else. . . . Suddenly a vast panoply of divine deeds and events recorded in Scripture are no longer regarded as having actually happened. . . . Whatever the Hebrews believed, we believe that the biblical people lived in the same causal continuum of space and time in which we live, and so one in which no divine wonders transpired and no divine voices were heard. To us, theological verbs such as "to act," "to work," "to do," "to speak," "to reveal," etc., have no longer the literal meaning of observable actions in space and time or of voices in the air.[27]

And, if they do not have that literal meaning, he went on to wonder, what do they mean? Gilkey formulated the problem in a characteristically post–seventeenth-century way: for the most part, he assumed the world runs itself, and the question (as Clarke and Leibniz debated it) concerns whether or not God occasionally interferes. Such occasional interference then gets plausibly portrayed as the sort of thing modern, scientific folk cannot believe, and references to God's actions turn into nonsense.

If, however, as earlier theologians held, God is an agent in *all* the world's events—if, in Aquinas's terms, the nature of any created thing "would collapse . . . were God's power at any moment to leave the beings he created to be ruled by it,"[28] or, as Calvin said, "If God should but withdraw His hand a little, all things would immediately perish and dissolve into nothing"[29]—then the picture changes. There is not an independent causal continuum in which it is puzzling how God could intervene. The only causal continuum is one whose every event God sustains. Divine action is not an interruption in or a violation of the normal course of things, but precisely *is* the normal course of things. The circling of the planets, the leap of a squirrel outside my window, and my own writing of this book are all also results of divine agency, and to claim that

---

27. Langdon B. Gilkey, "Cosmology, Ontology, and the Travail of Biblical Language," in *God's Activity in the World: The Contemporary Problem,* ed. Owen C. Thomas (Chico, Calif.: Scholars Press, 1983), 31–32. See also Gordon Kaufman, *God the Problem* (Cambridge: Harvard University Press, 1972), 248.

28. Aquinas, *Summa Theologiae* 1a.8.1.

29. John Calvin, *Commentaries on the First Book of Moses Called Genesis* (on Gen. 2:2), vol. 1, trans. John King, *Calvin's Commentaries,* 1:103.

this is so at another level of agency does not come into conflict with natural science's accounts of causal continua.[30]

Gilkey might reply that such an argument avoids the issue. Whether or not all events are the result of divine agency, the Bible seems to present some events as the result of divine agency in a special sense. The Red Sea permits the Hebrew people to pass as on dry land. The prophet hears the voice of the Lord. Jesus is raised from the dead. As noted in chapter 8, the idea of a "natural order" independent of God and there to be "violated" is a modern one, and it would therefore be anachronistic to impose it on ancient texts. It is also, as I have been saying, important to think of God as at work in all times and places. Yet aren't some of these dramatic events differently related to God than the normal course of the world's affairs? And isn't that what many people today find hard to believe?

But what is that difference? H. Richard Niebuhr offered one account of it: "Sometimes when we read a difficult book, seeking to follow a complicated argument, we come across a luminous sentence from which we can go forward and backward and so attain some understanding of the whole. Revelation is like that."[31] So the revelatory "mighty act of God" might be simply that event that enables us to see with particular clarity how we had daily been surrounded by God's mighty acts, the "wonder" the event wherein we recognized the work of a divine agent we could in principle have seen in all things.

To me, Niebuhr's account makes the distinctions seem too subjective. If last evening's sunset helped you see a kind of order in all things, and the intricacy of the spider's web in the corner of the barn did the same for me, then each could be, on his account, "revelatory" for one of us. The Bible seems more firmly to say that some particular events are clues to the meaning of the whole. If we understand the Bible as narrating God's identity as an agent, this should not be surprising, for other agents we know most fully enact their identities only in particular acts that best reveal who they are. I had cereal for breakfast this morning, and am even now breathing and digesting my dinner, but anyone who found one of these events, rather than my central acts of work and love or my moral failures, the luminous key to interpreting my life would get me wrong.

Gilkey, however, seems to me to have gone too far in the other direction. Faith has to claim, he wrote, that an "act of God" is not "indistinguishable from other events" but "objectively and ontologically different. . . . Otherwise, there is no mighty act, but only our belief in it, and God is the God who in fact does not act."[32] But this assumes the characteristically modern view that most of the time God is not acting, so that an act of God has to intervene in a normally

---

30. See Kathryn Tanner, *God and Creation in Christian Theology: Tyranny or Empowerment* (Oxford: Basil Blackwell, 1988), 84, 89.
31. H. Richard Niebuhr, *The Meaning of Revelation* (New York: Macmillan Co., 1941), 68.
32. Gilkey, "Cosmology, Ontology, and the Travail of Biblical Language," 37.

independent causal continuum. Fair enough, one can imagine Gilkey responding—but does not the Bible, even if it lacks our modern concerns, assume some different-than-normal form of divine activity as it describes the great acts of God? Answering this question turns out to be complicated. Parts of the Bible describe, at the very least, quite dramatic divine activity. Plagues get sent, seas parted, apostles freed from prison. In other stories, however, no such wondrous interventions occur. In most of the narratives about King David, for instance, nothing takes place that the most secular historian could not accept. One cannot explain these differences in terms of some sort of "development," for the divine wonders return, after the time of David, in the Elijah stories; much later they appear in some sections of Acts but not in others, and so on.

Neither the Deuteronomic historian who edited Israel's history nor the author of Acts, however, comments on these differences. No one ever says, "God didn't do miraculous things for David the way God did for Moses and Elijah." The texts as we have them assume that God is at work in *all* of this history and do not reflect on the different modes of divine action they report in different periods. If one were to try to extract a "biblical point of view" from these texts, therefore, it would have to be something like, "God works in history—sometimes more dramatically and sometimes through the more ordinary behavior of natural forces and human actors—and the differences do not much matter." What seems central is an understanding of God as sustaining *all* history. The narratives can thus function as Calvin saw scripture doing, as "spectacles" that help us see what, absent sin, would be visible to us in the whole theater of God's creation—although even then we would discern patterns in which some events would play a more important role than others.[33]

If we reflect on the narratives in this way, some questions that the biblical writers could, as it were, naïvely leave unasked come naturally to our minds. But we might do well to preserve a certain reticence in these matters, even if in our case doing so has to be more self-conscious. Theologians can teach us that we do not at all understand *how* God acts—I said something about this in chapter 7 and will say a bit more in a few pages. Therefore we are not in a position to make judgments about how God acts differently in some cases than in others.[34] Modern science provides us with lawlike generalizations that describe

33. "Having dispersed our dullness," the scriptures "clearly show us the true God. . . .Therefore, however fitting it may be for man seriously to turn his eyes to contemplate God's works, since he has been placed in this most glorious theater to be a spectator of them, it is fitting that he prick up his ears to the Word, the better to profit. . . . We must come, I say, to the Word, where God is truly and vividly described not by our depraved judgement but by the rule of eternal truth." John Calvin, *Institutes of the Christian Religion* 1.6.1–3, trans. Ford Lewis Battles (Philadelphia: Westminster Press, 1960).

34. "The truth to which we refer we cannot state apart from the biblical language which we employ to do so. And belief in the divine authority of Scripture is for me simply that we do not need more. The narrative description there is adequate. 'God was in Christ reconciling the world to himself' is an adequate statement for what we refer to, though we cannot say univocally how we refer to it." Frei, *Theology and Narrative*, 210.

the behavior of things in the world, but cautious scientists will admit that we do not know enough about the whole of things to know when one might expect variations in normal patterns. The cosmologists, for instance, tell us that many of the usual laws of physics did not operate in the first few seconds of creation. Perhaps, for one who saw the whole of the universe's history, quite abnormal events at key turning points in that history would seem utterly "natural."[35] We lack enough understanding *either* of God's modes of action *or* the pattern of things as a whole to know how to evaluate such an anomalous case.

If God "acts" revelatorily, in short, I am proposing this: (1) Some historical events can provide a luminous key to understanding all things. (2) They do not just happen to do so for some people, but there is something about the events themselves such that in them was the special disclosure of the transcendent beginning and end of all things we call God. (3) When we ask how God was acting differently in such events, however, we quickly realize that we lack the categories to describe such differences.

For Christians, of course, Jesus Christ represents the culmination of God's self-revelation, and here many of the usual problems about "God's action" disappear. In Jesus Christ, God was acting to reconcile the world, and Jesus had a voice and a body. We can understand what it means to say that he "acted." "The Father," Calvin wrote, "himself infinite, becomes finite in the Son."[36] "He shows us only in his Son—as though he says, 'Here I am. Contemplate me.'"[37] Illustrative anecdotes or key events from the life of Jesus as narrated in the Gospels render the enaction of God's love for the world and thereby disclose the one God is. Christians can point to the pattern of enacted intentions that make up this particular human life and say: "He is the image of the invisible God" (Col. 1:15). See how Jesus has compassion for the poor and the outcasts. See how he takes the risks of vulnerable love. Though "no one has ever seen God," yet "God's love was revealed among us in this way: God sent his only Son into the world so that we might live through him" (1 John 4:12, 9).

Appealing to Christology does not, however, provide a way of dodging the questions I have just been discussing. The Gospels identify Jesus as the self-revelation of the God Israel had already come to know in its history.[38] And

35. See Robert Merrihew Adams, "Theodicy and Divine Intervention," in *The God Who Acts,* ed. Thomas F. Tracy (University Park, Pa.: Pennsylvania State University Press, 1994), 36–39; Barth, *Church Dogmatics,* vol. 2, part 1, 540–41.

36. Calvin, *Institutes* 2.6.4.

37. John Calvin, *Congregation on Eternal Election,* trans. Philip C. Holtrup, in Philip C. Holtrup, *The Bolsec Controversy on Predestination from 1551 to 1555,* vol. 1, book 2 (Lewiston, N.Y.: Edwin Mellen Press, 1993), 717.

38. Calvin, indeed, argued that even the "holy men of old knew God only by beholding him in his Son as in a mirror" (Calvin, *Institutes* 4.8.5). Since the Son is the self-revelation of the Father, all revelations must be in some sense christological. Jonathan Edwards thus stood firmly in the Reformed tradition in thinking that the beatific vision would be a vision of Christ. See the quotations cited by Paul Ramsey in "Appendix III: Heaven Is a Progressive State," in Jonathan Edwards, *Ethical Writings* (New Haven: Yale University Press, 1989), 719.

they offer the fact that God raised Jesus from the dead as the decisive evidence that Jesus is the one they proclaim him to be. So we cannot simply point to the actions of the human Jesus to identify the activity of the God revealed in Christ and avoid all problems about divine action in history. The Gospels, however, turn out to reinforce patterns for thinking about these issues I have already noted in other parts of the Bible. The Gospel of John begins with a bold, cosmic account of divine activity. The birth narratives in Matthew and Luke are full of "divine wonders," and in all the Gospels miracles continue in Jesus' ministry. But in the passion narratives, there is only the human figure of Jesus, and virtually no event a secular historian could not report. Yet the logic of the story implies that here God's action in Jesus Christ is culminating. As Hans Frei continued the story:

> In his passion and death the initiative of Jesus disappears more and more into that of God; but in the resurrection, where the initiative of God is finally and decisively climaxed and he alone is and can be active, the sole identity to mark the presence of that activity is Jesus. God remains hidden, and even reference to him is almost altogether lacking. Jesus of Nazareth, he and none other, marks the presence of the action of God.[39]

At the climax of the story, we have no picture of "God acting" other than the presence of Jesus. For Christian faith, then, in Jesus of Nazareth, who "humbled himself and became obedient to the point of death—even death on a cross" (Phil. 2:8), we encounter the self-revelation of God. As Luther saw, whenever we try to think clearly about these matters, we unfortunately find ourselves imagining a hidden God behind the God revealed in the crucified Jesus. Yet we trust that, when all things are revealed, we will see in a way we cannot now imagine that the crucified Jesus was the self-revelation of the only God there is.[40] Christians reflect on the narrated identity of a loving person whom we take to be the embodiment of a God so transcendent as to be knowable only through self-revelation. We note the signs and wonders the Gospels describe while also noting that, here as elsewhere in the Bible, the text does not focus as much as we might expect on the differences between these and other parts of the story.

Christian reading of the Bible, then, takes Christ as a clue to the shape of the whole of scripture. We see the "character traits" exemplified in Jesus in the way other parts of the Bible describe God at work—even, albeit more tentatively, in the work of God throughout the one world in which we live and move and have our being—and these stories thus begin to shape the way we

---

39. Hans W. Frei, *The Identity of Jesus Christ* (Philadelphia: Fortress, 1975), 121.

40. Martin Luther, *Lectures on Genesis,* trans. Paul D. Paul, *Luther's Works,* vol. 6 (St. Louis: Concordia Publishing House, 1970), 45 (on Gen. 26:9), 148 (on Gen. 32:31–32).

live our lives.[41] Living within the framework of these narratives, however, as Aquinas put it, "does not tell us what God is, but thus joins us to him as to an unknown."[42]

Self-revelation and Transcendence

Talk of divine revelation, however, raises another question, as it were, from the other side. I have been discussing Gilkey's worries that divine action would interfere in what we understand of the created order. But what about its implications concerning God? *Does a God who acts in the world and whose character traits we can identify thereby cease to be radically transcendent?* Not surprisingly, I want to answer no. For one thing, we can attribute actions to God without claiming to understand how God performs those actions. In Austin Farrer's phrase, "The causal joint (so to speak) between infinite and finite action plays and in the nature of the case can play no part in our concern with God and his will."[43] Otherwise, we will "degrade" God's agency "to the creaturely level and place it in the field of interacting causalities."[44] God's creating is so unlike any form of human making, Aquinas said, that we use terms like "create" or "make" "equivocally in reference to this . . . and in reference to other productions."[45] We simply do not understand how God acts, and thus what it means to say *that* God acts.

In other cases, however, our lack of understanding of causal mechanisms does not prevent us from attributing agency. As a noneconomist, for instance, I can talk about the fact that the Hunt brothers tried to corner the silver market, and can draw some conclusions about their ambition and greed, even though I would not know how to go about purchasing a share of silver, and so do not really understand how they carried out their scheme. In reading a science fiction story about the inhabitants of Mars or a horror story about people who can read minds or take over the bodies of others, I can identify the character traits manifested in what they do while bracketing any sense of how they do it. In the latter cases, of course, I also bracket belief in the truth of these stories, but, for my purposes here, the point is that we can understand the stories' meaning, and their implications for the character of a person whose identity they narrate, without understanding the mechanism of the person's action. Similarly, we can reflect on the "character" manifested in a pattern of

41. See Karl Barth, *Church Dogmatics,* vol. 4, part 3, first half, trans. G. W. Bromiley (Edinburgh: T&T Clark, 1961), 64–65; Niebuhr, *The Meaning of Revelation,* 113.
42. Aquinas, *Summa Theologiae* 1a.12.13 ad 1.
43. Austin Farrer, *Faith and Speculation* (New York: New York University Press, 1967), 65.
44. Ibid., 62.
45. Aquinas, *Commentary on Aristotle's Physics* 8.2.974, trans. Richard J. Blackwell, Richard J. Spath, and W. Edmund Thirkel (New Haven: Yale University Press, 1963).

divine activity without understanding the mechanisms of how God acts. As Thomas Tracy puts it, any appropriate account of God's agency

> involves extending the concept of an agent of intentional actions beyond its familiar instances, stripping away the limitations that attach to finite agents (including, for instance, the limitations associated with embodiment). This process, I contend, does not break down the basic logical structure of the concept; we can coherently affirm that God is an agent. But it does leave us unable to spell out *what* it is to be such an agent and to act as this agent acts.[46]

The knowledge we infer from God's self-revelation, therefore, can leave us quite ignorant of the nature of God. If I have communicated with you by way of computer program, I conclude that you are, let us suppose, intelligent and kindly disposed toward me. You help me with my math problems in a way that gets me the right answers, and I cannot think that you derive any benefits from my mathematical successes for yourself. But I may not know your race, sex, age, or appearance. Imagine that my computer is connected to the intergalactic version of Internet, and I may not know your planet or species. Perhaps, given the sort of realities the science fiction imagination can conjure up, you do not even have a body. It is tempting to say that I know how you are disposed toward me without knowing how you are in yourself, but that makes the distinction too sharp, for I believe that your kindness toward me, for instance, must really manifest some quality you possess, even if I cannot imagine enough about the nature of your emotional life to understand what it would mean for you to feel kindness. Much more is all this the case with reference to a transcendent God.[47]

In short, our language about God's action is, in precisely Aquinas's sense, "analogous": it enables us to say something true while not understanding what we mean.[48] George Lindbeck has, by way of Victor Preller, in this connection recovered Aquinas's distinction between the "mode of signifying" and the "thing signified." When we use language about God, we do not understand how it applies to God (its *modus significandi* or mode of signifying), but we believe that, in a way we cannot understand, its meaning (its *significandum* or the thing it signifies) does apply to God. "Thus, for example, when we say that God is good, we do not affirm that any of our concepts of goodness (*modi*

---

46. Thomas F. Tracy, "Divine Action, Created Causes, and Human Freedom," in Tracy, *The God Who Acts,* 82. See also Robert H. King, *The Meaning of God* (Philadelphia: Fortress, 1973), 87–96; William Alston, "How to Think about Divine Action," *Divine Action,* ed. Brian Hebblethwaite and Edward Henderson (Edinburgh: T. & T. Clark, 1990), 68.

47. See Gregory of Nyssa, *Against Eunomius* 1.38, trans. H. A. Wilson, in *Nicene and Post-Nicene Fathers,* 2d sermon, vol. 5 (Peabody, Mass.: Hendrickson, 1994), 88.

48. "However friendly or adverse one may be to recognizing analogous uses of language, it is quite impossible, I should think, to deny that 'acting' must be so construed." David B. Burrell, *Freedom and Creation in Three Traditions* (Notre Dame, Ind.: University of Notre Dame Press, 1993), 69.

significandi) apply to him, but rather that there is a concept of goodness un-available to us, namely, God's understanding of his own goodness, which does apply."[49] Thomas Torrance makes an analogous point with reference to Calvin's hermeneutics by saying that images of God are there taken to be *ostensive* and *persuasive* but not *descriptive:* they direct us toward God and invite us to shape our lives as lived in a world created and sustained by this God, but they do not tell us how God is God.[50] I believe as a Christian that, if I were to know God as God is, I would know a kind of love that would make any human love seem a hopelessly pale reflection—but I cannot imagine the character of such a love.

The Inner Testimony of the Holy Spirit

If thinking of the events narrated in scripture as revelation does not pose insoluable problems about divine action or necessarily undercut the transcendence of God, a third question still remains. *Why should we believe that these particular stories do in fact reveal the transcendent God?*[51] The question demands our attention for at least three reasons. First, one would need to ask this question about any stories proposed for such a central role in our life and thought. Second, to take the life of this crucified teacher of love, and the deeply ambiguous history of this small country, as the revelation of the beginning and end of all things so challenges many of our ordinary assumptions about what is important and what is of most value as to make the question all the more pressing. Third, whatever pieces of confirmation archeological evidence or extrabiblical sources provide, they do not suffice to give us anything like a character portrait of a self-revealing God, so that we have this life and this history only through the witnesses to it of a variety of sometimes discordant and generally unsupported texts. Why believe them?

Important as these questions are, if they concern the particular arguments or psychological processes that lead Christians to such beliefs, then Christian

49. Lindbeck, *The Nature of Doctrine,* 66.

"Although the referential character of theological discourse is crucial to the whole enterprise (what would be the point of doing theology if one were not really talking about God?) the informational vacuity of such talk should shift the focus of someone investigating it away from epistemological questions of truth and meaning. Theologians . . . have no way of actually specifying what they are talking about (the *res significata* of their statements) apart from the meanings of the terms they use and it is just those meanings whose applicability to God they admit to failing to understand. The attention of the investigation is directed consequently to the practical effects of theological statements: as proposals for talk, these statements are helping to build a distinctive Christian practice of discourse and, by extension, forms of life congruent with it." Tanner, *God and Creation in Christian Theology,* 12.

50. Thomas F. Torrance, *The Hermeneutics of John Calvin* (Edinburgh: Scottish Academic Press, 1988), 92.

51. James Gustafson has regularly pressed this question. See James F. Gustafson, *Ethics from a Theocentric Perspective,* vol. 1 (Chicago: University of Chicago Press, 1981), 30.

theology has no systematic answers to offer. Once again, I would advise that theological wisdom calls for reticence. To quote David Kelsey, "The reasons for adopting just these writings as 'authority' are as complex, unsystematic, and idiosyncratic as are the reasons individual persons have for becoming Christians."[52] Moreover, their persuasive force involves, so a Christian will claim, the work of grace that partakes of the mystery of the transcendent God. Therefore, as Ronald Thiemann has written,

> Theology ought not seek to devise an explanatory theory for the subjective conditions for the possibility of faith, for such theories obscure both the diversity and the mystery of human response to the gospel. . . . the ultimate explanation of that mysterious movement from unbelief to faith lies beyond theology's descriptive competence. If a person comes to believe the gospel's promises, the theologian, as member of the Christian community, can simply join the chorus of witnesses in glorifying God for his miracle of grace.[53]

Calvin identified this aspect of grace's work as "the inner testimony of the Holy Spirit." "The word itself," he wrote, "is not quite certain for us unless it be confirmed by the testimony of the Spirit."[54] The Spirit is "the inner teacher by whose effort the promise of salvation penetrates into our minds, a promise that would otherwise only strike the air or beat upon our ears."[55] This is another point I have argued got lost in the seventeenth century, as prologomena about the authority of scripture replaced accounts of the Triune God as the starting point of theological systems, and rational arguments for the Bible's reliability took the place of appeals to the inner testimony of the Spirit. Theologians before the seventeenth century often better understood, first, that our coming to faith is also not our own work but something for which we must be grateful to God, and, second, that, since God is transcendent, this work of God too remains ineluctably mysterious. In Luther's words:

> Knowledge of Christ and of faith is not a human work but utterly a divine gift. . . . What the Gospel teaches and shows me is a divine work given to me by sheer grace. . . . This sort of doctrine which reveals the Son of God . . . is revealed by God first by the external Word and then inwardly through the Spirit.[56]

"No one," Paul wrote, "'can say 'Jesus is Lord' except by the Holy Spirit" (1 Cor. 12:3). Not only can we not find God on our own, but even our response to God's self-revelation is God's work.[57]

---

52. Kelsey, *The Uses of Scripture in Recent Theology*, 164.
53. Thiemann, *Revelation and Theology*, 147–48.
54. Calvin, *Institutes* 1.9.3.
55. Ibid., 3.1.4.
56. Luther, *Lectures on Galatians* (1535), *Luther's Works*, 26:64 (on Gal. 5:16), 26:72 (on Gal. 5:17).
57. See Barth, *Church Dogmatics*, vol. 1, part 1, 535.

If Christians believe in God's transcendence, it follows that we will remain cautious about all efforts to explain a process itself embedded in the work of a God we recognize remains unknowable to us. We recognize the way in which the biblical narratives keep illuminating our understanding of our lives and shaping the worshiping communities in which we live those lives. Sometimes our own experience drives us back to the Bible to discover a more complex meaning than we had earlier discerned. Sometimes we cannot figure out how some things the Bible seems to say could be true in the light of other things it says or other realities of our lives. We encounter passages that demean women or seem to foster anti-Semitism or speak joyously of the slaying of large numbers of Amalekites. Sometimes we see ways of reinterpreting these passages in the light of other biblical texts, but sometimes we cannot explain them away. Yet reflecting on our world in biblical terms keeps proving so enriching that we are willing to keep coming back to the Bible and leave many questions unanswered, many puzzles unresolved.[58] This is what it is like to acknowledge the mysterious work of the Holy Spirit. As when, having stared at a puzzling image, we suddenly "see" it as the picture of a human face, so with the way we "see" the world biblically: once the pattern has emerged, we cannot choose to "unsee" it. But the fact of our seeing feels more like being chosen than choosing. The experiences that keep driving us back to scripture do not add up to decisive argument for its authority, and our conclusions indeed often hardly seem matters of argument at all. Apart from the inner testimony of the Holy Spirit, Calvin insisted, "it will be vain to fortify the authority of Scripture by arguments, to establish it by common agreement of the church, or to confirm it with other helps."[59]

Given the place of God's self-revelation in Christ and the testimony of the Spirit in Christian claims to speak of a transcendent God, it follows that a Christian understanding of God needs to be embodied in Trinitarian reflection. We cannot give an account of God or of how we come to know God and then add the Trinity later, for the God we come to know is the God self-revealed in the Word and known through the Spirit. It is through the narratives of the humanity of Christ (and, as Calvin argued, God's already christological self-revelation in the history of Israel) that we are given the way of talking about the God who remains unknown to us. And it is through the testimony of the Spirit that we trust in those narratives.[60] Thus the way in which we appropriate this self-revelation is also at once immediate to us and ineluctably

---

58. See Phyllis Trible, "The Pilgrim Bible in a Feminist Journey," *Princeton Seminary Bulletin*, n.s., 11 (1990): 232–39. I have discussed these concerns at greater length in William C. Placher, *Narratives of a Vulnerable God* (Louisville: Westminster John Knox Press, 1994), chap. 4.

59. Calvin, *Institutes* 1.8.1.

60. "Though the Son does enact the Father's intentions, the very fact that we can identify those intentions as the *Father's* curbs any attempt to conceive of the Father as eternally hidden. The distinction between hiddenness and presence must rather cut across the entire conception of God as Father, Son, and Spirit. That is, of course, what the Cappadocian fathers attempted to do in

mysterious. The Spirit brings us to see God hidden in suffering in Christ, and joins us to this God as to an unknown.[61] Thus, by way of initiatives from God, we come to know a God who remains utterly transcendent.

When most seventeenth-century theologians tried to talk about "God," therefore, of course they got it wrong. Whether reflecting about the action of God in creation or the interplay of divine grace and human freedom, they were trying to domesticate God's transcendence into the categories of human understanding. Absent a Triune God, they had only human efforts to account for our internal appropriation of faith, and only human categories for our understanding of who God is. And therefore, they lost God's transcendence.

---

devising the distinction between the 'immanent' and 'economic' trinity. That distinction guards both the hiddenness and the presence of God's identity, because it asserts that the self-differentiated unity we observe in God's narrative relations is a reiteration of God's inner but hidden identity. The narrative description of God is reliable, because it shows us God's 'immanent' identity through 'economic' depiction. God's hiddenness is not some elusive self lurking behind or beyond the narrative depiction. God's hiddenness is simply a quality of God which the shape of the narrative itself indicates." Thiemann, *Revelation and Theology*, 139.

61. Martin Luther, "Heidelberg Disputation," trans. Harold J. Grimm, *Luther's Works*, vol. 31 (Philadelphia: Muhlenberg Press, 1957), 52; Aquinas, *Summa Theologiae* 1a.12.13 ad 1.

12 Evil and Divine Transcendence

One of the themes of this book has been that, for much of theology since the seventeenth century, God ceased to be the transcendent, sustaining beginning and end of all things and became one player among others on the stage of history, with unfortunate consequences for everything from the relation of theology and science to the way people thought about the place of grace in the accomplishment of salvation. Earlier chapters have discussed how and why that change took place in the seventeenth century in particular, but the hard realities of evil and human sin raise questions in any age about belief in a sovereign God. This concluding chapter steps back a bit from the historical issues to consider some of those questions.

We live in a world full of tragedies. Natural disasters and horrible diseases bring painful deaths and leave behind the grieving. Human beings seem capable of evils so appalling as to be almost beyond imagining. All of us, if we are honest, have to confront not only our fears and doubts but our deep moral failings. How can the God in whom Aquinas, Luther, and Calvin believed—a God at once the sovereign One who sustains and directs all things and the gracious One known in Jesus Christ—be Lord of such a world? As David Hume wrote two centuries ago, "Epicurus's old questions are yet unanswered. Is he willing to prevent evil, but not able? then is he impotent. Is he able, but not willing? then is he malevolent. Is he both able and willing? whence then is evil?"[1] In such a world, one could argue, faith in *any* God comes hard. Perhaps belief in a sovereign judge could serve to frighten people into ethical improvement, though the sort of world we have might bring that judge's moral authority into question. But trust in a God of overflowing grace might well seem incomprehensible.

In a characteristically dense and illuminative essay titled "The Demythization of Accusation," Paul Ricoeur has dreamed of a "theology of love" that would combine the "sublimation of consolation" with the "sublimation of accusation."[2] The sublimation of consolation would manifest the kind of trust in God that does not expect exemption from life's tragedies. The sublimation of accusation would lead the relation between faith and ethics beyond thoughts of reward and punishment. Together, they might form the basis for a critical

---

1. David Hume, "Dialogues concerning Natural Religion," in *On Religion* (Cleveland: Meridian Books, 1963), 172.
2. Paul Ricoeur, *The Conflict of Interpretations,* trans. Peter McCormick et al. (Evanston, Ill.: Northwestern University Press, 1974), 352.

retrieval of belief in a radically transcendent God, and I will keep returning to Ricoeur's language in the course of this chapter.

Against Theodicy

One "solution" to "the problem of evil" is to think of God as one limited force among the others in the world. In many ways, it is an empirically plausible approach. Our world does *look* more like an arena of conflict between good powers and evil ones than the creation of a sovereign and gracious God. The early church confronted such ideas in Marcion's contrast between the different gods of the Old and New Testaments and in the cosmic dualism of the Manicheans. Most recent books on "theodicy" or "the problem of evil," often influenced by process thought, conceive of a God with limited powers engaged with created beings in a cooperative venture of world-making.[3]

I have been arguing that thinking about God as one actor among others in the cosmic drama gets theology into trouble. The idea that God does some things but not others forces theologians in a secular age into defensive efforts to find some things for God still to do and negotiations between too much limit on God's power and too much limit on human freedom. It leads to explanations of what God does and does not do, and these explanations lose the mystery of radical transcendence.

Another solution is to think, as James Gustafson does, of God as a transcendent other, "the power that bears down upon us, sustains us, sets an ordering of relationships, provides conditions of possibilities for human activity and even a sense of direction,"[4] but without special concern for humankind, and of whom the language of personal agency can be used only very cautiously if at all. "Anthropocentrism," a sense that creation is ordered for the benefit of human beings, is Gustafson's enemy. "I do not say God is against man," he remarks, but he cannot accept it when Barth says, "vividly and categorically: 'God is for man.' "[5] The ordering of things sustains our existence, but it is not designed to our good.

This way of thinking about God indeed preserves God's transcendence and, as Gustafson argues, draws on elements in the Reformed tradition that appear in Calvin, Edwards, and H. Richard Niebuhr, among others. But it has little room for strong doctrines of revelation, Christology, or the work of the Holy Spirit. Its austere vision of things does not domesticate God, but it does follow the seventeenth-century trends I have been criticizing in thinking of God pri-

---

3. See for instance David Ray Griffin, *God, Power, and Evil: A Process Theodicy* (Lanham, Md.: University Press of America, 1990); John B. Cobb, Jr., *Encountering Evil: Live Options in Theodicy* (Atlanta: John Knox Press, 1981).

4. James M. Gustafson, *Ethics from a Theocentric Perspective*, vol. 1 (Chicago: University of Chicago Press, 1981), 264; see also 271.

5. Ibid., 181.

marily as unitary sovereign rather than as Triune source of grace. Absent more appeal to revelation, it raises questions about whether it can justify, out of a piety based on human reasoning and the experience of this often tragic world, even the claims it makes about God's direction of things and the "respect and gratitude" we owe to God.[6] We might be awestruck before the order of things, but why grateful? Tragedies, Gustafson says, "can be occasions for human *responses* that are beneficial to others," but cannot be seen as part of some divine plan for human good.[7] Has such a theology left us with enough of a personal divine agent to permit a relation like gratitude?

In a bleak moment, Freud once remarked that it is as if "obscure, unfeeling, and unloving powers determine men's fate."[8] Perhaps such a claim goes too far, but, in the midst of the world's tragedies, it is hard to think, just on the empirical evidence, of the world's sustaining power or powers as "good." It is Christ, H. Richard Niebuhr once wrote, who makes Christians

> suspicious of their deep suspicion of the Determiner of Destiny. He turns their reasoning around so that they do not begin with the premise of God's indifference but of his affirmation of the creation, so that the *Gestalt* which they bring to their experience of suffering as well as of joy, of death as well as of life, is the *Gestalt,* the symbolic form, of grace.[9]

A theology like Gustafson's, suspicious of claims to revelation and with a limited Christology, has an admirably rigorous integrity, but it is not clear that it has the resources to overcome that "deep suspicion" that so much of our experience of the world generates.

Calvin, risking the dangers Gustafson would see of anthropocentrism but guided by biblical claims concerning God's providence, and with a much fuller Christology and account of revelation, made bolder claims:

> Christ, when he declared that not even a tiny sparrow of little worth falls to the earth without the Father's will, immediately applies it in this way: that since we are of greater value than sparrows, we ought to realize that God watches over us with all the closer care; and he extends it so far that we may trust the hairs of our head are numbered. What else can we wish for ourselves if not even one hair can fall from our head without his will?[10]

---

6. Ibid., 61. See Gordon D. Kaufman, "How Is *God* to Be Understood in a Theocentric Ethics?" in *James M. Gustafson's Theocentric Ethics,* ed. Harlan R. Beckley and Charles M. Swezey (Macon, Ga.: Mercer University Press, 1988), 25.

7. Gustafson, *Ethics from a Theocentric Perspective,* 1:181.

8. Sigmund Freud, *New Introductory Lectures on Psychoanalaysis,* trans. James Strachey (New York: W. W. Norton, 1965), 147.

9. H. Richard Niebuhr, *The Responsible Self* (New York: Harper & Row, 1963), 175–76.

10. John Calvin, *Institutes of the Christian Religion* 1.17.6, trans. Ford Lewis Battles (Philadelphia: Westminster Press, 1960).

Gustafson would ask whether such claims about God's relations to the particulars of creation can be reconciled with the conclusions of modern science, and I briefly addressed such questions in the previous chapter. But the hard reality of evil also leads a critic like Gustafson to a different set of questions. Belief in a God like the one Calvin was praising can lead to the view ridiculed by Spinoza: One comes to think of God as designing all the universe for the benefit of humankind, even for the sake of our "blind cupidity and insatiable avarice." Such a belief is self-preoccupied to start with, and, in the face of the world's evil, it seems obviously untrue. As Spinoza continued, in the face of storms, earthquakes, diseases, and the like, "The attempt . . . to show that Nature does nothing in vain (that is to say, nothing which is not profitable to man) seems to end in showing that Nature, the gods, and man are alike mad."[11]

Ever since the seventeenth century, these issues have led theologians and philosophers to write "theodicies," to try to "solve the problem of evil." Accepting that God is powerful and gracious and that we understand what these terms mean, they have then often argued that what looks evil is not so bad after all, or that one can explain how apparent evils serve some greater good. So for instance, in a standard recent work on theodicy, Richard Swinburne proposes that if we hear someone screaming in pain, their pain may not be "nearly as great" as the screams "might suggest," and may provide someone else the opportunity to come to their aid so that the good of generosity and compassion thus brought into the world outweighs the evil of the pain that occasioned it.[12]

D. Z. Phillips understandably remarks that the ability to talk this way about the screams of the innocent "is the sign of a corrupt mind,"[13] and Kenneth Surin says that it reflects "an irremissable moral blindness."[14] Similarly, in *Evil and the God of Love,* John Hick proposes that a world without pain "would lack the stimuli to hunting, agriculture, building, social organization, and the development of the sciences and technologies, which have been essential foci of human civilization and culture."[15] Like right-wing politicians urging reductions in welfare benefits to force people back to work, such a theodicy seeks to justify God in the face of starving children by pointing out that their hunger constitutes a stimulus to agriculture and hunting. This seems to manifest a kind of moral tone-deafness. My point is not to launch personal attacks on particular writers of theodicy, but to suggest that something about the enterprise of theodicy itself drives even thoughtful, decent folk to morally unacceptable conclusions.

---

11. Benedict de Spinoza, *Ethics,* trans. William Hale White, rev. James Gutmann (New York: Hafner Publishing Co., 1949), 73–74.
12. Richard Swinburne, "The Problem of Pain: I," in Stuart C. Brown, ed., *Reason and Religion* (Ithaca, N.Y.: Cornell University Press, 1977), 92.
13. D. Z. Phillips, "The Problem of Pain: II," *Reason and Religion,* 115.
14. Kenneth Surin, *Theology and the Problem of Evil* (Oxford: Basil Blackwell, 1986), 84.
15. John Hick, *Evil and the God of Love* (New York: Harper & Row, 1978), 359.

Much of modern religious thought, however, takes it for granted that theodicy is a necessary part of reflection on belief in God. After all, the propositions

> God is sovereign.
> God is good.
> Evil exists.

do seem to imply a contradiction, and it would therefore seem one of the tasks of theology or the philosophy of religion to resolve the puzzle. If one wants to defend the first proposition against some form of process thought and the second—if we take "good" to mean "concerned for human welfare" and ignore Gustafsonian suspicions of anthropocentrism, for example—then one apparently has to whittle away at the third. In fact, however, the tradition of writing theodicies or trying to "solve the problem of evil" began only in the seventeenth century, particularly in the English tradition of "natural theology" developed in succeeding Boyle lectures and in a German tradition that reached its high point in Leibniz's *Theodicy*.[16]

Obviously, earlier theologians had worried about evil and its relationship to their faith in God, but they did so in different ways. Only in the seventeenth century, when theologians and philosophers began to assume that they had clear concepts of what "sovereign," "power," and "good" meant as applied to God, that beliefs about God ought to fit together in a logically coherent system, and that talk of the Trinity was marginal to our understanding of God did theodicy in its modern form emerge. That modern tradition continues down to contemporary figures like Hick and Swinburne, and it tends to read its own project back into earlier writers, on the assumption that they of course were engaged in the same enterprise.

But earlier Christian writers were doing something different. They were not trying to produce logical arguments that would "solve the problem of evil." First, they acknowledged that reflection on evil particularly calls attention to what Barth called "the necessary brokenness of all theological thought and utterance."[17] We do not understand what our words mean when we apply them to God. We find ourselves called to say things even as we have to admit that we cannot explain how they all fit together. We trust that our talk as Christians makes sense in a way that we do not yet see, and so there are things we are willing to leave unexplained. Second, they did not think about evil in relation to an abstract God, but with reference to the Triune God and therefore in the context of the cross of Christ and the comforting work of the Holy Spirit. The cross surely makes a difference when one thinks about whether God is

---

16. See Surin, *Theology and the Problem of Evil,* 4; Terrence W. Tilley, *The Evils of Theodicy* (Washington, D.C.: Georgetown University Press, 1991), 221.

17. Karl Barth, *Church Dogmatics,* vol. 3, part 3, trans. G. W. Bromiley and T. F. Torrance (Edinburgh: T&T Clark, 1961), 293.

indifferent to our pain. It is often the inner testimony of the Holy Spirit that makes it possible to trust what one cannot understand. But neither offers an "explanation" of how to fit God's power and love and the existence of evil together in a coherent account, so they have virtually disappeared from much of the modern literature on theodicy.

Third, earlier responses to these questions were rhetorical. That is, they addressed the particular concerns of victims of evil in particular situations. Alvin Plantinga, the author of an important recent work on the problem of evil, honestly admits that his sort of theodicy is of little help in pastoral counseling or in helping people think about particular cases of suffering. It rather tries, he says, to solve some problems of logical inconsistency that might pose an intellectual challenge to Christian faith.[18] But this would have seemed to many theologians before the seventeenth century to answer trivial questions and ignore the important ones. They were willing to live with apparent logical inconsistencies, but they wanted something one could actually say about evil to its victims.

Let me illustrate the form such Christian discourse in the presence of evil might take if it stopped attempting theodicy. Consider the story in John's Gospel of how Jesus "saw a man blind from birth. His disciples asked him, 'Rabbi, who sinned, this man or his parents, that he was born blind?' Jesus answered, 'Neither this man nor his parents sinned; he was born blind so that God's works might be revealed in him' " (John 9:1–3). He then healed the man. One could think of this as a horrifying story: this poor fellow has suffered his handicap until adulthood simply so that, at a particular moment, he might serve as a sort of human audiovisual aid to illustrate the power of God. Indeed, it seems to me that anyone not at least momentarily horrified by the story has not yet taken it seriously. But I do not think horror need have the last word.

Jesus' interlocutors wanted an explanation of the evil. Like preachers today condemning those who are HIV-positive, they wanted to get God off the hook by blaming the victim. Did the fault lie with the blind man, or his parents? Jesus' response rejected human efforts to understand such matters. No one, encountering this blind man the day before, could have figured out, Oh, he must have been born blind so that the Messiah could turn up tomorrow and cure him. Yet, in a way that no one could have expected, this man turned out not to have been forgotten by God, but to have his place in God's promised hope for all things. In contrast to the approach of theodicy, this seems to me the kind of thing Christian faith best says to the victims of suffering: (1) I don't understand, and I can't imagine why you should be suffering in this way, but (2) I trust that God has not forgotten you, and that you do not finally lie outside God's love.[19] The theodicist will correctly point out that this does not explain

---

18. Alvin Plantinga, *God, Freedom and Evil* (New York: Harper & Row, 1974), 28–29.
19. See the beautiful language along these lines in the Heidelberg Catechism, questions 26–28.

the evil, but it is not clear that victims want explanations. Indeed, offered an "explanation," they may feel affronted, or, even worse, internalize an account that puts the blame on them in a self-destructive way.[20]

So Jeremiah and the authors of many of the psalms do not explain their sufferings but lament them: They place their cries of pain and grief in the context of the praise of God.[21] They do not understand, but they can get on with their lives in a way that neither denies their pain nor abandons all trust in God to fall victim to despair. So Job never receives an "explanation" for his sufferings, but receives an assurance that God has not forgotten him, and a renewed sense of wonder in the face of God's self-revelation.[22] As Ricoeur puts it,

> No teleology emerges from the whirlwind; no intelligible connection is established between the physical order and the ethical order; what remains is the unforming of being within the fullness of word; what remains is only the possibility of an act of acceptance which would be the first step in the direction of consolation, the first step beyond the desire for consolation.[23]

Finding himself addressed by God, Job is willing to accept and give up trying to understand. Such a faith would take the form of that "love to Being in general" that Jonathan Edwards identified as true virtue.[24]

A sublimation of consolation, Ricoeur writes, "would be heir to the tragic faith of Job. It would adopt the same attitude in regard to the theological metaphysics of Western philosophy that Job adopted in regard to the pious words of his friends concerning the god of retribution."[25] Job is *not* condemned for his anger and impatience; God rather honors Job in contrast to the friends who tried to give explanations of why God had acted rightly (Job 42:8). Job accepts, but it is an acceptance without sentimentalism that therefore acknowledges mystery. If, in line with the themes I have traced in pre–seventeenth-century theology, one admits how little one can understand of God, then one can seek such trust.

In emphasizing the unsentimental character of such an acceptance, I mean to resist attempts to reduce the confession of mystery into a kind of aesthetic appeal, as if, for instance, the intricacies of the natural world could persuade

---

20. One can sometimes recognize educative or purgative value in suffering, Paul Ricoeur admits. "But we should immediately add that this meaning should not become the object of a specific teaching; it can only be found or rediscovered in each specific case. And there is a legitimate pastoral concern that this meaning taken up by a victim not lead him or her back along the route of self-accusation or self-destruction." Paul Ricoeur, "Evil: A Challenge to Philosophy and Theology," *Journal of the American Academy of Religion* 53 (1985): 647.

21. Ibid., 644–47.

22. See Ricoeur, *The Conflict of Interpretations,* 351.

23. Ibid., 461.

24. Jonathan Edwards, "The Nature of True Virtue," in *Ethical Writings* (New Haven: Yale University Press, 1989), 541.

25. Ricoeur, *The Conflict of Interpretations,* 460.

us that its beauty as a whole clearly justified the suffering in some of its parts. I do not think we can ever attain such a clear vision. Annie Dillard's unsentimental account of nature provides a helpful corrective against such attempts. Early in *Pilgrim at Tinker Creek,* for instance, she tells how, one day

> At the end of the island I noticed a small green frog. . . . His skin emptied and dropped; his very skull seemed to collapse and settle like a kicked tent. He was shrinking before my eyes like a deflating football. . . . Soon part of his skin, formless as a pricked balloon, lay in floating folds like bright scum on top of the water.
>
> I had read about the giant water bug but never seen one. "Giant water bug" is really the name of the creature, which is an enormous, heavy-bodied brown beetle. It eats, insects, tadpoles, fish, and frogs. . . . It seizes a victim, hugs it tight, and paralyzes it with enzymes injected during a vicious bite. . . . Through the puncture shoot the poisons that dissolve the victim's muscles and bones and organs—all but the skin—and through it the giant water bug sucks out the victim's body, reduced to a juice. This event is quite common in warm fresh water. . . .
>
> In the Koran, Allah asks, "The heaven and the earth and all in between, thinkest thou I made them *in jest?*" It's a good question.[26]

Later she reflects:

> It could be that God has not absconded but spread, to a fabric of spirit and sense so grand and subtle, so powerful in a new way, that we can only feel blindly of its hem. . . .
>
> Julian of Norwich, the great English anchorite and theologian, cited, in the manner of the prophets, these words from God: "See, I am God: see, I am in all things: see, I never lift my hands off my works, nor ever shall, without end. . . . How should anything be amiss?"[27]

Christians find themselves caught up in a biblically shaped whole that makes sense of the world around them and the way they live their lives, but always in a fragmentary way, with all sorts of questions still unanswered. In the tension between the mystery of radical transcendence, the God we know as one unknown, and the gracious God whose identity is narrated in the Bible, they do not find answers or explanations but *can* find, in Dorothee Soelle's words, that "The theodicy question is superseded here by an unlimited love for reality."[28]

Such faith lives in the light of the cross. As H. Richard Niebuhr put it, "We confront in the event of Jesus Christ the presence of that last power which brings to apparent nothingness the life of the most loyal man. Here we confront the slayer, and here we become aware that this slayer is the life giver. He

---

26. Annie Dillard, *Pilgrim at Tinker Creek* (New York: Harper Magazine Press, 1974), 5–7.
27. Ibid., 7, 177.
28. Dorothee Soelle, *Suffering,* trans. Everett R. Kalin (Philadelphia: Fortress Press, 1975), 91.

does not put to shame those who trust in him."[29] In the light of the cross, we may still not know how to tell the story of the world in which we live, but we cannot tell it as a story of God's indifference to our sufferings. We can live with the unanswered questions, Christian faith teaches, in a willingness to trust in the emergence of a pattern much of which we cannot discern. Our very willingness to live this way is mysterious to us, a mystery whose source we assign to the work of the Holy Spirit, thereby indicating that it too partakes of the transcendence of God. A Trinitarian context thus makes possible a classical Christian rhetoric about evil far more aware of what it cannot understand than is the discourse of theodicies. For the Bible, Niebuhr once wrote,

> Confidence in cosmic faithfulness held to the assurance that there was one self-consistent intention in apparent evil as well as in apparent good though how it was present often remained unfathomed. His ways were not man's ways, nor his thoughts man's thoughts; reasoning faith struggled to overcome anthropomorphism. It became clear that the righteousness of God was not like human justice. The suffering of the innocent, the prosperity of the wicked, brought faith to the edge of despair. But the postulate that God is faithful remained after every hypothesis about the mode of his faithfulness had broken down.[30]

The Irrationality of Sin

Problems of pain and suffering arise most dramatically when that pain and suffering is the result of human sin.[31] Here premodern Christian theology was most willing to acknowledge an exception to the rule of God's sovereignty over every event in creation. God permits sin, Christian theologians have agreed. They noted the possibility that the good of allowing human choice between good and evil outweighs the evil of sin, or that in the wake of sin's consequences God can bring about greater goods of compassion, transformation, and redemption, without ever claiming that any such concerns sufficed to explain God's permission—but God does not "cause" sin.[32] Indeed, sin has no

29. H. Richard Niebuhr, *Radical Monotheism and Western Civilization* (Louisville: Westminster/John Knox Press, 1993), 124–25.

30. Ibid., 47.

"What the problem of evil calls into question is a way of thinking submitted to the requirements of logical coherence, that is, one submitted to both the rule of non-contradiction and that of systematic totalization." Ricoeur, "Evil: A Challenge to Philosophy and Theology," 635.

31. A good many theodicies distinguish with some confidence the evils caused by human sin from natural evils. There are surely relatively clear cases, but we are not in a position to judge which cases of cancer have been caused by greed that led to unchecked pollution, which victims of AIDS would have been spared if bigotry had not discouraged early research, and so on. See Ricoeur, "Evil: A Challenge to Philosophy and Theology," 645.

32. Kant said that physical pain and suffering are only conditionally contrary to divine purposefulness, while sin is absolutely contrary. God could cause pain as a means to an end—but not sin. Immanuel Kant, "On the Failure of All Attempted Philosophical Theodicies," appendix to Michel Despland, *Kant on History and Religion* (Montreal: McGill University Press, 1973), 284.

cause. "The 'objective falsity' which is sin is not itself caused," David Burrell explains, following Aquinas, and "so has no part in a 'divine plan.' What remains unintelligible because it is irrational is the way we can 'remove ourselves from the order of the divine intellect' (*Summa Theologiae* 1.17.1), when that ordering takes in all there is."[33]

If this seems very strange, then Christian theologians will respond that it *ought* to seem very strange. As Kathryn Tanner puts it,

> The origination of sin is properly a mystery, properly inexplicable in a scheme of thought where God is the ultimate principle of explanation. Human beings must be the ones responsible for their own moral failing since God by definition brings to be only the good; but the *how* of that human-originated-sin is as Karl Barth says an impossible possibility, the surd of a creature turning against its own being given by God, as Bernard Lonergan avers, an inconceivable breaking off of the very relation to God that makes the creature all that it is.[34]

If sin had a cause, it would be part of a larger causal order, and ultimately part of the great plan of God's creation. It is the irrationality, the sense of things gone awry and off track, the fact of human creatures precisely *not* being and doing what they were meant to be and do that makes sin so terrible. Even the giant water bug seems to be fulfilling its destiny, however strange. A sinful human being is actually irrational. To insist on the impossibility of explaining evil is not just an abstract point or a theologian's excuse. To read histories of the Holocaust, for instance, is to become aware that attempted explanations—whether in terms of German history or social psychology or whatever—inevitably domesticate it and thereby deny its full evil.

Even while affirming the sheer aberrance of sin, however, Christian theologians have maintained that nothing ever simply escapes God's control. Calvin acknowledged, with biblical warrant, that God can use the deeds of evil folk for the doing of the divine will, even though the deeds remain evil. The Assyrians and Babylonians act out of greed and fury, but their victories serve God's purpose in chastising Israel.[35] More than that, *no* evil leads to the ultimate disappearance of anything that was for good, no part of creation ever falls altogether outside of God's sovereignty.[36] Even here, God remains the be-

---

33. David B. Burrell, *Freedom and Creation in Three Traditions* (Notre Dame, Ind.: University of Notre Dame Press, 1993), 157.

"When sin is understood positively, when it is esteemed and justified and established, when it counterbalances grace and is indispensable to it, it is not real sin." Barth, *Church Dogmatics*, vol. 3, part 3, 333.

34. Kathryn Tanner, "Human Freedom, Human Sin, and God the Creator," in *The God Who Acts*, ed. Thomas F. Tracy (University Park, Pa.: Pennsylvania State University Press, 1994), 112.

35. Calvin, *Institutes* 4.20.30.

36. For faith, "There is no evil in the city, but the Lord has done it; no crucifixion but the One has crucified. How and why these events fit in it does not yet know." Niebuhr, *The Responsible Self*, 125.

ginning and end of *all* things. Jonathan Edwards, in this as in many things, spoke for that earlier tradition, in his reluctance even to refuse without qualification to call God "the author of sin":

> If by "the author of sin" is meant the permitter, or not a hinderer of sin; and at the same time, a disposer of the state of events, in such a manner, for wise, holy and most excellent ends and purposes, that sin, if it be permitted or not hindered, will most certainly and infallibly follow: I say, if this be all that is meant, by being the author of sin (though I dislike and reject the phrase, as that which by use and custom is apt to carry another sense), it is no reproach for the most High to be thus the author of sin.[37]

One can never simply say, "This lies outside of God's purview," and we have these biblical tales where horrible human deeds do in some unexpected way work God's intent. Yet neither Calvin nor Edwards would offer any explanation of the "causal joint" at work between God and evildoers in the biblical stories or risk generalizing such analysis beyond biblical examples.

Theologians have often been justly criticized for announcing a "mystery" whenever they find themselves lacking a good explanation. But it is not intellectual cheating to refuse to explain something if you can give an account of why just this should not be explicable; and reflection on the nature of sin, I have been arguing, provides just such an account.[38] Christians therefore should say both that there is not a single point where God is absent or inactive or only partly active or restricted in action, *and* that there are irrational events that are somehow not caused by God. They should be willing to say both without worrying overmuch about how both could be true, for the attempt to resolve such worries leads inevitably to a search for sin's causes that makes it explicable, and it therefore loses its full irrationality.[39] Even worse, it starts to produce accounts of why those who have suffered somehow deserved it—the one thing biblical texts like Job and the Gospel healing stories so firmly reject. Sometimes, it must be admitted, not only modern theodicies but premodern theologies failed here, as when doctrines of original sin turned from reminders of what we cannot explain about the origin of evil to purported explanations—when, for instance, some sort of genetic theory "explained" the inheritance of original sin.[40] But premodern theologies generally did also keep in mind how

37. Jonathan Edwards, *Freedom of the Will* (New Haven: Yale University Press, 1957), 399.

38. It thus fits Karl Rahner's definition of "mystery": "A mystery is not something still undisclosed, which is a second element along with what is grasped and understood. . . . Mystery, on the contrary, is the impenetrable, which is already present and does not need to be fetched." Karl Rahner, *Theological Investigations*, vol. 4, trans. Kevin Smyth (Baltimore: Helicon Press, 1966), 108.

39. See R. Garrigou-Lagrange, *Predestination*, trans. Bede Rose (St. Louis: B. Herder Book Co., 1939), 104. See also Immanuel Kant, *Religion within the Limits of Reason Alone*, trans. Theodore M. Greene and Hoyt H. Hudson (New York: Harper Brothers, 1960), 38; Ricoeur, *The Conflict of Interpretations*, 435.

40. Ricoeur, *Conflict of Interpretations*, 286.

little they could understand about God. It was only in the modern era, with
the emergence of theodicies, that regrettable claims to explain too much turned
from being the exception to being the rule.

Chapter 4 discussed the rhetoric of Calvin's theology, and on these issues
rhetoric matters a lot: The way something is said and the context in which it
is said can matter as much as the truth-value of the propositions to its appropriateness to Christian theology. For example, in a moving memoir, H. B.
Deqhani-Tafti, the exiled Anglican bishop of Iran, speaks of the horrors he suffered during the Iranian revolution, culminating in the death of his son Bahram.
He includes in his book a prayer:

> O God
> We remember not only Bahram
>   but also his murderers;
> Not because they killed him in the prime of his youth
>   and made our hearts bleed and our tears flow . . .
> But because through their crime we now follow Thy footsteps
>   more closely in the way of sacrifice.
>   On the day of judgment
> Remember the fruit of the Spirit by which
>   they have enriched our lives,
> And forgive.[41]

This seems to me deeply moving, the sort of prayer a Christian might hope to
be able to pray and much admire in hearing another Christian pray. It also
seems, however, impossible to shift its "contents" from the mode of prayer to
the mode of didactic theology without turning it into something rather horrible. A calculation that weighs the death of Bahram against the fruit of the Spirit
multiplied in the souls of his loving survivors and confidently comes out with
a positive number has gone badly wrong.

A theodicist would argue that, if we can honor the prayer, then we *ought* to
be able to translate its implications into clear statements about God. A proper
understanding of transcendence, I have been arguing, permits Christians to preserve an appropriate reticence in such matters. We can pray in ways appropriate to Christians while admitting that, since we do not know the essence of
God, there is much about how the implications of those prayers fit together
that we cannot understand. Did God permit Bahram's murder? Was it part of a
divine plan? As Luther once wrote, "If . . . I could by any means comprehend
how this God can be merciful and just . . . there would be no need of faith."[42]

> For if his righteousness were such that it could be judged to be righ-
> teous by human standards, it would clearly not be divine and would

41. H. B. Deqhani-Tafti, *Design of My World* (Guildford, Surrey: Lutterworth Press, 1982), quoted
in Vernon White, *The Fall of a Sparrow* (Exeter: Paternoster Press, 1985), 183.

42. Martin Luther, *The Bondage of the Will*, trans. Philip S. Watson, *Luther's Works,* vol. 33
(Philadelphia: Fortress Press, 1972), 63.

in no way differ from human righteousness. But since he is the one true God, and is wholly incomprehensible and inaccessible to human reason, it is proper and indeed necessary that his righteousness also shall be incomprehensible.[43]

Seventeenth-century theologians and philosophers grew less accepting of such reticence, and their demands for better explanations have led to all too many insensitive efforts to "make sense" of the world's sin and evil. It is faith's willingness to live without such efforts that "sublimates" consolation.

From Accusation to Grace

Ricoeur wrote not only of a "sublimation of consolation" but also of a "sublimation of accusation." It was a commonplace of theology in the seventeenth and eighteenth centuries that, whatever doctrines one discarded, the role of religion as moral sanction survived. Early in the seventeenth century, in the first classic text of Enlightenment Deism, Lord Herbert of Cherbury wrote,

> There is no general agreement concerning rites, ceremonies, traditions, whether written or unwritten, or concerning Revelation; but there is the greatest possible consensus of opinion concerning . . . that moral virtue which . . . has been esteemed by men in every age and place and respected in every land . . . [and that] there is Reward and Punishment after this life. . . . In this sense there is no nation, however barbarous, which has not and will not recognize the existence of punishments and rewards.[44]

Those punishments and rewards then constituted one of the chief values of religion, and the reason for obedience to God too often shifted from simple awe before the divine glory to hope of due reward. "You who are virtuous," Nietzsche wrote, "still want to be paid. . . . Alas, that is my sorrow: they have lied reward and punishment into the foundation of things, and now also into the foundation of your souls."[45] By the eighteenth century, Joseph Addison only put it more bluntly than most in justifying Sunday worship:

> It is certain the country people would soon degenerate into a kind of savages and barbarians were there not such frequent returns of a stated time, in which the whole village meet together with their best faces, and in their cleanliest habits, to converse with one another upon indifferent subjects, have their duties explained to them, and join together in adoration of the supreme Being.[46]

43. Ibid., 290.
44. Edward, Lord Herbert of Cherbury, *De Veritate*, in Peter Gay, ed., *Deism: An Anthology* (Princeton, N.J.: D. Van Nostrand Co., 1968), 36–39.
45. Friedrich Nietzsche, *Thus Spoke Zarathustra*, in *The Viking Portable Nietzsche*, trans. Walter Kaufmann (New York: Viking Press, 1954), 205–06.
46. Joseph Addison, no. 112 (9 July 1711), in *The Spectator*, ed. Donald Bond (Oxford: Clarendon Press, 1965), 460.

The "accusation" of sin, with accompanying rewards and punishments, takes a central place in a rational religion that keeps the country people in line by providing divine sanction for their social duties. Religion in general becomes a way of maintaining the established social order—just the role I noted it often served in the seventeenth century in reaction to the English Civil War or Anne Hutchinson's rebellion in Massachusetts. When religion's *defenders* say this, its critics—the whole tradition in which Marx and Freud play such prominent roles, for instance—really have little to add.

All this, however, had little to do with the Reformation's good news of grace. The God known in Christ, Luther insisted, is "the God of the humble, the miserable, the afflicted, the oppressed, the desperate, and of those who have been brought down to nothing at all," the God whose character it is "to exalt the humble, to feed the hungry, to enlighten the blind, to comfort the miserable and afflicted, to justify sinners, to give life to the dead, and to save those who are desperate and damned."[47] The revelation of such a God comes not as accusation but as grace, and that, as earlier chapters have already indicated, has at least two consequences.

First, it makes Christians free. Christian freedom, Calvin said, is not some power to act independently of God—that would define freedom as equivalent to sin. Rather, it is "especially an appendage of justification."[48] Because Christians trust that they have been justified by grace, they need not worry about justifying themselves. That frees them to act boldly, to take chances, to risk the foolishness of love, in the confidence that God will sustain them—to "sin boldly," as Luther put it, knowing "that by the riches of God's glory we have come to know that Lamb that takes away the sins of the world."[49]

Second, it challenges the ultimacy of any human order or hierarchy. The human rules of success or virtue have nothing to do with the ultimate worth of persons in the face of Luther's God, who "loves sinners, evil persons, fools and weaklings."[50] When the good citizens of seventeenth-century Boston heard John Cotton preach that "God doth sometime pour out the spirit of grace upon the most bloody, and most haynous, and most desperate, and most prophane, and most abominable sinners,"[51] they recognized a threat to their civic order. This was not Addison's sort of preaching, which kept "the country people" in line, but an invitation to challenge authorities and the order they impose.

47. Martin Luther, *Lectures on Galatians* (1535) (on Gal. 3:19), trans. Jaroslav Pelikan, *Luther's Works,* vol. 27 (St. Louis: Concordia Publishing House, 1964), 13.

48. Calvin, *Institutes* 3.19.1.

49. Luther to Melanchthon, 1 August 1521, *Luther's Works,* vol. 48, trans. Gottfried G. Krodel (Philadelphia: Fortress Press, 1963), 281–82.

50. Martin Luther, "Heidelberg Disputation," trans. Harold J. Grimm, *Luther's Works,* vol. 31 (Philadelphia: Muhlenberg Press, 1957), 56.

51. John Cotton, "The Way of Life" (London: L. Fawne and S. Gellibrand, 1641), 109, in David D. Hall, *The Antinomian Controversy, 1636–1638; A Documentary History* (Durham, N.C.: Duke University Press, 1990), 171.

"I am not saying," Ricoeur writes in his meditation on the "sublimation of accusation," that faith in God in this mode will call for no obedience. Astonished gratitude calls for its own forms of obedience, done in freedom and full of joy,

> but it is a question of something completely different from the sacralization of moral obligation. As Kierkegaard realized, it is a matter of an obedience beyond the suspension of the ethical, of an "absurd" obedience, one related to the singularity of a call and to a need which renders the believer a stranger and a sojourner on earth. . . . This is what the author of the Epistle to the Hebrews calls, in almost Gnostic language, "the desire [for] a better country" (Heb. 11:16).[52]

A transcendent God does not follow human rules. Jesus' parables keep reminding their hearers of God's unexpectedness: those who worked the last hour get paid as much as those who struggled all the day. It is not the head of the hierarchy who speaks for such a God, Ricoeur reminds us, but the prophet, "the figure outside the family, outside politics, outside culture, the eschatological figure par excellence."[53] And the life of Jesus, the one who was more than prophet, provides the ultimate enacted parable of God's unexpected love, that this wandering prophet without a place to lay his head, who washes the feet of his companions, should be the self-revelation of God.

With respect to consolation, I suggested that Christians live in a tension between the biblical narrations of God's identity and God's transcendence: they trust in the love and faithfulness of this God but have to remember their inability to understand what that love and faithfulness mean. With respect to the theme of accusation, however, biblical narratives and the principle of transcendence come into concord, for *both* remind us of our inability to fit God into our categories and structures.

Many contemporary theologians protest against a transcendent God, that distant being who dwells on high, our stern judge, the culmination of the cosmic order. They are right to protest, but wrong simply to blame "the Christian tradition" or "classical Christian theism" for the faults they identify. The principal object of their complaint came to dominate the Christian understanding of divine transcendence only in the seventeenth century. Before that, theologians spoke more forcefully of a Triune God utterly beyond our understanding and full of unexpected grace. As I have said, we cannot simply return to that earlier theology, and would not want to if we could. But in its radical vision of divine transcendence, it may still have lessons to teach us.

---

52. Ricoeur, *The Conflict of Interpretations,* 343.
53. Ibid., 350.

Index